THE FALL OF THE
ROMAN
EMPIRE

ARTHER FERRILL

THE FALL OF THE
ROMAN
EMPIRE

THE MILITARY EXPLANATION

With 48 illustrations

THAMES AND HUDSON

To Ardis and J. Kelley Sowards
in Gratitude and Friendship

Frontispiece: Relief of a soldier with
spear and flat shield on a tombstone
in Istanbul, c. AD 214.

© 1986 Thames and Hudson Ltd, London

First published in the United States in 1986 by Thames and Hudson
Inc., 500 Fifth Avenue, New York, New York 10110

First paperback edition 1988

Reprinted 1994

Library of Congress Catalog Card Number 85-51117

Printed and bound in the USA

Contents

Preface

On one side of the frontier separating the civilized world from the land of barbarian darkness stood the mighty Roman legions, successors to the foot-soldiers who had stopped Hannibal and had carried Caesar to greatness; on the other side, the thundering horses of the savage Huns and the Germanic nations. In the clash we know as the fall of Rome, barbarian cavalry trampled the Roman infantry into the earth and planted the standards of the Early Middle Ages in Roman territory. Or so some would have us believe.

Actually, however, many twentieth-century historians have ignored or relegated to a secondary place the purely military aspects of Rome's fall. One of the foremost authorities on the period, E.A. Thompson, in a brilliant essay entitled 'Early Germanic Warfare', *Past and Present*, 14 (1958), 2–29, concludes with the following statement:

If we are asked how the barbarians ever managed to overthrow the Western Empire, we may reply that the question implies . . . that the fall of the Empire was essentially a military defeat; but in fact it is impossible to point to a series of military conflicts and say that these led to the destruction of the Empire. The process was less cataclysmic than that. . . . It would be superficial to look for the causes of the fall of the Western Empire simply in military techniques.

In fact, strictly military considerations must play a large part in any explanation of the fall of the Roman Empire. Many factors – political, social, religious and economic – shaped the unfolding of that story, but warfare did matter: much was decided on the battlefield. In this book, without denying the possible importance of other considerations, I hope to show that generals and their armies must be regarded as an essential component in the decline and fall of the Roman Empire.

In one respect twentieth-century scholars have made a significant contribution to the military history of the Late Roman Empire, by questioning the traditional nineteenth-century picture of the triumph of barbarian cavalry over Roman infantry. It is now commonly recognized by professional historians that the Germans and even the Huns of the fifth century were not the horse warriors of popular tradition. Generally they fought on foot, and the Roman Empire was lost by Roman infantry fighting barbarian infantry. One of the purposes of this book is simply to emphasize for the non-specialist reader the priority of infantry in the age of the barbarian invasions.

Some problems of definition are perhaps best treated here. Throughout the book it will be necessary to use the terms 'grand strategy', 'strategy', and 'tactics' and such expressions as 'strategic' or 'tactical' warfare. Military terminology is notoriously elusive. Grand strategy often shades into strategy and strategy into tactics, but normally grand strategy is the overall plan for defending the security and integrity of the state while strategy is the plan for winning a war and tactics for winning a battle. A state that has conventional tactical superiority, that is, the ability to defeat the enemy in individual battles, may nevertheless lose the war (or suffer strategic defeat) because it lacks sufficient manpower and matériel or because it is drawn into unconventional, guerrilla warfare where normal tactics no longer apply.

Another distinction that must be made clearly in a book on the fall of Rome is that the words 'decline' and 'fall' are not synonymous, although they are frequently interrelated. The Romans began their gradual decline at such a high level of wealth and power that they were able to decline for centuries before they were in danger of falling. In their case the reasons for decline need not be the same as the reasons for the fall, which can be sought in a somewhat different and more immediate context.

Many problems can be avoided by keeping the distinction between decline and fall sharp. One is the date of Rome's fall, which some historians confuse with the beginning of imperial decline and, as a result, place much too early in history, often in the third century AD or in the age of Diocletian and Constantine. Nor is the fall of Rome necessarily simultaneous with the beginning of the Middle Ages. *The Cambridge Medieval History* begins with Constantine, as do many standard textbooks on the history of the Middle Ages. This common custom is reasonable and necessary. Some of the most important ingredients of the medieval world were firmly in place at least by AD

395, but so was the Roman Empire in East and West. As we shall see, the traditional date for the fall of Rome in AD 476 is basically a good one, despite many efforts to debunk it.

I must thank several friends and colleagues for their help in the preparation of this book. Fritz Levy and Solomon Katz read each chapter as it was written and offered helpful criticism. John Eadie and Chester Starr read the completed typescript and saved me from many errors of detail and inconsistencies of argument. Ramsay MacMullen gave important encouragement as I began this project. Thomas Kelly, as always, helped in numerous essential ways. Needless to say, the remaining faults and errors are my own. Special thanks go to the firm of Thames and Hudson Ltd for their assistance throughout.

Arther Ferrill

Chapter One

The Decline and Fall of Rome

Rome created a mighty empire, the western world's most powerful one. Legions defending the frontiers of the 'immense majesty' of that empire guarded territory stretching some three thousand miles, from Britain to Egypt, and a border nearly six thousand miles long. What Poe called 'the grandeur that was Rome' has always impressed poets, historians and the general public. Colourful emperors and empresses, pageantry and power blend into a composite of military and administrative greatness, an empire of eternal strength. The Rome of Augustus and Nero, of Christ and St Paul, embraced the whole civilized world – emphatically not including the wild barbarians around the fringes, or the decadent world of Parthian Mesopotamia.[1]

The majesty of Rome has left its physical mark on the modern world in such impressive ruins as Hadrian's Wall in northern England, the aqueducts of France and Spain, the Colosseum in Rome itself and the splendid relics of Roman North Africa. Today one cannot travel in the countries around the Mediterranean without encountering constant reminders of bygone greatness, when the whim of an emperor could make men tremble.

Rome, emperors, legions and power – the cluster of words conjures up an image that is confirmed by the monuments and the literature of the ancient world, but there is one anecdote that in its own way illustrates the power of Rome as clearly as the Colosseum. A distinguished rhetorician by the name of Favorinus, a friend of the biographer Plutarch, got into an argument with the Emperor Hadrian (AD 117–138) over the proper use of a certain word. Favorinus, an authority on words, nevertheless yielded to the emperor. When chided by his friends for retreating from a position that was certainly correct, the scholar said: 'Who am I to argue with the commander of thirty legions?'

The Roman Empire at its height in the second century AD.

The Roman achievement, however, went beyond raw power and colossal architecture. The benefits of the *Pax Romana* included the development of one of man's most impressive codes of law and an administrative system that met the needs of men of varied languages, ethnic backgrounds and cultural traditions. The poet Virgil (70–19 BC) was not far wrong in claiming that his nation ruled the world in peace and justice. Although the Roman Empire was in many respects an exploitive structure, it retained for centuries the loyalty and often the enthusiastic approbation of its subjects.

The aesthetic, intellectual and literary contributions of Rome to the modern world are too well known to list. They are sometimes deemed inferior to those of ancient Greece, but the comparison is otiose – similar to one between two precious metals or gems. Although Virgil's *Aeneid* was influenced by Homer's *Iliad* and *Odyssey*, the Roman writer stands, alongside the blind bards Homer and Milton, at the head of a list of the world's greatest epic poets. Likewise, if Tacitus was no Thucydides, he was nevertheless one of antiquity's most powerful historians.

Although the Roman triumph of mind and intellect was grand by any standard, there was one respect in which they excelled without question beyond the exploits of the Greeks. That was in the creation of a basic standard of living that remains a marvel in the history of western civilization. Unlike most people before or since, until very recent times, the inhabitants of the Roman Empire had ample supplies of fresh water for drinking and bathing, often transported hundreds of miles in the famous systems of aqueducts. The reader should not pass lightly over the word 'bathing'. The fact is that Romans did bathe, in elaborate, publicly supported, heated baths, found all over the Roman Empire from Hadrian's Wall to the Greek East. That alone makes them nearly unique in western history. Furthermore their cities were serviced by sewers, and there were public facilities for the elimination of bodily wastes that were unmatched anywhere until the nineteenth century. The ruins of a flushing latrine for Roman legionaries still stand at Housesteads on Hadrian's Wall.

For all the reasons mentioned above, and for many more, Romans everywhere came to believe in *Roma Aeterna*, the eternal city. Yet the Roman Empire proved mortal after all, and the ghost of that great structure has haunted western man ever since. As one historian recently wrote: 'The best-known fact about the Roman Empire is that it declined and fell.'[2] And one might add that probably the best known modern work of history, when all is said and done, is Edward Gibbon's *The History of the Decline and Fall of the Roman Empire*. Although the topic has been popular, and a myriad of reasons has been offered to explain Rome's fall, no consensus has emerged, and historians of the twentieth century have multiplied the variety of explanations many times over. A recent book in German, almost 700 pages long, lists some 210 factors that have been adduced as causes of Rome's fall.[3]

Have we reached the stage that Mark Twain forecast when he said about another matter, 'We shall soon know nothing at all' because scholars 'have thrown much darkness on the subject'?[4] Students, confronted with a bewildering maze of theories, may legitimately wonder; yet, as we shall see, study of the problem is rewarding, and there may be some light at the end of the tunnel. To place the subject in perspective, as background to the narrative of events in subsequent chapters, we must first review briefly the major modern explanations of the fall of Rome.

From Gibbon to Today

Gibbon's *Decline and Fall* was published in six volumes from 1776 to 1788, before the birth of 'scientific' Roman historiography. If Gibbon's masterpiece lacks some of the refinements of modern historiography and seems at times an idealized product of the Enlightenment, it has at least two redeeming virtues. The great classic was written in a sublime and beautiful prose style so lofty that no historian, perhaps no prose author, has since matched it. It was, moreover, the work of an extraordinarily powerful intellect who was able to perceive and portray with considerable force the calamitous events that shook the Late Roman Empire – even without benefit of nineteenth-century advances in historiography. At the end of the nineteenth century one of the greatest of the 'scientific' historians in England, J. B. Bury, could still say, 'If we take into account the vast range of his work, his accuracy is amazing'.[5]

Gibbon begins with a majestic survey of the Roman Empire at its peak in the great age of the 'Five good emperors' from Nerva (AD 96–8) to Marcus Aurelius (AD 161–80). His encomium to the Rome of that period, often quoted, is somewhat exaggerated yet arguably sound, at least at the time Gibbon wrote it:

If a man were called to fix the period in the history of the world during which the condition of the human race was most happy and prosperous, he would without hesitation, name that which elapsed from the death of Domitian [AD 96] to the accession of Commodus [AD 180]. The vast extent of the Roman Empire was governed by absolute power, under the guidance of virtue and wisdom. The armies were restrained by the firm but gentle hand of four successive emperors, whose characters and authority commanded involuntary respect. The forms of the civil administration were carefully preserved by Nerva, Trajan, Hadrian, and the Antonines, who delighted in the image of liberty, and were pleased with considering themselves as the accountable ministers of the laws.[6]

Gibbon then proceeds to a more difficult stage in the history of the Roman Empire – the extraordinary reign of Marcus Aurelius' off-balance son, Commodus, who 'attained the summit of vice and infamy'[7] and was finally strangled in his sleep by a wrestling companion on the last day of the year 192. The reign of the Antonines was succeeded after a brief civil war by that of the Severans (AD 193–235), a dynasty founded by the forceful Septimius Severus (AD 193–211), whom Gibbon describes as 'the principal author of the decline of the Roman Empire'.[8] As his narrative spills over into the events of the third century, Gibbon's treatment of the decline and fall begins in earnest.

Septimius, in some ways a strong and effective emperor, was justly excoriated by Gibbon for ignoring the republican principles that had been woven into the fabric of the principate; for parading his absolute power; and for allowing the military a too prominent role in Roman public life. The emperor's sons and their successors had only the weaknesses of Septimius and lacked his redeeming strengths. As Romans entered the third century under the stifling influence of the Severans, the full range of their ancient civilization began to suffer from a debilitating lethargy and staleness. In literature and philosophy the vitality of the classical period had been sapped, and art and architecture, with few exceptions, revealed the same stagnation.[9]

The murder of the effete Alexander Severus in 235 inaugurated an age of trouble in Roman history, the so-called period of the Barracks emperors (235–84), when in fifty years Romans witnessed a succession of twenty-one emperors and numerous unsuccessful aspirants to the purple. Most of them were generals, some of them commoners who had risen through the ranks. In the anarchy of frequent civil wars the Empire nearly fell. At one point around 260 the emperor in Rome only ruled over Italy and North Africa – the rest of the Empire in the West and East was in the control of rebels. Barbarians crossed the frontiers, and one emperor (Valerian) died in Persian captivity. Of the twenty-one emperors of the period only two (Claudius and Tacitus) died a natural death.[10]

In gruesome and colourful detail Gibbon worked his way through the Barracks emperors until finally coming to the age of Diocletian and Constantine (284–337), two strong emperors who restored peace and stability to the Roman world and gave the Empire a new lease of life. Diocletian, in the words of Gibbon, was 'the founder of a new empire'.[11] Throughout most of the fourth century Rome was militarily strong. The conversion of Constantine the Great in 312, however, the ultimate adoption of Christianity as the official Roman religion, and the construction of Constantinople as the centre of empire did invest the period with a distinctly new flavour.

In the last half of the fourth century began the wave of barbarian invasions, starting with the victory of the Visigoths over the Emperor Valens at Adrianople in 378, that eventually overwhelmed the Roman Empire in the West. The Empire ceased to exist altogether almost a hundred years later in 476. In the *Decline and Fall* Gibbon described variously and not always consistently what he once referred to as 'the triumph of barbarism and religion'. In that respect, incidentally, his judgment was similar to Voltaire's, who wrote: 'Two flails at last brought down this vast Colossus: the barbarians and religious disputes.'[12] In one passage Gibbon said that 'the stupendous fabric' of the Roman Empire 'yielded to the pressure of its own weight'. When he says that 'the Roman world was overwhelmed by a deluge of Barbarians' in one section of the work, he seems to contradict the view elsewhere expressed that 'If all the Barbarian conquerors had been annihilated in the same hour, their total destruction would not have restored the Empire of the West.'[13] He did believe that the construction of Constantinople and the division of the Empire into West and East weakened the West, as 'the Byzantine court beheld with indifference, perhaps with pleasure, the disgrace of Rome, the misfortunes of Italy, and the loss of the West'. The introduction of Christianity buried 'the last remains of the military spirit . . . in the cloister'. Still, the conversion of the barbarians softened the blow of the invasions: 'If the decline of the Roman Empire was hastened by the conversion of Constantine, his victorious religion broke the violence of the fall, and mollified the ferocious temper of the conquerors.'[14]

The quotations above can be pressed too far. More than anything else Gibbon was a narrative historian who wove into 'the stupendous fabric' of his story, often without direct analysis, the various ingredients of Rome's decline and fall; because so many details impinge upon the whole picture, one must read him to get the full force of his interpretation. Nevertheless, it is generally true that Gibbon identified Christianity as the source of the most important internal weakness in the Empire and saw barbarian pressures on the frontier as the decisive force in the fall of the Western Roman Empire. If a multi-volume masterpiece may be abridged to a few words, 'the triumph of barbarism and religion' is probably the best one can do.[15]

Although Gibbon's explanation of the decline and fall of Rome has had its adherents to the present day, the twentieth century has produced many alternative versions. Indeed, there have been so many that the last generation of professional ancient historians has seemed bored by the recurrent problem. One major historian has recently dismissed the fall of Rome as simply 'inevitable' and another has ridiculed as 'simplistic' the historians of the fall who proceed 'as does a detective investigating a crime, pursuing the forces responsible for it, to arraign them before the bar of history'.[16]

Perhaps the most popular approach to the period in the last generation has been to deny the fall altogether – to emphasize the continuity between Rome and the Middle Ages. Peter Brown in his book, *The World of Late Antiquity* AD *150–750* (1971), generally ignores the fall and the barbarians (or at least the implications of the word, 'barbarians').[17] He concentrates instead on the transformation from Roman to Byzantine history in the East and to a certain extent from Roman to early medieval history in the West. On the whole the emphasis of the 'Late Antique' school is positive and up-beat – it is on change rather than collapse and cataclysm, on spirituality in religion rather than superstition. 'Savage barbarians' and 'Germanity' have little role to play in the world of 'Late Antiquity', and Brown's approach has attracted many followers.

It is not difficult to understand the ennui now felt by historians confronted with the fall of Rome. There is a feeling of hopelessness, that no one will ever find an answer that will satisfy the majority of scholars. Nor has there been any significant 'new evidence' since Gibbon's day. There have been relatively few important literary discoveries, and, although some interesting archaeological work on the Late Empire has been undertaken, archaeologists generally are more attracted to the romantic fields of Egypt and Mesopotamia, the Minoan and Mycenaean world, and Periclean Athens.[18]

Another reason for discontent with the 'problem' of Rome's fall is that many of the best-known explanations, even in some instances those offered by otherwise outstanding ancient historians, are frivolous or absurd. Michael Rostovtzeff's monumental, two-volume *Social and Economic History of the Roman Empire* (originally published in 1926) deserves for many reasons the high repute it has enjoyed, but Rostovtzeff's explanation of the fall of Rome – a class struggle in which the army became involved on the side of the peasants – is nonsense. So too is Tenney Frank's view that race mixture, or the debilitating influence of the East on the West, caused the fall of Rome, although Frank was in other respects one of the greatest Roman historians in the first half of the twentieth century.[19]

Then there are the 'seed' or 'germ' theories which trace the reasons for the fall of Rome so far back into the period of Roman greatness that they become remote from the events of the fourth and fifth centuries (the 'Downhill-all-the-way' school). Gibbon began with the Antonines and regretted after he finished his work that he had not begun even earlier.[20] Apparently simple explanations, usually variations of the 'Downhill-all-the-way' approach, such as climatic changes, the decline of population, and lead poisoning have had some popular appeal but few adherents among professional historians.[21]

Likewise some historians are undoubtedly troubled by the polemical or 'topical' nature of attempts at explanation: 'reflecting the problems of those who propounded them,' wrote F. W. Walbank, 'and designed to illuminate what was dark in contemporary life.'[22] In the fifth century Christians blamed the pagans and pagans blamed the Christians. In the twentieth century writers concerned with growing bureaucracy or immorality in modern life commonly see bureaucracy or immorality as the cause of Rome's fall. The obvious absurdity of some of the arguments seems to make little difference. Morality, in the Christian sense in which the word is normally intended, was much greater in the fourth and fifth centuries than it had been before. If immorality contributed to Rome's fall, why did it take so long?

The main line of substantial scholarly research into the fall of Rome, however, particularly in England but elsewhere as well, has emphasized that the fall of the Western Empire in the fifth century was a cataclysmic event, a sharp break in European history, and that the invasion of the barbarians was the chief act in the story. In the last two hundred years, three works in particular stand out: Gibbon's *Decline and Fall*, J. B. Bury's two-volume *History of the Later Roman Empire, 395–565* (1923), and A. H. M. Jones' multi-volume *The Later Roman Empire, 294–602* (1964). All three emphasize the role played by the barbarians in the fall of Rome. Even in languages other than English, that view has been a significant one. One of the most respected accounts of the Late Empire in French, Andre Piganiol's *L'Empire Chrétien (325–395)* (2nd ed., 1972) concludes:

> It is too easy to say that upon the arrival of the barbarians in the empire 'everything was dead, it was a powerless corpse, a body stretched out in its own blood', or that the Roman Empire in the West was not destroyed by a brutal blow, but that it was 'sleeping'.
> Roman civilization did not die a natural death. It was killed.[23]

In German scholarship the age of the barbarian invasions, the so-called *Völkerwanderung*, has understandably attracted somewhat more attention, and there is a kind of nationalistic bias in favour of change rather than continuity.[24] The idea that 'Germanity' combined with Christianity to add a strikingly new dimension to Graeco-Roman classical civilization has naturally had a strong appeal and indeed has influenced scholars outside Germany.[25]

In many ways A. H. M. Jones' panoramic treatment of the fall of Rome is most representative of the mainline tradition.[26] One of his greatest contributions to the problem was an important and obviously correct distinction – the Roman Empire did not fall in the fifth century: it continued to survive in the East in what we know as the Byzantine Empire until the Turkish conquest in the middle of the fifteenth century. Therefore, when we speak of the fall of Rome, a perfectly legitimate expression as long as everyone understands exactly what is meant by it, we refer only to the western half of the Roman Empire, and any explanation of the fall of the West must take into account the survival of the East.

'These facts are important,' Jones wrote, 'for they demonstrate that the empire did not, as some modern historians have suggested, totter into its grave from senile decay, impelled by a gentle push from the barbarians. Most of the internal weaknesses which these historians stress were common to both halves of the empire.'[27] If Christianity weakened the Empire internally, since the religion was stronger and more divisive in the East, why did the West fall and the East continue to stand? The evils of bureaucracy, of social rigidity, of the economic system, were all present in the East as well as the West.

The main difference, as Jones accurately saw it, was that 'down to the end of the fifth century' the East was 'strategically less vulnerable' and 'subjected to less pressure from external enemies.'[28] In short, the barbarian invasion of the West was the main cause of the fall of Rome. The Western emperors of the fifth century could not stop attacks from both the Rhine and the Danube whereas the Eastern emperor more easily held Constantinople, a superbly fortified capital. Trouble with Persia threatened the East, but Romans for various reasons found the Persians easier to deal with than the barbarians. For one thing Persians were not migratory. They had their own internal problems, and they could be dealt with according to the well developed protocol of ancient diplomacy.

In a somewhat less persuasive section Jones dismisses civil war and rebellion as major causes of the decline and fall because the fourth and fifth centuries saw less of them than the earlier period of imperial history. That is debatable, and so is Jones' view that the Roman army had not been neglected and that in certain respects it was superior to the more famous army of the Early Empire. It was larger, and it had more cavalry, but whether after Constantine it pursued a 'wiser strategy' in abandoning preclusive security along the frontiers is much less certain than Jones believed. On the whole his survey of the 'fighting quality' of the late imperial army was too optimistic. The frontier garrisons were inferior to the central reserve and 'barbarization' of the Roman army was a serious problem, not, as Jones saw it, a source of strength. When he wrote that 'No career officer of German origin . . . is ever known to have betrayed the interests of the empire to his countrymen', he may have been correct, but the loyalty of barbarian officers is not really the issue, as we shall see.[29]

On the other hand, Jones correctly argued that the decay of trade and industry was not a cause of Rome's fall. There was a decline in agriculture and land was withdrawn from cultivation, in some cases on a very large scale, sometimes as a direct result of barbarian invasions. However, the chief cause of the agricultural decline was high taxation on marginal land, driving it out of cultivation. Jones is surely right in saying that taxation was spurred by the huge military budget and was thus 'indirectly' the result of the barbarian invasions.

The evidence for another often mentioned problem, depopulation, is not very strong. The existing statistics are notoriously unreliable, and not many figures are available anyway, but population probably did decline. After reviewing the evidence Jones concludes that the city of Rome had a population of 500,000 to 750,000 around AD 300 (down from perhaps 1,000,000 at the death of Augustus in AD 14); that Constantinople was the same size by the sixth century; and that Alexandria in the sixth century was half as large as Constantinople. Antioch may have had somewhere between 150,000 and 200,000 inhabitants. On the whole Jones sees 'no significant difference' between the birth and death rates of the Early and Late Empire (both of which were high).

Strangely, there is much evidence for manpower shortages, as opposed to depopulation, in the Late Empire. That is why workers were bound to their occupations under Diocletian, Constantine and their successors, and it is why tenants (*coloni*) were tied to the soil. Plague and famine, compounded by the disruptions of the barbarian invasions, also took their toll. After paying rent and taxes the peasants of the Empire simply could not afford to support all their children at a subsistence level. Infanticide and malnutrition had their effect, on the urban poor as well as the peasantry, and the population shrank, but, according to Jones, 'it was not in most areas catastrophic'.[30] The increasing demands of the church, the governmental bureaucracy, and the army, however, exacerbated the manpower shortage. Yet no matter what the number of people in the Roman Empire, it was certainly much greater than the barbarians who invaded.

One result of the decline of population was that the number of producers sank while the number of 'idle mouths' stayed the same or possibly increased (particularly with the demands on manpower created by the increases in military forces). Social regimentation more or less guaranteed that there would be idle mouths to feed, since regimentation puts people firmly at the top of society as well as at the bottom. On the other hand, the rigidity of the law tying Romans to their occupations was accompanied by a laxity in enforcement, and there were many escape valves. The frequency of such laws in the Late Empire reminds one of the laws against bribery and corruption in the days of Caesar and suggests that in this case it was easier to legislate than to police. It is also true that many more commoners rose to high position in the Late Empire than in the days of Augustus.

Although corruption in government was a greater problem in the Late Empire than it had been earlier, partly because the civil bureaucracy had grown larger, Jones argues convincingly that relative to the size of the Empire the number of governmental officials (which he estimates at about thirty thousand) was not great and that this expense was small. More significant than corruption as a sign of the times was what Jones called the 'absence of public spirit' or the 'decline of morale'. Pride in the Empire and in the cities certainly diminished, and the lack of public spirit showed itself in the passive manner in which Romans in the West faced the barbarian invasions. There are some notable exceptions, of course, but Romans generally seem simply to have fled when they did not meekly submit. The apathy and docility of the Roman population need not reflect a grave societal malaise; for centuries unarmed Romans had relied on the protection of a great professional army.

Finally Jones notes that there were two ways in which the East was stronger than the West. The East was 'richer and more populous', and wealth was more evenly distributed; there were more peasants, more 'medium landowners' and fewer aristocrats. In the West the aristocracy was incredibly wealthy, and it was more influential in its region of the Empire than the eastern aristocracy was with the emperor in Constantinople, where imperial autocracy reigned. Because the economic resources were greater in the East, governmental revenues were less limited. In the fifth century emperors at Constantinople paid enormous sums in bribes to the barbarians to go west, whereas western rulers faced crushing fiscal burdens.

In the end, however, according to Jones, the 'major cause' of the fall of Rome in the West was that the West 'was more exposed to barbarian onslaughts'. The concluding sentence of his massive study of the Late Roman Empire reads: 'The internal weaknesses of the empire cannot have been a major factor in its decline.' This view carries respected authority; it was in fact the internal structure of the Roman Empire that Jones knew best. One of the ironies of his work is that in a multi-volume book dealing in intricate detail with the internal social, economic and administrative structure of the Empire, the author argued that external pressure caused its fall.

Naturally, we need not slavishly follow Jones' views. He was often more circumspect in stating them than the paraphrase above might suggest. Furthermore, he was not invariably correct; for example, his assessment of the Roman army in the fourth and fifth centuries requires significant modification. But, on the whole, the emphasis on barbarian pressures rather than on internal weakness is surely justified, and his careful analysis of all the symptoms of decay highlighted by other historians is generally persuasive.

Jones' arguments, of course, do not dispose of the advocates of continuity, as opposed to change, in the transformation from the Roman Empire to the Middle Ages. Peter Brown and the 'Late Antique' school (along with those historians who see in the West the perpetuation of Roman economic, social, administrative and legal patterns into the sixth and seventh centuries) generally deny the reality of the cataclysmic fall of Rome. The fact is, however, that the two points of view are not necessarily contradictory, and their adherents need not clash as much as they seem to.

It is quite possible that many significant features of Roman life survived the overthrow of the last emperor in the West, Romulus Augustulus, in 476. Obviously they did in the East, and in the West too one would expect to see major Roman survivals in the economy, in society and in law. The advocates of change are much too strident in their insistence that the fall of Rome destroyed everything Roman. Likewise, the advocates of continuity all too often ignore the obvious fact that not everything survived the barbarian invasions of the fifth century, that indeed dramatically significant changes occurred in the West from AD 400 to 500.

In fact the Roman Empire of the West did fall. Not every aspect of the life of Roman subjects was changed by that, but the fall of Rome as a political entity was one of the major events of the history of western man. It will simply not do to call that fall a myth or to ignore its historical significance merely by focussing on those aspects of Roman life that survived the fall in one form or another. At the opening of the fifth century a massive army, perhaps more than 200,000 strong, stood at the service of the Western emperor and his generals. In 476 it was gone. The destruction of Roman military power in the fifth century AD was the obvious cause of the collapse of Roman government in the West.

Chapter Two

The Grand Strategy of the Roman Empire

'In the second century of the Christian Aera,' wrote Gibbon in the opening sentences of the *Decline and Fall*, 'the Empire of Rome comprehended the fairest part of the earth and the most civilized portion of mankind. The frontiers of that extensive monarchy were guarded by ancient renown and disciplined valour.'[31] Modern historians have less eloquently restated the point insofar as the 'majesty' of Rome is concerned, but in the purely military sphere modern scholarship has diverged from Gibbon's opinion.

In a highly significant article written in the late nineteenth century the 'father' of all modern Roman historians, the great German scholar Theodor Mommsen, argued that the most important development in the history of Roman grand strategy came when the emperors created a strategic central reserve. Mommsen believed that the creation of a central mobile striking force, a *Feldheer* or *Bewegungsheer* (in French an *armée de manoeuvre* or *armée de campagne*) was the joint work of the Emperors Diocletian and Constantine – though he conceded that the evidence for this view was shaky.[32] Most scholars flocked to follow in Mommsen's footsteps.[33] No one but a professional classicist or ancient historian can imagine how influential Mommsen's views have been. Almost all modern studies of Roman history begin with his work (as this one does) and go on from there.

In fact Mommsen's basic assumption has never been questioned although there have been attacks on the details of his dating. It is now generally agreed that the mobile central reserve was the work of Constantine the Great and that Diocletian had little to do with its creation.[34] There has been almost no criticism of the main assumption in Mommsen's article, that the development of a central reserve was a long-needed strategic change. The view has been canonized. A restatement (by a modern military systems analyst) with the aid of

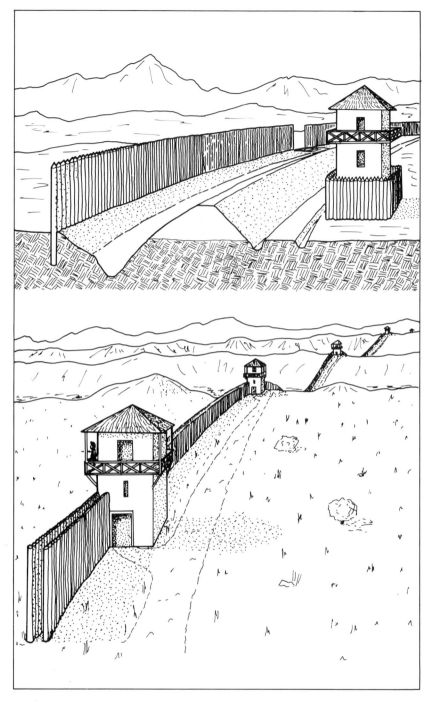

In this reconstruction of the frontier (limes) in Germany and Raetia one can clearly see how the emperors of the second century tried to defend the Empire with a grand strategy of preclusive security. No central mobile army was necessary in such a strong, frontier defence system.

elaborate military jargon has in recent years attracted considerable attention (Edward N. Luttwak, *The Grand Strategy of the Roman Empire*, 1976), and the idea that Romans of the early imperial period relied on a theoretically flawed defensive system until they turned to defence-in-depth supported by a large, mobile central reserve has become standard.

Amazingly this is so despite the fact that the only important ancient author to comment on this change in Roman grand strategy (for which there is remarkably little literary evidence) took a view directly opposite to that of modern scholars. Zosimus, writing in the fifth century, said:

Constantine abolished this [frontier] security by removing the greater part of the soldiery from the frontiers to cities that needed no auxiliary forces. He thus deprived of help the people who were harrassed by the barbarians and burdened tranquil cities with the pest of the military, so that several straightway were deserted. Moreover, he softened the soldiers, who treated themselves to shows and luxuries. Indeed (to speak plainly) he personally planted the first seeds of our present devastated state of affairs.[35]

In the remainder of this chapter we shall examine the Roman grand strategy of the second century, the collapse in the third century, and the resurgence of imperial power under Diocletian and Constantine. There is considerable reason to believe that the ancient commentator was closer to the truth than his modern detractors and that the grand strategy of Constantine the Great was defective.

From Preclusive Security to Third-Century Collapse

In the days of Hadrian and his successors down through the Severans (AD 117–235) Roman emperors pursued a grand strategy based on preclusive security – the establishment of a linear barrier of perimeter defence around the Empire. The legions were stationed in great fortresses around the frontiers, along some of which was actually a cordon of vast stone walls – none more famous than Hadrian's Wall in northern England.[36] The static frontiers of the Empire were impenetrable, or at least were intended to be. Consistent with this system of strong frontier defence the emperors maintained no central reserve in the heart of the Empire.

This military defensive system had many advantages not the least of which was its cost. Although the Romans are considered to have been among the most militaristic people in the history of the western world, they ruled over a vast stretch of territory with an economy of force that is remarkable. Their superb military organization and disciplined tactics made it possible for them to defeat northern barbarians even when the Roman army was greatly outnumbered. Rigorous Roman discipline itself is not the only reason. The Romans thoroughly mastered the art of military support and logistics. By way of example – though it comes from a later period, in the fourth century – when Constantius acted to suppress his nephew Julian, his agents gathered three million bushels of wheat along the borders of Gaul and another three million further east, so that the emperor's troops might have plenty to eat. As one historian observes, 'When an army of northern barbarians undertook a campaign, its leaders did not think in terms of millions of bushels of wheat.'[37]

Such obvious advantages, reflecting organization of war-making capacity far beyond that of Rome's potential opponents, gave the Roman armies a psychological edge, a superiority in morale, often sufficient in itself to deter hostile military action. In the great days of the second century, with an army of about 300,000, the Romans defended an empire of some 50,000,000 people living in the Mediterranean basin.

In monetary terms as well the costs were low. A recent estimate puts the annual military budget of the Roman Empire in the second century at 450,000,000 to 500,000,000 sesterces.[38] Although there is no way in which ancient Roman coinage can be converted into its equivalent in modern US dollars, some idea of the amounts involved here can be derived from a few comparisons. Perhaps the most telling one is that there were *individual* Romans in the first century who had private fortunes of nearly this amount. In the first century BC Crassus had a private fortune of 200,000,000 sesterces, and Caesar and Pompey eventually probably had much more.[39] The wealthiest individuals in the United States today could not come close to supporting the US military for a year!

As late as the early third century the grand strategy adopted by Hadrian and modified gradually by his successors over the decades was still in force.[40] Legions were stationed in permanent fortresses around the frontiers. By the death of Septimius Severus (211) there were more legions than there had been earlier, thirty-three altogether, and they were openly more important in the Roman world: when

Septimius died the advice he gave to his sons – 'Work together, enrich the soldiers, and scorn everyone else' – reflected the prominence of the military in the Roman Empire.[41]

Septimius introduced one change that would have far-reaching effect. He significantly strengthened the garrison of Rome (which included the Praetorian Guard and other special units) by increasing it almost threefold, from 11,500 to 30,000. By doing so he anticipated the later acts of Gallienus and the reforms of Constantine, but to argue that Septimius used this force as a central reserve or as a mobile field army is to go beyond the evidence. He paid his troops more and permitted them to marry, forsaking the older ban, but otherwise made no major changes in the legions.[42]

The Roman imperial defensive system was based on a network of roads and other interior lines of communications (rivers and the sea) so that troops could be transferred from their base along the frontier to help protect a point in jeopardy.[43] It is usually assumed that the great flaw of the system was that it could not function when there were large-scale, simultaneous attacks on two points or more around the imperial frontiers.[44] Once invaders penetrated the frontier defences, the soft inner shell of the Empire was easy prey. Some historians have even talked about a 'Maginot-line mentality' in the Roman Empire.[45]

On the whole, this modern analysis is not persuasive. A war on two fronts is almost always a military catastrophe for any nation; to prepare for such an event militarily probably costs more, financially and politically, than it is worth. Governments traditionally rely on diplomacy (as an instrument of their grand strategy – which need not be entirely military) to avoid that problem. Generally the Roman Empire managed rather well on that score. Furthermore, it is not altogether clear what a central reserve might have done to improve Rome's military position around the Mediterranean. Military history actually shows that reserves, tactical and strategic, are not invariably the best use of manpower. It is sometimes much better to maximize strength by deploying almost all forces than to maintain a strategic or tactical reserve.

In the case of the Roman Empire how would a strategic reserve have helped? It is true that such a force (based centrally in northern Italy) might move faster to a trouble spot on the frontier than troops transferred from other frontier fortresses. But, as events in the third century proved, the advantage normally would have been only a matter of days and in most cases simply not critical.[46] If there were a war on two fronts, the central reserve, presumably deployed on only one of those fronts (or, alternatively, weakened by division) would be useless on the other. The most important consideration was for Rome's rulers to avoid war on two fronts. Furthermore there *was* a small central reserve in Italy, the garrison at Rome – or at least it could have been used as a central reserve. By the time of Septimius Severus it numbered thirty thousand, equal in manpower to about five legions. That was enough. As we shall see, the larger mobile field armies of the Late Empire were created at the expense of frontier defence.

More than anything else Roman grand strategy in the High Roman Empire was based on the tactical superiority of the Roman army against all potential foes. To that extent the famous walls and fortresses can be misleading. The army, not the walls or forts, defended the frontiers. Walls and forts could be useful to fall back upon when the fighting became too difficult or to provide an important form of psychological security for Rome's troops, in the manner of the famous marching camps, but they could not keep a determined foe out of the Empire. Only the army fighting in the field could hope to do that.[47]

Twentieth-century writers on the Roman army have been mainly concerned with the administrative, institutional, and social structure of Rome's military arm, from legionary quarters to pay and food, from the men in the ranks through NCOs and higher officers.[48] They have been somewhat less interested in the army on the battlefield. For that we must turn to nineteenth-century authors, particularly Ardant du Picq, author of a French military classic, whose insight into ancient battle was striking. Du Picq understood why Roman armies did so well in the field. While emphasizing 'the heart of man' in warfare, or what Marshall Foch called 'la force morale', du Picq knew that *esprit* came from tactical organization and training!

The determining factor, leaving aside generals of genius, and luck, is the quality of troops, that is, the organization that best assures their spirit, their reliability, their confidence, their unity. . . . We have seen that man will not really fight except under disciplinary pressure. . . . The purpose of discipline is to make men fight in spite of themselves. No army is worthy of the name without discipline. . . . Discipline cannot be secured or created in a day. It is an institution, a tradition.[49]

Du Picq clearly believed, and probably rightly, that the Roman tradition of military discipline combined with their system of tactical organization, was the most effective in the history of the world. The point is well illustrated by a speech put into the mouth of the Roman general and future emperor Titus by the first-century Jewish author, Josephus:

> Now these Jews, though they be very bold and great despisers of death, are but a disorderly body, and unskilful in war, and may rather be called a rout than an army; while I need say nothing of our skill and our good order; for this is the reason why we Romans alone are exercised for war in time of peace, that we may not think of number for number when we come to fight with our enemies; for what advantage should we reap by our continual sort of warfare, if we must still be equal in number to such as have not been used to war! Now it is not the multitude of men, though they be soldiers, that manage wars with success, but it is their bravery that does it, though they be but a few; for a few are easily set in battle array, and can easily assist one another, while over-numerous armies are more hurt by themselves than by their enemies.[50]

Romans normally fought in close order in waves of thin lines, avoiding the use of the so-called 'heavy battalions' such as the Greek phalanx.[51] The advantage of the Roman tactical system was that all available manpower could be brought into direct action along this line. There was no wastage at the rear of a deep formation. Furthermore Roman soldiers were not expected to fight to the death before being replaced by men from the rear. There was a regular rotation of fighting waves. Obviously such a system demanded good fighters throughout. In heavy battalions, weak troops can be put in the centre of the formation with good troops in front and rear (panic almost always starts in the rear). There was no place for weak troops in a Roman legion.

Although the efficient use of manpower in the Roman army was obviously important, the psychological advantages of such a system were enormous. Because Roman soldiers in the front of the line could expect to be reinforced in the course of fighting, they fought confidently, and knew in the depths of their souls that their comrades-in-arms to the rear would not leave them in the lurch. As a result, contrary to the usual rule in pre-modern military history, Romans inflicted heavy casualties even when they were defeated. Normally Romans did not run (which is when the heaviest casualties are taken). Against untrained troops, they simply could not be defeated, even when they were greatly outnumbered. Only when a Roman army was caught by surprise on unfavourable terrain did barbarians have a chance to win a tactical victory. It was this tremendous tactical superiority that made the Roman grand strategy of preclusive security a reasonable use of military manpower.

The strength of the Roman army is most clearly revealed in comparison with the tactical organization of the Germanic tribes, which seems to have been basically the same from the first century to the Visigoths, Vandals, Suebi and Alamanni in the fourth and fifth centuries. There may have been some slight differences between Germanic barbarians on the one hand and Huns or Alans on the other, particularly in cavalry tactics, and in the use of specialized weapons and armour, but on the whole there is a detectable sameness of organization – or lack of it – in all barbarian armies, at least in comparison with the refined drill and training of the Roman legions.

Ever since Caesar's campaigns in Gaul in the first century BC the Romans had been familiar with the advantages their training gave them against barbarian armies. Germanicus had told his legionaries that the Germans were so disorganized that they 'fled shamelessly and with no concern for their commanders'. Their traditional fighting formation the Romans called a *cuneus*, which literally means 'wedge' but seems in practice to have been an irregular group of warriors attacking in deep, loose formation with some at the front rushing ahead of the others, not in a genuine, ordered wedge formation, a boar's head (*caput porci*) formation.

Germanic barbarians were not trained to fight in a line, either in the first century or in the fifth. Delbrück was correct in saying that 'the deep column, the squared formation, was the original formation of the tactical body of the Germans', but to use such military terminology (which is unavoidable) implies more cohesion and organization than there was. In any event disciplined Roman lines normally out-flanked and enveloped the deep bands of attacking barbarian infantry, giving the Romans genuine tactical superiority under normal conditions.[52]

Grand strategy is an elusive concept. It includes more than the purely military, often involving politics, diplomacy, economics, and sometimes religion. Roman grand strategy of the second century was predicated on political stability – preclusive security requires the presence of the legions on the frontiers. Civil war and rebellion, especially when they became endemic, diverted legions from the frontiers to the interior, creating marvellous opportunities for enemies across the border. That is what happened in the third century.

From Chaos to a New Order

In the middle of the third century, when the system of succession broke down during the period of the Barracks emperors, the fabric of the Empire began to shred. As legion fought legion in internecine war, barbarians poured across the undefended frontiers.[53] Goths and Alamanni crossed the Danube, while Franks penetrated the defences of the Rhine, and Athens was sacked by Herulian attackers in 268. Saxons crossed the Channel into Britain. In the East the newly revived Sassanian Persian Empire, which toppled the last lethargic Arsacid Parthian king in 227, showed strength and aggressiveness at a time when Rome was drastically weakened, and the greatest threat of all, the war on two fronts, became a reality. One analyst (Luttwak) has suggested that the near collapse of central authority in the third century destroyed 'an entire conception of empire'.[54] Defence of 'remote frontiers' seemed much less important to the Barracks emperors than protection of the imperial regime. In the tragedy of this period the ideal of one united empire remained strong, but the reality of a fractured, sometimes defenceless, circle of civilization around the Mediterranean weighed heavily on men's minds.

From a military point of view two considerations stand out strongly: one was the abandonment of preclusive security in favour of an elastic system of defence, since emperors in Rome could not maintain large forces in frontier districts; the other, almost certainly a direct result of the former, was the appearance of a central large cavalry force – but not the mobile field army of the Late Empire (which was much larger and also included infantry).

In a situation in which the enemy can almost certainly pierce the defensive perimeter, defence-in-depth and 'elastic defence' are the two most likely military responses.[55] The idea of elastic defence is simply to seek out the enemy's attacking force and defeat it whenever possible. Such a system is elastic because it is not based on holding any specific positions or territory. But defence-in-depth permits limited retention of frontier territory in forts manned by small forces. Since many of the emperors of the third century did not control 'traditional' frontier territory, elastic defence was their only option. The ideal of preclusive security around the defensive perimeter of the old frontiers remained quite strong, but these were also times when confusion rather than grand strategy ruled supreme. 'Regional defence' under local rebels was a reasonably common feature of the period. Naturally in those troubled times, whenever an emperor had any choice in the matter at all, he preferred to have a strong military force nearby than scattered thinly along thousands of miles of frontiers.

A strong cavalry force was apparently deployed by the Emperor Gallienus (253–68) and his immediate successors though it may not have become a permanent feature of Roman defensive policy – it seems to have disappeared by the reign of Diocletian.[56] Gallienus based his newly mobilized cavalry at Milan for immediate strategic reasons – to guard against an invasion of Italy by Postumus, the rebel in Gaul. The emperor actually controlled so little of the Roman Empire that there is a sense in which Milan was a frontier outpost. To see his grand strategy as the deployment of a central army in support of a frontier system of defence-in-depth is a serious, though common, misunderstanding.

In fact, the Romans had always used cavalry, though their military strength usually rested on infantry. Scipio could not have defeated Hannibal at Zama in 202 BC without strong cavalry support, and in 48 BC at Pharsalus, Pompey the Great deployed several thousand horse against Caesar (to no avail). When it became clear, for whatever reason, that cavalry was tactically indispensable, the Romans turned to it, but never on a large scale except on an *ad hoc* basis (until the Late Empire). So it was with Gallienus, despite attempts by modern historians to read permanent policy into his actions.[57]

After Gallienus his successors began to restore the military strength of the central government in the Roman Empire, but it was a gradual process. Aurelian (270–5) was especially important in the reconsolidation of imperial power. It was he who suppressed Zenobia of Palmyra and regained control of the East. The princess graced the emperor's triumph in Rome, and her captivity justified Aurelian's claim to be 'Restorer of the World' (*Restitutor Orbis*). On the other hand Aurelian, probably wisely, permanently abandoned the province of Dacia (roughly modern Romania) on the northern side of the Danube and the so-called *Agri Decumates*, the area between the Rhine and Danube. Yet political instability continued to plague the Empire and threaten the general peace, and Aurelian was assassinated.

1   *Hadrian's Wall near Cawfields in Northumberland showing one of the famous mile forts.
Built in the second century* AD, *Hadrian's Wall is the most famous remnant of the
imperial grand strategy of preclusive security, though there were other walls with mile posts
elsewhere in the Empire.*

2   (Above) *The Aurelian Wall in Rome was built in* AD *272 as the Romans were beginning to recover from the darkest days of the mid-third century. It was twenty feet high and the battlements were even higher. Extending for twelve miles, the wall was designed for repelling attackers. It was repaired later by Honorius and by Valentinian III.*

3   (Above right) *These walls were built by the Emperor Theodosius II around 413 and are part of the defensive system of Constantinople. Barbarians were unable to penetrate Constantinople's walls, and they turned instead against the Roman Empire in the West.*

4   (Right) *In this detail from Trajan's Column, dedicated in* AD *113, barbarian Dacians are shown attacking a fortified Roman camp. Roman superiority over the barbarians in siege warfare was one of the Empire's greatest advantages.*

5   (Above) A famous chaotic battle scene on a sarcophagus found near Portonaccio. Dating from the reign of Marcus Aurelius, it shows a mounted Roman general in the thick of fighting, holding his sword high. Although it is an overcrowded composition, the details of armour and equipment are considered to be authentic.

7   A barbarian captive from a relief on the Arch of Diocletian, Rome, c.300.

6   (Left) A scene from the so-called Great Trajanic Frieze that was probably removed from the temple of the Divine Trajan and incorporated into the Arch of Constantine, AD 312. Trajan, whose appearance has been changed to make him resemble Constantine, is shown fighting on horseback in the Dacian War.

8   (Above left) This rock relief from
Bishapur shows the Roman Emperor
Valerian (253–60) kneeling in submission
before the Persian King, Shapur I. Valerian's
defeat and capture number among the most
humiliating military losses in Roman history.

10   (Above) The outer wall of Diocletian's
fortified palace at Split, near Salona in
modern Yugoslavia. Built around AD 300, the
palace had massive walls sixty feet high and
seven feet thick. It occupied an area of about
eight acres.

9   (Left) A Persian clibanarius, shown here
from a graffito at Dura-Europus on the
Euphrates, was a heavily armoured
cavalryman. Romans may have developed
their heavy cavalry (or cataphracts) from
ancient Near-Eastern models. A clibanus was
an oven for baking bread, and in the
Mesopotamian deserts the Persian
clibanarius must have been rather warm in
his scale or chain armour.

11 (Left) The Tetrarchs, Diocletian and his colleagues, c.300. A sculpture in porphyry at St Mark's in Venice. The statues reveal the intense, military spirit of the age of Diocletian, when order had been restored and the Empire reorganized. Much greater vigilance was required for the defence of the Empire than in the more relaxed days of the first and second centuries.

12 (Right) A medallion showing the people of London welcoming the Caesar Constantius, who had returned Britain to imperial rule after the revolt of Carausius (c.296). The legend reads 'Restorer of Eternal Light'. Under the tetrarchy of Diocletian the Roman Empire was again united.

When Diocletian came to power in 284, there was no particular reason to believe that he would be much different from his predecessors, the Barracks emperors. He had risen through the ranks to be a general of the army, and his seizure of the purple was no less violent than others had been. It is true that the Empire had become stronger since the darkest days of Gallienus, but emperors of the third century, as a rule, did not last very long. In that sense, perhaps the greatest contribution Diocletian made was to rule for over twenty years (284–305), the longest reign since the death of Antoninus Pius in the second century.

The Army of Diocletian

In politics, economics, religion and warfare, Diocletian's re-organization of the Empire was far-reaching. This is not the place to survey his entire achievement, but some comments about the political and administrative reforms are necessary as background to his defence policy.[58] Diocletian was able to restore the traditional frontiers (except for Dacia and the *Agri Decumates*) in a long series of campaigns on all fronts.[59] In order to do that it was necessary to appoint a colleague in the purple – another Augustus, Maximian – and the two of them eventually (293) took heirs-designate (Caesars), Galerius in the East and Constantius in the West, who were given their own districts to govern. The so-called tetrarchy, or government by four, proved stable as long as Diocletian, who held it together by the force of his strong personality, continued to rule.

In 293 Diocletian also reorganized the Empire administratively by creating many new provinces through the subdivision of the old ones.[60] He imposed a new level of administration in the creation of twelve imperial dioceses, each ruled over by a vicar, a deputy of one of the four Praetorian Prefects serving with the four rulers. This administrative rearrangement made defence of the Empire easier, since the emperor could no longer be tied down by attackers to only one part of the Empire. War on two fronts lost much of its sting. Furthermore the new provincial organization with its vastly increased bureaucracy made it easier to extract from Rome's reluctant subjects the taxes necessary to maintain the larger army required for defence of the old frontiers.

A much larger army it almost certainly was. One ancient source says that Diocletian quadrupled the size of the army, but no modern

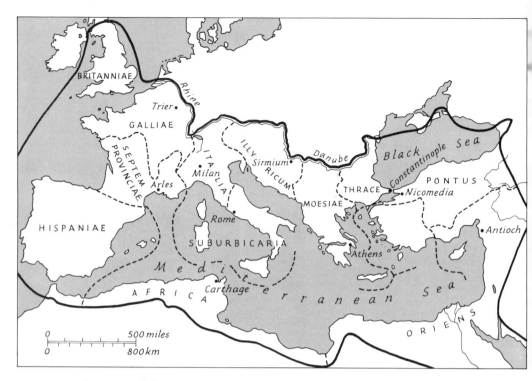

Dioceses of the Roman Empire in the fourth century.

scholar has been willing to accept such a statement. Estimates vary, and the exact size is in fact unknown, but it would probably not be far from the mark to assign to Diocletian and his associates an army of from 400,000 to 500,000.[61] That is significantly larger than the army of Septimius Severus (about 350,000), but in other respects Roman forces may not have changed a great deal. The legion probably still contained about 5000 men, and military tactics probably remained much as they had been before.

The most important change was the increasing importance of tactical variety in the skirmisher arms and in cavalry. Far more than had been the case in the Early Roman Empire we now find specialized units serving in the Roman army. Inscriptions attest the existence of highly regarded cavalry lancers (*Lanciarii*) and Companions (*Comites*). There were special shock troops, crack infantry divisions called the *Ioviani* and the *Herculiani*, who seem to have served in the personal following of the emperors. An imperial bodyguard appears, the *Protectores*, a corps of picked men who normally went on to higher commands. But there is no evidence of a *Feldheer*, a major, mobile striking force permanently maintained and centrally stationed.

42

As A. H. M. Jones wrote, 'In Diocletian's day, when an important expeditionary force was required, it was formed in the manner habitual in the second century by assembling detachments drawn from the frontier legions and auxiliary troops.'[62]

The cardinal feature of Diocletian's grand strategy is the return to firm frontiers and preclusive security.[63] His was not, however, the grand strategy of the second century. The more troubled conditions of the late third and early fourth centuries required a somewhat different approach to preclusive security. Diocletian reorganized the frontiers into four great military sectors, each under an Augustus or a Caesar, each with its own defensive and mobile units. The tetrarchs in Trier, Milan, Nicomedia and Sirmium in Pannonia offered much closer military supervision of the frontiers than emperors had done previously. Diocletian was a vigorous builder of roads and forts. Naturally, restoration of the frontiers came at great cost, and recruitment, especially, was a problem. There is no definite evidence that Diocletian introduced the practice (which can be clearly associated with Constantine) of requiring the sons of veterans to serve in the army. He did introduce a system of annual conscription in which recruits were levied from the cities in the same manner as the land tax, and large landowners had to give up men from their estates while smaller landowners were permitted to pool resources in order to provide a recruit. Later in the century the value of a recruit was set at thirty-six solidi, and that calculation made it possible for even the smallest landowners to pay a portion of the cost. There was, naturally, the corruption always associated with such conscription. Indeed the price paid by Roman society for the new, strong imperial defence may be compared with the cost to the Spartans of the creation of their famous army in the seventh century BC.

Constantine and his Sons

The big change in Roman grand strategy came with Constantine the Great.[64] As Zosimus claimed in the passage quoted above, Constantine organized a large mobile field army (probably 100,000 or more), stationed centrally, by withdrawing units from the frontiers, leaving them in a weakened condition.[65] Zosimus saw this modification of traditional Roman grand strategy as catastrophic, an interpretation endorsed by Gibbon:

43

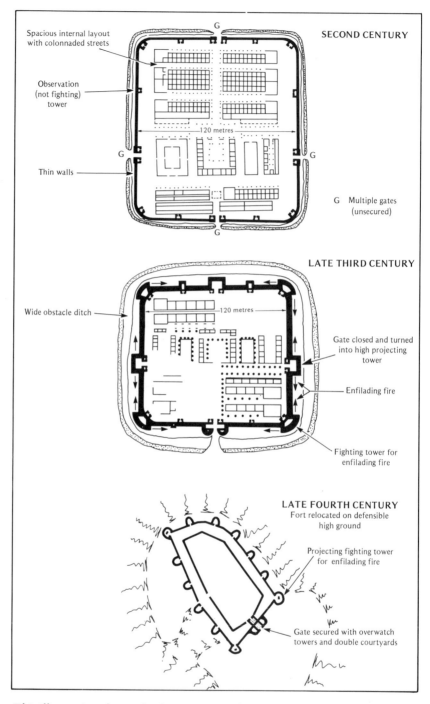

SECOND CENTURY

Spacious internal layout with colonnaded streets

Observation (not fighting) tower

120 metres

Thin walls

G   Multiple gates (unsecured)

G

LATE THIRD CENTURY

Wide obstacle ditch

120 metres

Gate closed and turned into high projecting tower

Enfilading fire

Fighting tower for enfilading fire

LATE FOURTH CENTURY
Fort relocated on defensible high ground

Projecting fighting tower for enfilading fire

Gate secured with overwatch towers and double courtyards

This illustration shows the deterioration of Rome's frontier troops from the second to the fourth century. In the second century the troops were not expected to fight from behind their fortress walls but to meet the enemy in the field. By the fourth century small bands of frontier garrisons (limitanei) tried to hold strongly fortified, hilltop positions.

The memory of Constantine has been deservedly censured for another innovation, which corrupted military discipline and prepared the ruin of the empire. . . . Though succeeding princes laboured to restore the strength and numbers of the frontier garrisons, the empire, till the last moment of its dissolution, continued to languish under the mortal wound which had been so rashly or so weakly inflicted by the hand of Constantine.[66]

As we saw earlier in this chapter, Mommsen and virtually all modern analysts since his time have ventured to overturn the judgment of antiquity and of Gibbon. According to them the strategy of preclusive security along firm frontiers was no longer valid (indeed, according to some, had always been flawed). Protection of the Empire in the trying times of the fourth and fifth centuries required a new grand strategy relying on a central mobile army and a system of defence-in-depth.[67]

Defence-in-depth is based on the assumption that the frontiers cannot be made impenetrable (at least not at a reasonable cost) and that attackers will inevitably succeed in piercing the defensive perimeters. Such invasions can be thwarted, however, by maintaining relatively strong forts in a fairly deep band along the frontiers and a mobile army (or several scattered regionally) within the Empire. The forts must be strong enough to withstand attack and yet not so strongly defended as to become a drain on manpower weakening the mobile army. Since barbarian invaders of the Roman period normally knew little about the techniques of siege warfare and could not place forts under blockade for fear of being caught by the mobile army, defence-in-depth was in some respects theoretically realistic.

During an invasion the forts served as pockets of resistance for storing food and fodder. Later, as the mobile army coordinated its efforts against the enemy with the small defending frontier forces, supplies could be denied to the invader while they were made available to the central reserve. When situated at strategic points such forts might also hold river crossings and passes thereby impeding the enemy's movements. From them it was easier to maintain intelligence operations, and in emergencies they offered temporary protection for the mobile army.

To what extent Constantine had thought all this out is debatable, but in practice, with some important exceptions (for example under Valentinian I), it is a fair reflection of what happened in the Late Empire, consciously or not. The question is whether it was wise insofar as it was policy. Here, as we have seen, modern historians have agreed with Constantine. There are two major reasons for the nineteenth- and twentieth-century enthusiasm for defence-in-depth. One of them is the belief that preclusive security is simply impossible over an extended period. As a grand strategy it has too many inherent faults. The other is that the maintenance of a central reserve is in keeping with modern military science and is therefore good. A common criticism of ancient generals is that they never learned the proper use of reserves – at least in the Late Empire on the strategic level there was finally an appropriate recognition of the importance of a mobile reserve.[68]

But are these reasons valid? They are certainly rarely questioned. If we examine them a little more closely, however, we may find that they are less compelling than is commonly assumed. Preclusive security around the frontiers of the Roman Empire in fact worked well from the time of Hadrian to the end of the Severan dynasty – over a century, with the exception of Marcus Aurelius' reign. War on two fronts was a potential problem, as we saw above, but not an impossible one even under Marcus Aurelius, and it is actually no less a problem in defence-in-depth than in preclusive security. It has been suggested that soldiers stationed on the far frontiers became enervated by the monotony of border patrol, but there is virtually no evidence that Roman armies of the Early Empire were so affected. The army of Septimius Severus was as effective as the army of Trajan. Furthermore, the difficulty of shifting troops from a central reserve to a trouble spot on the frontier was greater than most modern analysts assume. It would have taken more than sixty days to march troops from Rome to Cologne.

Indeed the criticisms that can be made against defence-in-depth are far more damning. Although the emperor might be comforted by the nearby presence of a mobile army, the inhabitants of the frontier provinces, through which invaders were expected to pour, understandably failed to appreciate his position. Obviously, the worst feature of defence-in-depth is that inevitably the central mobile army will become an élite force and the frontier defenders merely second-rate actors in defence policy. Troops that are not expected to defeat the enemy can hardly be blamed for wanting to avoid him altogether. Indeed as time went by, the frontier troops of the Roman Empire (the so-called *limitanei* and *ripenses*) became virtually worthless while the mobile army (*comitatenses*) was expected to do all the fighting. The result was that Rome's effective combatant manpower was drastically reduced, even though the overall army was larger than in the Early Empire. That is why battles of the Late Empire normally involved fewer men than those of the Late Republic.[69]

Ultimately the worst feature of the new grand strategy was that it undermined Roman infantry. Naturally in a mobile army the most mobile units, cavalry, will tend to be favoured. With the emergence of cavalry and the decline of infantry (precipitous along the frontiers) Rome's military position went into a tailspin, for, as we shall see, the great battles of the coming decades were decided by infantry. Traditional Roman infantry tactics, driven by harsh discipline and constant training, simply disappear.

The mobile army of Constantine was commanded by two Field Marshals, the commander of the infantry (*magister peditum*) and the commander of the cavalry (*magister equitum*). Ironically, although Constantine was the creator of the field army, there are few contemporary references to it, and most information comes from a later period. It consisted of some of the specialized units introduced by Diocletian (the *Lanciarii*, *Ioviani* and *Herculanii*) and a number of new ones enrolled by Constantine. Many were ethnic units from Gaul or across the Rhine. Constantine's fondness for German troops led to the charge that he had barbarized the army.[70]

Generally Constantine and his sons retained the reform launched by Diocletian which separated military command from civilian, and eliminated senators from the armies. The new provincial commanders – called *duces* (sing., *dux*) – sometimes commanded troops in more than one province, while in the dioceses a ranking general (*comes*) had jurisdiction over several *duces*. (Ironically in English a duke – from *dux* – outranks a count – from *comes*.) There is in fact little evidence that the separation of civilian and military authority led to greater efficiency in the army. Governors and generals were certainly less powerful than their predecessors in the Early Empire, and there were in some ways more opportunities for corruption, as generals resorted to various devices to extort money from the governors and financial officers. Politically, however, the advantage was that the new governors and generals, reduced in power, were much less likely to lead rebellions. Indeed it is difficult to escape the conclusion that Constantine's reforms were dictated by political perhaps more than by military considerations. Insofar as they rested on the earlier work of Diocletian it must be remembered that he shared imperial authority

(Above right) A Roman soldier at the beginning of the third century. This legionary still carries a rectangular, curved shield (scutum) although new flat oval shields were in use. He carries his sword on the left and still wears metal breastplate and helmet. His equipment is basically similar to that of the first-century legionary.

(Above left) A fourth-century Roman auxiliary with flat oval shield and boss in centre. He is wearing a leather helmet and carries a long sword. There is virtually no metal armour for protection.

with three other colleagues. What was intended to promote efficiency in the tetrarchy merely added to the emperor's already great authority in the autocracy of Constantine.

Constantine was responsible for other important reforms of the army. He reduced the size of a legion from about five thousand to one thousand fighting men. He disbanded the old Praetorian Guard since the new mobile army made it obsolete, and he maintained Diocletian's logistical system based on taxation in kind. That system provided for military pay in rations with occasional (but fairly regular) cash bonuses. Special imperial guards (called the *Scholae Palatinae*) consisting of élite cavalry regiments (five hundred strong), recruited mainly from Germans, served at Constantine's pleasure and replaced the disbanded Praetorian Guard.[71] The frontier troops (*limitanei* and *ripenses* – literally border and river guards) in the new, smaller legions, supported by modest cavalry contingents and commanded by a *dux*, may have served as a kind of regional police force in the somewhat wilder and more lawless conditions prevailing in the late-imperial frontier provinces. On the whole, under Constantine and his sons the mobile army fought with the spirit and discipline of the famous legions of bygone days, though politics and urban life eventually led to some decay. The *limitanei* probably went into immediate but gradual decline – the evidence for their tactical deployment is nearly non-existent.

A Roman cavalryman of the fourth century. He carries a round shield and wears metal armour and helmet. In the Late Empire, Roman cavalry was better armed and better trained than Roman infantry.

As tactics and military organization changed, so did weapons and armour. The famous *scutum* or rectangular shield of the second century had been replaced by the mid-third with an oval shield. Except for heavy cavalry (the so-called cataphracts) body armour was almost abandoned by the Roman army. While cavalry wore mail shirts and metal helmets, infantry had only leather caps. By the end of the fourth century weapons and weapons training had deteriorated drastically from earlier standards, undoubtedly because the new strategic role of the frontier troops gave them less significant responsibilities and did not demand as much of them tactically. The grand strategy of Constantine took a terrible toll in military efficiency and *esprit de corps*. The increasing centralization and militarization of the Roman Empire in the fourth century did not necessarily produce a better army.

A Roman cavalryman from the Arch of Galerius, Salonika, in the early fourth century. He is armoured and wearing a pointed, conical helmet influenced by a barbarian style that goes back at least as far as Trajan's Dacian Wars.

Chapter Three

Crises on the Frontiers in the Fourth Century

In the last half of the fourth century the mobile army of the East fought two great campaigns – one against Persia and the other against Germanic barbarians. The result in each case was humiliating defeat. Neither of the emperors involved, Julian and Valens, returned alive from their abortive efforts. In this chapter we shall examine these initial failures in the collapse of Rome's military might and analyze the impact they had on the Roman imperial army.

Following the chaos of civil war after Diocletian's abdication, Constantine abandoned the tetrarchy and returned to the dynastic principle: he was succeeded by his sons, Constantine II (337–40), Constans (337–50), and Constantius II (337–61). Ultimately Constantius II survived an intricate and brutal power struggle to emerge as sole emperor of the Roman world. As the legions became involved in political strife, barbarians overran the Rhine frontier, and Constantius, concerned about the problems there, sent his cousin Julian as Caesar to Gaul (355).[72]

Julian, later called 'the Apostate' because of his return to paganism, was an extraordinary success in the West. He reduced taxes, streamlined the bureaucracy, and defeated the barbarians in a famous battle at Strasbourg (357). Naturally this achievement generated tensions between the young, popular Caesar and his jealous, suspicious uncle, Constantius II. Finally, when the emperor became committed to a war with Persia in the East, Julian rebelled (360). Before Constantius could meet the rebel in the field, the eastern ruler died a natural death, and Julian became sole emperor (361).

Immediately he 'came out of the closet' and revealed himself as a pagan; his quaint effort to overthrow Christianity has always been the focus of attention on his reign. As we shall see, however, the new emperor's military policy was fundamentally more important to the fate of the Empire. The attempted restoration of paganism can be dismissed as an anachronistic impossibility and therefore of little genuine historical significance. The loss of parts of northern Mesopotamia was another matter.

Julian the Apostate in Persia

In the third century Rome's relations with the newly revived Persian Empire of the Sassanians had been hostile and tragic. Shapur I (240–72?) had defeated and captured the Emperor Valerian in 260, and Roman territory in northern Mesopotamia, conquered under Marcus Aurelius and Septimius Severus, was lost, apparently for ever. Diocletian, however, tipped the scales again in Rome's favour during his successful reign, and by the time the soldier-emperor abdicated in 305 Rome had organized new provinces in northern Mesopotamia. The great city of Nisibis served as a Roman thorn in the side of Persia, a bastion from which the Romans could dominate Armenia to the north and flank any attempt by Persia's kings in the east and south to threaten the imperial frontier.

For more than fifty years Rome maintained this strong position in the East, but in 359 Shapur II (309–79) attacked imperial territory and stormed Amida in Roman Mesopotamia. Constantius rushed to the area (360), but before the crisis was resolved, Julian rebelled in the West, and Constantius died. Naturally, the first main task Julian faced, after consolidating his power, was the problem of Persia. What happened in the war that followed had a tremendous impact on Roman power generally and on the morale of the Roman army. It was a precursor of the tragedy that befell Rome on the field at Adrianople in 378, only about fifteen years later.

In 362 Julian took up quarters in Antioch to supervise from that ancient eastern city – largely Christian – the preparations for the war against Persia. A vast army of some 65,000 men, consisting mainly of units from the mobile army reinforced to a certain extent by frontier troops, assembled in the East. Julian's pro-pagan policies had not been popular in Antioch, and both the city and the emperor were relieved when he finally set out for northern Mesopotamia in March of 363.[73]

The army had been drilled intensively, because Julian was not convinced that the troops of the East were as effective as his forces in the West had been. The necessary logistical support for an army of

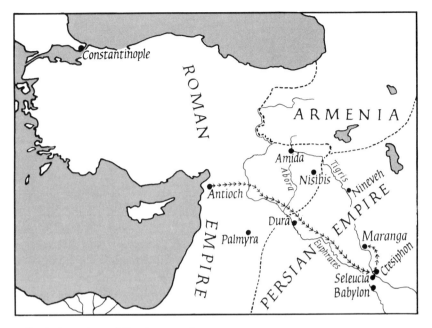

Julian's invasion of Persia, AD *363.*

that size was massive and can best be illustrated by an anecdote that says more, in its own way, than a statistical list of supplies might tell us. Shortly after crossing the Euphrates, cavalry grooms were getting fodder from a great depot where it had been stacked high. As they took what they needed (presumably from near the bottom of the stack), the pile collapsed and the crash killed fifty men.[74]

In this war against Persia Julian's strategy was to divide his army, leaving a force of 30,000 under the general Procopius in northern Mesopotamia with instructions to join with Rome's ally, the King of Armenia, and to guard the rear of the main Roman army as the emperor led it down the Euphrates towards the Persian capital, Ctesiphon. If Shapur tried to strike against Julian's advancing column, the two Roman armies in a combined operation could take him in a pincers movement. In the meantime, Procopius was to prevent Shapur from seizing the Roman base in Julian's rear. In the beginning Julian did everything he could to keep his plans secret from the Persians in order to achieve as much surprise as possible. To this end he feinted a move towards the Tigris before turning south down the Euphrates.

One eminent modern authority on this period has recently argued that Julian actually relied upon 'strategic surprise' against the Persians.[75] Surely this cannot be. Recent hostility between Rome and Persia plus the elaborate preparations of the Romans for the campaign made 'strategic surprise' impossible. Shapur knew that the Romans were coming. Of course he could not know exactly what they planned to do, but he had sufficient mobility to watch their every move, which is precisely what he did. In the end it was Julian who was taken off guard by a surprise strategy. The Roman emperor did what many of his predecessors had done before – darted down the Euphrates, supported by a fleet of more than a thousand ships, in a dash towards Ctesiphon. It was, of course, necessary to move from the Euphrates to the Tigris in Lower Mesopotamia.

Apparently Julian expected Shapur to advance with the Persian field army between the Romans and the capital. Presumably then, after defeating the Persian army in battle, Julian would take Ctesiphon. What happened is that Shapur refused to fight, though he harassed the Romans along the way, and, when Julian got to within one mile of the walls of Ctesiphon, the emperor had to halt his attack. The Roman army could not afford to get pinned down in a siege of the well-defended Ctesiphon while the Persians had freedom of movement in the field.

At this point Julian and his generals faced up to strategic failure and tried to decide how to extricate the Roman army. Although the situation was bleak, it was not hopeless. The army was intact and still strong. In the council of war that convened at this time the majority wanted to return back up the Euphrates as fast as possible, but Julian ruled that out. On the advance the Romans had stripped the Euphrates route of supplies and to go back by the same way was madness. Besides, the emperor added, there was no glory in it. The huge number of ships could not return upstream and was therefore destroyed simply to deny its use to the Persians.[76]

Instead Julian took his army, which had already crossed the Tigris towards Ctesiphon, and marched up the Tigris, hoping to dart into Persia proper to the east where he might find Shapur. Procopius presumably could reinforce the emperor although Julian had probably lost contact with his general. Unfortunately for the Romans, as they made their march, the Persians resorted to a scorched-earth policy and burnt everything in Julian's path.

Finally Shapur arrived with the main Persian army, but he refused to engage the Romans. Persian cavalry kept up a constant pressure but avoided Roman infantry and fell back whenever Roman cavalry sallied out to meet it. In such circumstances it is not surprising that the Roman army became demoralized and ridden with tension. The elephants used by the Persians heightened Roman fears. In much earlier times Roman infantrymen had faced elephants firmly, but in the fourth century they were again a new, fearsome force in warfare.

On 22 June 363, there was a battle a few miles from Maranga on the Tigris. To prevent envelopment Julian adopted a crescent formation and attacked his foe on the double (to thwart enemy missiles by closing fast). After costly, drawn-out fighting the Persians retreated, but the Persian army had not been destroyed, and tactical victory had merely weakened the Roman army further. Adrift in a distant land, Julian had lost the strategic initiative and was completely at the mercy of the Persians. Marching always on ready alert, the Romans were heading for Samarra when early on 26 June Julian learned that his rear was under attack. In a frightful hurry to help his men, the emperor dashed off without his breastplate and into the thick of the fighting. His appearance at a critical moment seems to have turned the tide of battle, and the Persians began to retreat, when suddenly, from out of nowhere, a flying spear brought Julian down. (To this day no one knows whether the assailant was a bitter Christian Roman or a Persian.) Later that night the emperor of Rome died in his tent – like Alexander, not yet thirty-three years old.

Age was perhaps the only characteristic Julian had in common with Alexander. As a strategist, although Julian had performed reasonably well along the Rhine, the emperor was incompetent in the much more sophisticated East. He divided his forces and seems to have lost contact with one half of his army. Whether he had a strategic plan at all as he advanced towards Ctesiphon is uncertain, but in any event he broke one of the fundamental rules of warfare by striking at the enemy's capital rather than his main force – a mistake Alexander had consciously avoided in the campaign against Darius III almost seven hundred years earlier.

The fault does not rest with the Roman army.[77] In the early 360s it was still quite capable of tactical victory on the field, and Shapur clearly respected its abilities. There had been a failure of leadership, of strategic conception, and in the end the cost was staggering. The new emperor, Jovian (363–4), a Christian, selected by the army from among the generals on the campaign, negotiated a humiliating and expensive settlement with the Persians. Rome abandoned part of northern Mesopotamia, including the great city of Nisibis. The pitiful inhabitants of the city watched helplessly as the flag of Rome was replaced by that of Persia. Although the 'real' cost in territory was enormous, the psychological price of defeat, as it spread through the population at large and the army in particular, was even greater.[78]

The Battle of Adrianople

After a reign of less than eight months the Emperor Jovian died (accidentally, of fumes from a bedside fire) before he reached Constantinople on the return from Persia. He was replaced by another general, Valentinian I (364–75), who stands out among the emperors of the Late Roman Empire as a man of remarkable ability though he was unlettered, boorish and occasionally violent.[79]

Immediately Valentinian realized the need for two emperors, partly because the soldiers actually demanded a co-ruler and partly because strategic pressures required it. His brother Valens (364–78), who was appointed to rule over the East from Constantinople, lacked Valentinian's vigour and ability – he was a mediocre man (at best) in a period that demanded more than mediocrity. The days were gone when the Roman Empire could survive the folly of a Nero or a Commodus (although Valens was not in their mould). If there was ever a time that cried out for great men, yet failed to produce them, it was the (late) fourth and fifth centuries. Valentinian in the West was by far the best of the lot.

The collapse of Roman power in northern Mesopotamia and the resultant blow to Rome's prestige led to a resurgence of hostile action along the northern frontiers of the Rhine and the Danube. Valentinian struggled heroically and with some effect to restore the integrity of those frontier regions against the attacks of barbarians while Valens spent most of his time in the East in usually fruitless attempts to restrain the growing power of Persia.

From his western capital at Trier in Gaul Valentinian fought the Alamanni on the Rhine, and supervised action against Picts and Scots near Hadrian's Wall and against raiding desert tribes in Africa. Through vigorous annual conscriptions the emperor maintained and probably increased the size of the army, but to keep up the numbers he reduced the minimum height requirement from five feet ten inches to five feet seven inches. In 375 when Valentinian shifted his attention to the Quadi and Sarmatians along the Danube, the emperor was so offended by the insolence of barbarian ambassadors that he died from a stroke in a fit of temper. His soldier's qualities had been the tonic the Empire needed after the fiasco of Julian and Jovian, and his efforts to restore strong frontiers were generally successful.

Earlier, in 367, Valentinian's eight-year-old son Gratian had been proclaimed co-emperor, and he had served, insofar as a mere youth served at all, with his father in the West. Upon the death of Valentinian, Gratian was sixteen, and he assumed the reins of government from Trier. In the meantime, however, troops on the Danube had proclaimed as western co-emperor the four-year-old Valentinian II, and to guarantee the support of the Danubian legions Gratian acquiesced in the choice of the child, his half-brother.

Tragically for the Empire its finest emperor-soldier since Diocletian and Constantine died on the brink of one of the greatest military crises in Roman history, perhaps in the history of the western world. In the very next year (376) began the chain of events that led to the battle of Adrianople and the triumph of Gothic over Roman arms. Whether events would have been different had Valentinian I restrained his anger in 375, no one today can say with certainty, but most historians agree that it was by far the weaker of the two imperial brothers – Valens – who survived to face the Visigoths.

As background to the story of Adrianople and to the barbarian invasions that followed, we must briefly examine the Germanic nations that threatened Rome's northern frontiers. Except for the Alans and the Huns, who came from Central Asia, Rome's barbarian enemies were 'Germanic', but the word covers a wide range of people north of the Rhine–Danube line from the North Sea to the Black Sea. They were by no means monolithic in culture, and those living on the North Sea coast – the Saxons, Jutes and Danes – spoke languages completely unintelligible to the Goths on the Danube, probably even to one another. Naturally, the economic structures of the western coastal tribes differed drastically from those of central, forested Germany and from the plains tribes north of the Danube and the Black Sea.

Although the linguistic classifications are controversial, scholars frequently divide the fourth- and fifth-century Germans into three broad groups – the North, East and West Germanic dialects, corresponding geographically roughly to the three different regions mentioned above. In the North Germanic group one finds Old Norse and its derivatives. The East Germanic dialects include Gothic, and the languages of the Burgundians and Vandals appear to have been closely related. Angles, Saxons, Franks, Alamanni and Frisians spoke West-German dialects. If it was rare for Germanic tribes to know one another's languages, it is nevertheless likely that Vandals spoke almost the same language as the Goths.

Romans had had some contact with the Germans at least as early as the second century BC, and the works of Caesar and Tacitus from a later period show an increasing Roman awareness of Germanic culture. In the third century AD, as we have seen, there were important Germanic invasions of the Empire, but the invaders had ultimately been beaten back or assimilated. In the last half of the fourth century, before the coming of the Huns, the Ostrogoths (literally, East Goths) inhabited the area of southern Russia north of the Black Sea. Possibly they had come originally from Scandinavia, as the sixth-century Gothic historian, Jordanes, claimed, but that is not certain. Next to them, north of the Danube in the former Roman province of Dacia, lived the Visigoths (the West Goths). The Goths had subjugated other tribes, such as the Skiri, a tribe that later produced Odovacer, who toppled the last Roman emperor in the West in 476. The Goths generally lived a rough, village, semi-agricultural existence in which hunting and food gathering were also important. The material level of their civilization was not high, and they had been economically and politically less influenced by their civilized Roman neighbours than is sometimes assumed.

In religion, however, Barbarian and Roman came to share a common faith – Christianity – though the Germans were Arian heretics. Arius (died 336), a priest in Alexandria, had preached the doctrine that Christ, as the Son of God, was not truly God. Though the details of his theology remain uncertain, undoubtedly Arius emphasized the human nature of Christ and the importance of Christ's sacrifice for man. In any event, he attracted a large following in the Eastern Roman Empire, and in AD 325 the Emperor Constantine assembled the bishops in the first ecumenical council at Nicaea where they rejected Arianism and affirmed in the Nicene Creed that Christ was truly God. Arians were excommunicated, anathematized, and banished from the Roman Empire.

One of the Arians, Ulfilas (*c.* 311–83), converted the Goths and translated the scriptures into Gothic, thereby turning the barbarian tongue into a literary language. The conversion of the Goths to Christianity before the invasions, albeit in an heretical Arian form, was an act of great significance. From the Goths Christianity spread to other barbarian tribes such as Vandals, but not to all of them. The Angles and Saxons, for example, remained Germanic heathens until long after their invasion of the British Isles. Still, many of the barbarians who invaded the Roman Empire were Christians, and the shared religion ameliorated, to a certain extent, the impact of Rome's fall.

To continue the survey of Rome's northern frontier, Vandals, Burgundians, Suebi and Alamanni threatened the Upper Danube and the Upper Rhine while Franks were on the lower Rhine, and Angles, Saxons, Jutes, and Danes faced Britain across the North Sea. This then was the 'line-up' of barbarian nations as the first act in the age of invasions began, and the Romans prepared to face the Visigoths at Adrianople.

Although the story of the battle is relatively well known, some elements of it are controversial, and in any event it bears retelling.[80] The fearsome Huns from the Asiatic steppes of South Russia, riding on their fat-headed, peculiar-looking plains horses, swept down on the Ostrogoths living north and east of the Black Sea.[81] In one of the few genuine examples of 'billiard-ball history' this set in motion a chain reaction as the Ostrogoths fled in panic westward against the Visigoths who were driven hard against Rome's Danubian frontier. Two Visigothic chieftains, Fritigern and Alavivus, sought Valens' permission to settle in the Empire, and on condition that the Visigoths give up their arms the emperor agreed to let them cross the border. Valens hoped that they would farm deserted land in Thrace and expected to recruit heavily from them for the imperial army.

Late in 376 the river crossing began. The Visigoths, perhaps 200,000 strong, were starving, and insensitive, grasping Roman officials exploited them unmercifully.[82] To avoid starvation the Visigoths traded their children into Roman slavery for dog's meat at the rate of one child per dog. There were other stories of rape and robbery by Roman officials, one of the sorriest chapters in the long history of governmental exploitation. Possibly the truth is less dramatic than the legend. Surely some Romans tried to alleviate the distress of the Goths, but clearly the crossing of the Danube was badly mishandled.

In the meantime some Ostrogoths, who did not have permission to cross the river, did so anyway, and to add to the confusion the Roman Field Marshal of Thrace, Lupicinus, killed some of the followers of Fritigern and Alavivus during a truce with the Visigoths. This was more than the barbarians could bear, and they began to ravage the area and then to gather in the general vicinity of Adrianople where they had been resisted and denied food by the local authorities. Vainly the Goths tried to storm the walls of the city until Fritigern returned them to the plunder of the countryside, 'reminding them that he kept peace with walls', a reasonable policy for a warrior with no capacity for siege warfare.[83]

In Antioch the Emperor Valens decided that the problem required his imperial presence, and after sending up troops to Constantinople, he arrived there himself on 30 May 378. Earlier Gratian had despatched troops from the West, and in 376 and 377 the Romans had conducted a desultory campaign in which they won and lost some battles and skirmishes but generally succeeded in their strategy of sealing the Visigoths into Thrace, thereby protecting Moesia and Macedonia.

The Goths are sometimes assumed to have been a mounted, nomadic people, but in fact they are unlikely to have had many horses. That there were some is certain, but Ammianus' account of the skirmishes leading up to the battle of Adrianople suggests that for the most part Gothic warriors fought on foot as infantry. To the extent that Fritigern deployed cavalry, it was a small force used mainly for scouting, skirmishing, and, presumably, pursuit. The old view that Adrianople was a 'medieval' battle involving large numbers of cavalry is simply not sound. Indeed, one recent authority has said categorically that the Gothic victory 'was essentially infantry over infantry'.[84]

Valens moved out of Constantinople in the summer of 378 and headed for Adrianople where he stopped to wait for the arrival of the slow-moving Western emperor, Gratian. There were reports that only ten thousand Goths were under arms, and though Gratian was at last

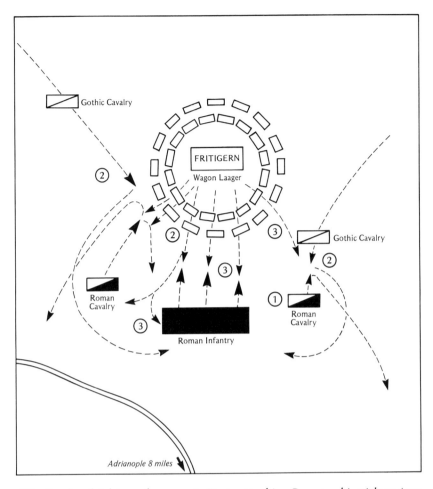

The Battle of Adrianople, AD 378. First, attacking Roman skirmishers (not shown) were thrown back in confusion against the Roman line of battle, which was not yet firmly placed. 1 Roman cavalry on the right tries to protect the line while the legions deploy. 2 Visigoths counterattack from the laager as their cavalry arrives and drives Roman cavalry from the field. 3 Visigothic cavalry and infantry turn the Roman left and encircle the Roman centre and right. Roman losses were heavy, and the Emperor Valens died in the fighting or shortly thereafter.

nearby, Valens decided to attack immediately and win all the glory for himself. Thus it came to pass that one of the world's most decisive battles was fought by a Roman emperor driven by jealousy into a hasty and precipitous assault.[85] Our sources agree that the day, 9 August 378, was a 'scorcher', and from the descriptions it sounds as if the temperatures must have been near 100°F, as they often are in August in the same vicinity to this day.[86]

In this terrible heat Valens led his army of nearly sixty thousand in line of column over uneven terrain with cavalry in front and rear. Around two in the afternoon, before the Roman forces had eaten their midday meal, they were as surprised as the Goths when the two armies began to come together. The Roman army had not yet deployed from line of column into line of battle. Such a failure of military intelligence on the part of the Roman army is nearly incredible, but it seems to have occurred, perhaps through overconfidence on Valens' part.

The Visigoths had formed their wagons into the traditional circular laager (a 'perfect' circle according to Ammianus), and Fritigern, caught equally by surprise, sent out a call for his mounted Ostrogothic and Alan allies who were probably foraging nearby.[87] Both sides began negotiations to gain time for the proper deployment of their forces, but it was not long before fighting began. The leading contingent of Roman cavalry moved over to take a place on the right wing while the infantry straggled behind, eventually to form the centre of the line. With difficulty the cavalry in the rear had to charge ahead, somewhat in disarray, to its position on the left. Before the Romans, suffering from heat and thirst, had actually drawn up their line, the Goths set fire to the grasslands around their enemy to intensify Roman discomfort.

Unfortunately at this point Roman skirmishers – archers and cavalry from crack units belonging to the emperor's bodyguard – made a classic mistake.[88] It is the role of skirmishers to engage the enemy at a distance with intermediate or long-range weapons at the outset of battle. Effective skirmisher fire can have a devastating impact on the enemy especially when it is directed against officers.[89] But skirmishers must be careful not to become engaged with the foe. They are not trained to fight in formation (except sometimes as very small teams), or to hold a line. As the two main forces come into contact, skirmishers must fall back to the sides or the rear of their own army and get out of the way. Furthermore, if regular troops advance against them in force, the skirmishers must retreat into the protection of their line. As a general rule they cannot hold their ground and are not supposed to.

Professional military historians have long known that fear on the field drives men to peculiar actions. One overwhelming instinct before battle is the desire to start fighting, to get it over with. Generals have resorted to many devices to control this instinct for premature attack ('Don't shoot until you see the whites of their eyes'), but it is not easy under the best of circumstances. In the heat and confusion at Adrianople, Roman commando-like skirmishers moved against the Visigoths and with so much spirit that, before the Romans realized what was happening, they had committed themselves too strongly. In such a situation there is only one possible result – panic, complete and irredeemable. The Visigoths' counterattack threw the Roman skirmishers in disorder back against their own line, and it was at this point, so fortuitous for the Visigoths, that their cavalry returned to the laager and proceeded immediately to charge, 'as a thunderbolt near the mountains', against the Romans.[90]

In the face of this assault, surprised equally by their own fleeing skirmishers and the Gothic cavalry, the Roman line yielded, but Roman discipline was too strong to give way so easily. The troops rallied, and outside the laager raged a violent battle, according to Ammianus, swaying back and forth like the 'waves of the sea'. On the left Roman cavalry advanced too far, creating a gap between cavalry and infantry that Fritigern's troops penetrated. This permitted encirclement of the Roman cavalry and a subsequent attack against the left wing of Roman infantry, drawing Roman foot-soldiers together in a confused mass so tightly compacted that they could not use their weapons properly.

Noise and dust were a greater problem for the Romans than for the Visigoths, because the laager served as a focal point for the Germanic warriors in the chaotic conditions. Fritigern had turned the Roman left, and his troops poured around to hit their enemy in the rear in a hammer-like attack, pounding the Romans against the anvil of the Gothic troops and laager. The Roman right apparently held out longer against attack, but it was eventually pressed by the troops in the Roman centre and the attacking Gothic left into a tight ball – an inviting target for Gothic archers. Valens, trapped in his own army, was temporarily protected by a body of crack troops. At the darkest moment of the battle one of the ranking Roman generals tried to bring in the Batavian reserves only to find that they had run away. All was lost, and all that remained was the killing. Perhaps as many as two-thirds of the Roman army perished (or were captured) in the fighting.[91] Piles of fallen warriors and horses impeded Roman attempts at flight. Finally a moonless night engulfed the battlefield and brought an end to the bloody tragedy. Not since Cannae in the war against Hannibal had a Roman army been so badly beaten.

The Emperor Valens' body was never found, and there were two versions of his death. According to one story, he was felled by an arrow and perished with the masses of his men, lost in the heap. Another tradition held that Valens was carried wounded by a few retainers to a nearby cottage, later surrounded by Goths who did not know that the emperor of Rome was inside. When they were unable to break down the doors and were shot at by archers from within, the Goths fired the house which inadvertently became Valens' funeral pyre. Thus ended in some uncertainty the reign of an emperor whom Ammianus described as 'equally ignorant of war and literature'.[92]

In the aftermath of Gothic victory Fritigern marched on the following day to Adrianople where Valens had left the war treasury, equipment and supplies. Jammed with fugitives from the Roman army the city remarkably found the resolve to resist. Firing catapults and other weapons from their walls, glutted with the supplies of the imperial army, the citizens of Adrianople forced the Goths to abandon direct assault in favour of ruse. Some Roman captives taken by the Gothic army agreed to cooperate with Fritigern's force and to flee from the attacking army towards the gates of the city in feigned escape. Once inside, they volunteered to set fire to the city. For whatever reason, however, they were kept under arrest after their entry, and the plot failed.

After another abortive assault the Goths withdrew and marched on Constantinople. Lacking a fleet they had no chance at all to take the strongly fortified city, and they were easily repulsed in some disorder and confusion. The Visigothic deficiency in siege warfare, typical of all Rome's barbarian invaders, limited the strategic effect of tactical victory over Roman forces in the field. In the next few years the Visigoths, rampaging at will within the Balkans, concentrated on plunder and booty.

The Effect of Defeat on the Roman Army

In the following chapter we shall take up the story of the military recovery of the Roman Empire in the aftermath of Adrianople. First, though, we must have a closer look at the military machine that suffered, in the space of only about fifteen years, two devastating defeats – in Persia under Julian and at Adrianople under Valens. In both cases the army was led by the emperor in person, and in both cases the surviving Roman soldiers, in humiliating circumstances, saw their emperor fall mortally wounded on the field of battle.[93] It is reasonable to assume that the psychological impact on Roman morale of two such catastrophic losses so close together must have been demoralizing.

Although the American military establishment of today knows something of the impact of defeat on morale, as a result of the experience in Vietnam, that experience pales in comparison with the rout of Roman arms in 363 and in 378. In the twentieth century only the German army has suffered a similar fate. Yet, surprisingly, despite the disappointing loss in World War I, the German army recovered, and its morale remained very high until early 1945 when defeat in World War II had become a certainty.[94] One prominent authority has claimed that the two best armies in all military history were the German army in World War I and the German army in World War II.[95] The way those armies coped with defeat is merely a reflection of their greatness. (Obviously, the justice of German war aims is not the issue here.)

To a certain extent, although it cannot in many ways be compared with modern German armies, the Roman army in the last half of the fourth century proved remarkably strong. As we shall see, it did make at least a partial recovery under Theodosius the Great to offer, for a while, reasonable protection for the Empire. Despite the vast changes introduced in the early fourth century by Constantine, and the unfortunate effect of his strategy of defence-in-depth, the fighting quality of Rome's fourth-century army was high. The defeats it suffered in Persia and at Adrianople were the result of a failure in leadership, not a lack of training, discipline or *esprit*. Significantly, at Adrianople the army stood its ground and fought. It was still fighting when the sun set over the countryside. Most defeated armies run. In Persia the Roman army was not actually beaten tactically in any major engagement. Foolish strategy and the untimely death of Julian combined to force it out of Mesopotamia.

Still, the defeats were costly. At least twenty thousand new troops had to be found for the mobile army after Adrianople, and replacements made in haste on such a scale simply cannot take the place of seasoned veterans.[96] The army remained much the same as it had been in the days of Constantine, at least in its general organization and in the grand strategy it pursued, but some signs of deterioration begin to appear after Adrianople, partly because of the effect of defeat, partly because Constantine's system was flawed.

Nevertheless Constantine's military reorganization of the Empire resulted in a more flexible army than many scholars have realized.[97] The most obvious change was that, since there were often multiple emperors at any one time, there was usually more than one mobile army. It follows that there was a substantial duplication of major military commands. In short, there were many generals, far more than in the days before Constantine and significantly more than the great emperor himself had intended. Both Julian and Valens would certainly have commanded larger armies if there had not been essentially separate military commands in the West. To a certain extent they could draw on the western armies, but there were administrative limitations that could have effects going beyond purely military considerations.

Constantine had created the ranks of Field Marshal of the Infantry (*magister peditum*) and Field Marshal of the Cavalry (*magister equitum*). Under Constantius II we find a single officer, Field Marshal of the Infantry and Cavalry for the Orient (*magister equitum et peditum per Orientum*). Here we have an increase in rank combined with a restriction of the area of command. Similar examples abound. By the end of the fourth century there were Field Marshals of Illyricum, Gaul and Thrace in addition to the Orient. Sometimes the emperors allowed these posts to go vacant for months or even years; at least once the Field Marshal of the Orient was transferred to Gaul only to serve alongside the newly appointed Field Marshal of Gaul (in what capacity remains a mystery).[98]

Much of this apparent fluctuation was caused by political rather than military considerations. The great generals were potential rivals for the throne, and emperors were naturally jealous and sought to restrict military authority. Strangely this may have led to an improvement, though unintended, in Roman grand strategy. Insofar as the tendency after Constantine was to restrict geographically the authority of the great marshals (and this was intensified by the frequency of multiple emperorships), the result was to create several mobile armies throughout the Empire. Militarily this meant that smaller mobile armies were able to respond much faster to problems on the frontier. The army that Julian led to victory at Strasbourg on the Rhine in 357 was only thirteen thousand strong.

On the other hand the dispersion of mobile field armies throughout the Empire made it much more difficult, militarily and politically, to mobilize a grand army for an extraordinary campaign. When Constantius attempted to bring the army of Gaul east against Persia, the troops rebelled and proclaimed Julian emperor. Julian's promise not to use them in Mesopotamia obviously reduced the strategic force he could bring to bear against Persia. Likewise, Valens' jealousy made it impossible for him to wait for assistance from Gratian though it was near at hand.

Other changes characterize the army of the last half of the fourth century. The palace guards (*scholae palatinae*) created by Constantine were naturally crack units, and, instead of being used simply to protect the emperor, by the time of Adrianople they served as shock troops at decisive points in battle. On another front, as the mobile armies operated in closer conjunction with the frontier troops (*limitanei*) the distinctions between *comitatenses* and *limitanei* began to break down. *Limitanei* were used in the great armies of Julian and Valens, and *comitatenses* occasionally did frontier duty.[99] This departure from the policy of Constantine was probably militarily sound – though there is no reason to assume that it reflected conscious change in imperial grand strategy – but, unfortunately for Rome, it was not the wave of the future. In the fifth century frontier troops were separated more than ever from the mobile armies and rapidly deteriorated.

On balance, then, in the fourth century it is fair to say that Diocletian restored Roman military strength. Constantine retained that strength but reorganized the Roman army and adopted a new grand strategy (defence-in-depth) leading ultimately to an unfortunate distinction between the central mobile army and the frontier forces. Still, the Roman army and Empire remained strong. Foolish mistakes led to serious defeats in Persia (363) and at Adrianople (378), but these were not the result of tactical weaknesses in the Roman army. Potentially, as Rome entered the 380s and 390s, there was a military basis for recovery. The Roman army, recently battered and beaten, might yet regain its ancient strength.

Chapter Four

Theodosius the Great
AD 378–395

After Adrianople the Western Emperor Gratian named the Spanish general Theodosius (born *c.* 346) as Augustus in the East. The formal ceremony was celebrated on 19 January 379. Theodosius eventually became known as 'the Great' mainly because of his Christian piety rather than his secular achievement. He was the son of a famous general of the same name, a man who had served as Count (*Comes Rei Militaris*) and as Master of the Cavalry in Britain (367) under Valentinian I and who smashed a revolt in Africa (373–5). Then he was executed for treason in circumstances that suggest he may not have been guilty.[100] In any event the statesmanlike decision of Gratian to elevate to the purple the competent son of a convicted traitor was of great significance in Roman history. Ultimately the dynasty of Theodosius presided over the dismemberment of the Roman Empire in the West.

The Reunification of the Empire

At the accession of Theodosius the most pressing problem was the Gothic threat and the urgent need to rebuild the army in the face of it. Rigorous conscription was enforced. Valentinian I had ordered 'draft dodgers' who cut off their own thumbs to escape service in the army to be burnt alive. Theodosius, who needed all available manpower, made them serve without thumbs but stipulated that any group sending such recruits for service had to send two for every one recruit demanded.[101] The new emperor also enrolled barbarians in the army.

During the next several years, from 379 to 382, Theodosius and his generals tried to hunt down and defeat barbarian forces that had divided into several groups and scattered throughout the Balkans.

Finally, in the autumn of 382, the emperor agreed to terms with the Visigoths that set the standard for barbarian settlement in the Empire for the next hundred years, until the fall of Rome in the West. In the words of A. H. M. Jones, 'The settlement was, in fact, a grave breach with precedent'.[102] Essentially Theodosius and Gratian agreed to allow the Visigoths to settle in Moesia in the northern Thracian diocese along the Danube, and the native inhabitants of the region, insofar as it was still inhabited, were probably required to provide food, clothing and housing for them. In return the Visgoths promised to fight for the emperor as allies (*foederati*) of the Roman Empire.

The so-called 'federate' status of barbarians within the Empire eventually became a device for carving up the Empire, and this settlement was controversial even under Theodosius. The important point is that the Visigoths were recognized by the treaty as an independent people under their own rulers and were allowed to retain their arms. This 'federate' relationship should not be confused with the treaties made by the United States government with 'sovereign' Indian tribes in the nineteenth century. There were certainly some technological differences between the Romans and the Visigoths (for example, siege machinery) but they were not as great as those separating the white man from the Indian in the American West. Furthermore Roman citizens generally were disarmed, and the presence of armed barbarians in the Empire not even under the control of a 'Visigothic agent' sent out by the central government made them quite unlike the later American Indians. They were not even required to stay on their 'reservation'. Their numbers were relatively large: in 394 there were twenty thousand Visigoths in Theodosius' army. It is unlikely that the Visigoths paid taxes to Rome or subjected themselves to Roman civil and criminal law. In the end this legal barbarian penetration was never repulsed.

In the following year, 383, the famous rhetorician Themistius, tutor to Theodosius' son, Arcadius, gave a speech honouring the emperor for the Gothic policy:

After that terrible Iliad of ours by the Danube [the crossing of the Visigoths], fire and sword were carried wide over Thrace and Illyricum; our armies vanished like a shadow: no Emperor presided over the State, and no mountains seemed high enough, no rivers deep enough, to prevent the barbarians from swarming over them to our ruin. Then . . . Theodosius . . . first dared to note this fact, that the strength of the Romans now lies not in iron, not in breastplates and shields, not in countless masses of men, but in

Reason . . . Do you complain that their race has not been exterminated? . . . Still, I say, which of the two is better, that Thrace should be filled with corpses or with cultivators of the fields; that we should walk through ghastly desolation or through well-tilled grain-lands?[103]

The speech reveals controversy and dissent. Not all Romans believed that the pacific policy of Theodosius was the wisest way to defend the Empire. Some simply wanted the barbarians expelled, and indeed, it proved impossible to control them with 'Reason'. Another contemporary of the period, the Bishop Synesius of Ptolemais (*c.* 365/375–415), in his *de Regno* (14–15), later respectfully attacked the emperor's strategy and saw it merely as a reflection of weakness.[104]

It is difficult today, however, to judge whether Theodosius the Great might have dealt more successfully with the Visigoths. The Roman army, recovering from the defeat in Persia, had suffered a shattering blow at Adrianople; the military rebuilding programme launched by the emperor required time for recruitment and training but mainly for the infusion of a new spirit to overcome the demoralizing depression of defeat. Furthermore, Theodosius could not have known that future barbarian invaders would use 'federate' status as a way of taking over vast stretches of the Western Roman Empire. In any event, he probably had no choice under the circumstances. Had he been another Valentinian I, or better, a truly inspirational leader of men, such as Alexander or Caesar, he might have marshalled Roman strength and driven the barbarians from the Empire. But he was not, and the emperor who yielded to Ambrose, the Bishop of Milan, could hardly have held his ground against the Visigoths. It was as much a question of personality as of policy. The consequences, however, were drastic.

At about the same time (probably 384–7) the emperor also tried through negotiations to secure the eastern frontier against Persian aggression. The accession of a new Persian king, Shapur III (383–8), made diplomacy possible. The two powers agreed to partition Armenia under terms that gave by far the larger share of the country (about four fifths) to a king nominated by Persia while some of the former territory of Armenia was annexed outright by both Rome and Persia. This settlement with the Persians in the East was generally more successful than the one with the barbarians on the Danube, partly because the Persians were more inclined to keep their word once having given it.[105]

In the end internal strife proved a greater problem for Theodosius than pressures on the frontiers. His relationship with the literate, virtuous but impolitic Gratian in the West remained good, but in 383 Gratian's soldiers, angered by his preference for barbarian Alans, killed him and supported Magnus Maximus, Count in Britain (*Comes Britanniarum*). Maximus rapidly gained control of Gaul and Spain as well as Britain while the rest of the West – Africa, Italy and Pannonia – remained loyal to Valentinian II, the child emperor who in 383 was still only thirteen and under the domination of his mother Justina. Theodosius, who had negotiated settlements with the Goths and the Persians, found it consistent to acquiesce in the usurpation of Maximus and to recognize him as an Augustus.

Then, in 387, Maximus marched into Italy to seize the ancient seat of Roman power from Valentinian II. The young emperor and his mother sought and received the protection of Theodosius, who invaded Italy and defeated and killed Maximus at Aquileia. Valentinian was sent to Gaul while Theodosius stayed on in Italy for the next three years. (It was at this time that Ambrose, Bishop of Milan, forced the emperor to surrender and repentance after attacking him from the pulpit on several points of disagreement.)[106] When the elder emperor returned to Constantinople in 391, Valentinian reacquired Italy and Illyricum. The next year, at Vienna in southern Gaul, Valentinian quarreled with his Field Marshal, Arbogast, a zealous pagan and a Frank by birth, who killed the young emperor and elevated a certain Eugenius, a pagan rhetorician, to the purple.

In the East Theodosius could not tolerate this attack upon Christianity and the House of Valentinian I since he was much too attached to both. Inevitably, in 394 he brought his army west again to face the pagan team of Eugenius and Arbogast at the Frigid River (the ancient Frigidus, the modern Vipava in Yugoslav Slovenia near the border with Italy). Fighting began on 5 September in a low Alpine pass some thirty-five miles from Aquileia at the head of the Adriatic. Surprisingly, this battle is not as well known as it ought to be. The armies were large (more than 100,000 on each side), and the clash was the last between the armed forces of Roman paganism and Roman Christianity.[107]

The Field Marshal Arbogast was a formidable foe.[108] He had been a Count (*Comes Rei Militaris*) for about eight years (since 380, originally under Gratian) before he simply assumed the position of

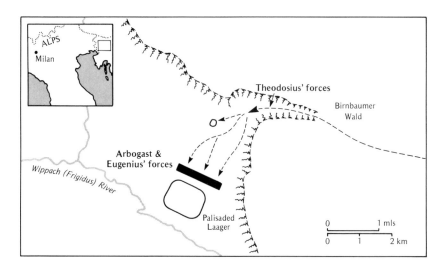

The Battle of the Frigid River (AD 394). On the first day of the battle Theodosius' Visigothic allies came down the mountain pass in line of column against the army of Arbogast and Eugenius, which was strongly protected behind laager and palisade. Of the 20,000 Visigoths, 10,000 lay dead at the end of the day. Next morning Theodosius' army defeated the enemy with the help of a cyclonic wind, the 'Bora'.

Field Marshal of the Army (*Magister Militum*) under Valentinian II around 388. He was popular with his troops and had served in the war against Maximus. His domination of Valentinian II had been so complete that, when the emperor attempted to dismiss him, the great Marshal said, 'I did not get my command from you, and you cannot take it away'.[109] Whereupon he threw down the letter of dismissal and walked out, subsequently murdering Valentinian, as we have seen.

With his puppet Eugenius the pagan Arbogast held a commanding place in Italy. As Theodosius approached Aquileia he found that Arbogast had taken a strong defensive position outside the city on the road from Sirmium across the Julian Alps. Although Theodosius had apparently moved west more rapidly than expected and as a result had secured strategic surprise by taking the pass, the troops of the West had built a large palisade, or laager, with high towers to serve as a base along the Frigidus. They had seized other critical highpoints in the vicinity, so Theodosius had little alternative but to drive headlong against Arbogast's army which was in battle order outside the palisade. There was no room for flanking movements and a combat of manoeuvre. The battle of the Frigid River was a 'battle of rats', a head-to-head confrontation in which there were heavy casualties on both sides.

Theodosius had mobilized his barbarian 'federate' allies from the Danube – perhaps as many as twenty thousand. At the summit of the pass looking down on the valley of the Frigidus and the army of Arbogast stood a pear tree at a station known in antiquity as *Ad Pirum* (in a plateau called in modern German the Birnbaumer Wald). From the pear-tree station Theodosius could gaze down upon the strong position of Arbogast and Eugenius. Having reached the summit at about mid-afternoon on 5 September, Theodosius ordered his army to proceed in line of column against the enemy. The twenty thousand Gothic allies were in the van of the emperor's army, and they surged up against the strongly entrenched troops along the Frigidus.

A direct assault in line of column against a strong enemy position violates most of the rules of modern warfare, especially those laid down by the adherents of the so-called 'strategy of indirect approach', such as Liddell Hart, but actually the history of warfare has witnessed many successful direct attacks.[110] In fact the route taken by Theodosius may have been too narrow to permit deployment into line of battle. This time, in any event, the forces of Arbogast and Eugenius held, and by sunset some 10,000 of the emperor's allied Goths lay dead on the field – more fatalities than the US Marines suffered (fewer than 7,000) in a month of fighting on Iwo Jima, one of the bloodiest battles of World War II. That night Eugenius celebrated an apparent victory, feasting and distributing rewards and compliments to his men.

In Theodosius' camp, in contrast, the mood was gloomy. His generals urged him to withdraw under cover of darkness to conserve his strength, and to return to fight another day. But the emperor, who spent most of the night in prayer and fitful sleep, would not retreat, and the next morning, at daybreak, he moved his army down against an enemy now somewhat off its guard. Arbogast's forces were still in the comfortable glow of a victory celebration. Despite the surprise of this renewed offensive and the defection of some troops that had been stationed on the flanks of Theodosius' army to impede his movements, the army of Arbogast and Eugenius rallied and held its ground in furious fighting. The battle swayed back and forth, suggesting incidentally (since neither army broke) that the morale of the Roman army so near the end of the fourth century was still remarkably high.

Thousands fell on both sides, and the outcome was in doubt until nature intervened (some said it was the Christian god) on the side of Theodosius.

In that region to this very day there are sometimes great cyclonic gusts of wind that rage from the Alpine passes down into the northern Adriatic. The scientific cause, unknown to the soldiers of Theodosius and Arbogast, is that the cold air of the Alpine passes, when it is moving too fast to be warmed by the warmer air of the Adriatic, is drawn down by the difference in pressure in gusts that frequently reach 60 miles per hour and occasionally 125 mph.[111] The wind is known as a 'Bora' (from *Boreas* – north wind). At a moment when the battle between Theodosius and Arbogast was still uncertain, the Bora swept down the pass blowing dust into the eyes of the Western soldiers, driving Theodosius' army against the foe, and giving victory to the Christian emperor.

A contemporary, the poet Claudian (*c.* 370–*c.* 404), described the critical event.[112] His poem is addressed to Honorius, the young son of Theodosius, who was nowhere near the fighting, but since the eleven-year-old was consul for the year, Claudian, with some considerable poetic license, ascribed the victory to him:

> Down from the mountain, summoned by thy name
> Upon your foes the chilling north wind came;
> Back to the sender's heart his javelin hurled,
> And from his powerless grasp the spear-staff whirled.
>
> Oh greatly loved of heaven! from forth his caves
> Aeolus sends his armèd Storms, thy slaves.
>
> Aether itself obeys thy sovereign will,
> And conscript Winds move to thy bugles shrill.
> The Alpine snows grew red with blood: the Frigid stream
> Now, with changed waters, glided dank with steam.
>
> And, but that every wave was swoln with gore,
> Had fainted 'neath the ghastly load she bore.

Despite Claudian, 'Alpine snows' were almost certainly not a factor – not at two thousand feet in early September – but the Bora definitely tipped the scales of battle in favour of the Theodosian army. The butchery was great, and the victors penetrated the towers and palisades of the enemy and burnt them to the ground. Eugenius was captured (while he still expected to win) and was taken to Theodosius and decapitated. In a ghastly form of psychological warfare, not uncommon in antiquity, the fallen pretender's head, raised high on a pole as a standard, was displayed to the defeated army. Arbogast fled into the hills and committed suicide when he could not escape the emperor's forces.

The battle of the Frigid River had been decisive. Theodosius the Great was finally sole emperor of the united Roman Empire. The conqueror moved from the battlefield towards Rome, and there, before the ancient Senate, urged the Romans of Italy to abandon the traditional idolatry and paganism (which were still reasonably strong in Italy) in favour of Christianity. Later, in January of 395, only a few months after the victory at the Frigidus, Theodosius the Great fell ill at Milan and died, worn out, some said, by the war with Arbogast. His body lay in state for forty days until Ambrose delivered a funeral oration, and it was then taken to Constantinople for burial.

At the time no one knew that Theodosius would be the last emperor to rule over the entire Empire. At his death it was still an empire that Augustus and Diocletian would have recognized. It was bigger, in fact, than the Augustan Empire and only slightly smaller than Diocletian's. From a glance at the map one could hardly see the signs of imperial demise. But there was a cancer in the Empire – the 'federate' Visigoths under their new king, Alaric, who had fought for Theodosius at the Frigidus but bitterly resented the unwillingness of the great emperor to use him in an official military command, as the Frank Arbogast had been used in the West. Before the year was out Alaric was on the warpath.

Zosimus the historian, writing in the fifth century, looked back upon the age of Theodosius as the decisive turning point in Rome's history, but for a reason that modern historians cannot accept. Theodosius had cut funds from the imperial budget for support of the pagan sacrifices in Rome. 'The result of this has been,' Zosimus wrote, 'that the Roman Empire, cut short in every direction, has become the home of every barbarous tribe or else has been so utterly wasted of its inhabitants, that men can no longer recognize the places where its great cities stood.'[113] In other words, the pagan gods had punished Rome for forsaking them.

Although the explanation is unacceptable, the 'event' described by Zosimus was real, and there may be some justice in his view that Theodosius must be held accountable, at least in part, for the collapse of the Empire that followed his reign. It is true that the barbarians who settled in the Empire under Theodosius eventually played an important role in the fall of Rome. And Theodosius may be held partly accountable for another error not mentioned by Zosimus. The decision to divide the Empire between the emperor's two sons, Honorius in the West and Arcadius in the East, a division that became permanent, ultimately contributed to the fall of Rome in the West. At a time when the resources of the entire Empire were needed for defence of the West, only half of them were available. Although the division of the Empire had been a reality since the death of Constantine, it had not become official policy. In the last half of the fourth century only the years 353–64 saw the Empire united under a single emperor, but the last few months of Theodosius' life opened new possibilities for unity. Those possibilities were shattered by the emperor's dynastic settlement.

There is, too, another way in which the reign of Theodosius may have contributed to the fall of Rome. His policy towards the Goths and the division of the Empire take on greater significance when one considers the costly impact of civil war on the armed forces during his reign. The Roman army had suffered severely in 363 and in 378 before Theodosius came to the throne. Then the war with Maximus in the West and the great clash with Arbogast and Eugenius on the Frigidus led to heavy losses. There is a sense in which the best troops of the Empire were thrown at one another in bloody head-on engagements with losses greater than those of the humiliating Persian campaign – greater in total even than those at Adrianople. Because Gothic allies took heavy losses on the Frigidus on the first day of battle, they could legitimately claim a greater share of influence in imperial affairs than they had previously exercised, a result fraught with danger. So the battle was doubly costly.

Speaking of the effects of Theodosius' military policy, Gibbon wrote: 'The enervated soldiers abandoned their own and the public defence; and their pusillanimous indolence may be considered as the immediate cause of the downfall of the empire.'[114] It is not fair to the Roman troops who fought at the Frigidus to speak of 'pusillanimous indolence', but it is possible that the continuing disasters of the last half of the fourth century were having a cumulative effect that would become visible only in the fifth century. It is true that Rome had suffered losses earlier in her history of some considerable magnitude, but those against Hannibal had been in a short period from 218 to 216 BC and did not have the enervating effect that a long, drawn-out 'age of defeat' could cause. Later, when significant losses had been stretched out over a considerable period of time, as in the period AD 240–60, the effect had been a near collapse of the Empire. The Empire, to be sure, had rallied after the crises of the mid-third century, but Theodosius was no Diocletian, and the Christian emperor had compromised with Rome's foes whereas his pagan predecessor had resolutely planted Roman standards around the frontiers.

The Roman Army in AD 395

Although the barbarization of the Roman army in the fifth century may be traced back to the policies of Theodosius, the army at the time of his death in 395 was still a powerful instrument. To understand how destructive barbarian influences were to Rome's military might, we must examine the strong, purely Roman army that defended the Empire as it entered its twilight days of the fifth century.

Fortunately, it is possible to describe with reasonable accuracy the Roman army in 395 (or at least early in the fifth century under Honorius and Arcadius). The reason is the survival into modern times of a document called the *Notitia Dignitatum* (literally a *List of Positions*), a table of organization for the Roman Empire, East and West, civil and military. Needless to say it is a fascinating document that has exercised considerable influence on modern scholarship from Gibbon to today.[115]

Although scholars have strenuously debated the date and purpose of this extraordinarily thorough administrative description of the Empire (complete with illustrations), what follows seems to me to summarize a developing consensus. That part of the *Notitia Dignitatum* that describes the eastern half of the Empire was prepared near the end of the reign of Theodosius along with a similar description of the Western Empire, and the two parts were intended for use by Theodosius' sons, Honorius and Arcadius. The hope was that the two halves of the Empire would be governed in a more or less identical fashion. The document reflects a continuing sense of the 'unity' of the Empire even under two emperors.

The copy that has survived, however, is the one that was used in the West. The description of the Eastern Empire remains unchanged, much as it must have been in AD 395, but for the western provinces modifications were made reflecting changes in the administration of the West in the period from 395 down to perhaps AD 430. It seems then to have fallen from use, probably into private hands, perhaps because it seemed better to make an entirely new copy than to continue revising an older one of *c.* 395. Happily someone filed the old copy away, and what survives today is a reproduction of the original (which has disappeared), made in 1551 at a monastery in Speyer, Germany.

Obviously the *Notitia Dignitatum* is an invaluable primary source for the history of the Late Roman Empire, and it tells us a great deal about the Roman army at the end of the fourth century. First, it was a large army – in the neighbourhood of half a million men for the Empire as a whole.[116] There were still central mobile armies and border forces in both halves of the Empire; the eastern army was probably a bit larger than the western one, but the difference in size was not significant. Indeed from the time of Constantine on, the western army, particularly the Gallic units, became the major source of crack troops in the Roman Empire.[117] One can see in the *Notitia Dignitatum* the reflection of a great, ancient military machine, of an incomparable army, of a fighting tradition infinitely more elaborate and sophisticated than anything known to the barbarians on the frontiers. The collapse and barbarization of that machine are all the more significant when one realizes the extent of its complexity.

One development clearly revealed by the *Notitia* is the emergence in the Late Roman army of the specialized skirmisher arms and cavalry units. There were still simple infantrymen, soldiers of the line, and what might be called basic cavalry in the Roman army, but by the end of the fourth century a wide variety of specially trained and equipped forces were giving Roman generals far more tactical flexibility than they had had in the days of the Early Empire.[118] Based on the *Notitia* it appears that there were about seventy thousand specialized troops in the Late Roman army, perhaps one-sixth to one-eighth of the total strength.

A rapid (and necessarily incomplete) survey of such units reveals their importance in the military system of the Late Roman Empire. In the cavalry, Persian-style heavy units (the so-called *Catafractarii* or *Clibanarii*) were used much more extensively in the mobile army of the East than elsewhere, presumably for duty primarily on the Persian front. It is unlikely that such heavy cavalry, with its concomitant immobility, would have been as useful in the West, though there were a (very) few units there. Likewise the camel corps (*Dromedarii*) is found in Egypt and Palestine and obviously not in Gaul.

On the other hand mounted archers (*Sagitarii*) are found everywhere in the mobile armies as well as in the frontier forces. They are naturally more common in the desert areas of the East and in Africa, but they also appear in the western army in the frontier forces of the Upper Danube. Significantly there were more infantry archers in the mobile army of the East than mounted ones, but mounted archers were more useful on the frontier. The document reveals a few units of infantry pike-men (*Lanciarii*), and the catapult operators (*Ballistarii*) are all assigned to the mobile armies mainly in the East, except for a lonely unit at Bontobrica on the Rhine downriver from Mainz. Strangely there is only one unit of slingers (assigned to the mobile army in the Orient), but it is likely that all Roman troops took weapons training with the sling. Troops specializing in river warfare, trained in the use of inflated leather bags as flotation devices, were stationed on the Danube. In the West, especially, there were units of scouts (*Exploratores*) who somehow differed from *Praeventores* who are attested for Moesia and may have been scouts under a different name. The *Superventores* were probably trained as commandos for rearguard action.

The army that defended the Roman Empire in AD 395 was Napoleonic in its proportions and its degree of specialization. The French emperor led into Russia a force about the same size as the late-fourth-century Roman army, and the army of the Roman Empire probably required an even more sophisticated logistical support system. Napoleon's armies were famous for moving rapidly and living off the land. Roman armies generally moved more slowly and depended on a depot and convoy system of supply.[119]

We have considered in an earlier chapter the superiority of Roman logistics over the primitive logistical systems of barbarian armies. It is a point of difference, however, so enormous and so important that it requires elaboration and example. To understand the destruction wrought by barbarization, one must have some comprehension of what was destroyed. For that reason we shall examine by way of example some of the components of Roman logistics.

The complexity of the supply system is revealed, to take just one instance, through means of horse recruitment, though we shall also briefly consider the provision of wool, foodstuffs, and weapons to the army.[120] In horse recruitment the barbarians depended on stealing and breeding. One obvious source of supply of cavalry horses and pack animals for the Romans also was to capture those of the enemy, and this they had always done, but confiscation alone was not enough. In the Early Empire there had sometimes been critical shortages.[121] Relying on a highly developed horse-supply system the Roman army routinely purchased animals, even camels, from civilians in the Empire, and standards were sufficiently high that a veterinary examination was required before purchase. For special jobs, animals were sometimes simply hired rather than purchased. There is some evidence that soldiers occasionally actually took animals by threat of force without paying for them, but the central government generally frowned on confiscatory animal recruitment.

A bill of sale (on papyrus) for a Cappadocian horse purchased in AD 77 shows that it cost 675 *denarii* (more than twice the annual pay of a Roman legionary of the time); that it had passed a veterinary examination; and that it had some training for its duties. Yet this horse was not even destined for the cavalry; it was a pack animal.[122] In the third century cavalry commanders officially asked the governor of the province in question to provide a horse or horses. The officer's request was specific, listing the soldier or soldiers who would receive the animals. The governor purchased the horse(s) and ordered it entrusted to a single soldier, mentioning him by name. In the Late Roman Empire there were stipulations regulating the size, shape and age of military horses. There was a special premium on sure-footed, fast and obedient horses while sluggish or high-spirited ones were avoided. Training for a cavalry horse was intensive. Horses had to wheel, turn, circle, move in a straight line and at an angle, and they had to do these things at the walk, trot, and gallop. They were accustomed to swim, to kneel and lie down, and to stand still. In fact, of course, governors and other high-ranking administrators in the Roman Empire were too busy (or at least too important) to deal personally with individual horses, and the documents issued in their names must have been approved by lower officials. In the Late Empire a *strator* (groom) performed this duty. One such person, in the fourth century, was stoned to death for trying to profit from horses.[123]

Later, imperial stud farms in Cappadocia, Thrace and Spain bred horses for the army. The whole system was under the jurisdiction of a tribune of the stable, subsequently a *comes*, attached to the mobile armies, who supervised the grooms as well as the supply of animals. Generally, in the last half of the fourth century there are signs of greater and greater centralization of horse recruitment and a return to a monetary system of account in the imperial stables.[124] Incidentally, the cavalry used only mares and geldings since stallions could not be kept together without fighting or getting excited in the pursuit of the mares. Stallions tended to be too highly strung for cavalry anyway. On the other hand, cavalry mares were not used for breeding since that took them out of effective military action for too long. The stud farms, then, were quite independent of the regular cavalry remounts. Nothing that is known about the barbarian armies of the Huns or the Germans suggests the existence of such a highly organized horse-recruitment system.

In other ways, as well, Roman organization was superior to that of barbarian armies. The soldiers of the Late Empire, in the mobile armies and in the frontier forces, were paid primarily in two ways – in kind and in money. Payments in kind, rations, were made from governmental storehouses built near the military camps, which also held fodder for the horses. From the time of Diocletian, at least, soldiers began to receive money again on a regular basis but apparently only as a supplement to the more important system of payment in kind. The regular money payments were small, but in addition the emperor normally gave payments of money on special holidays (for example, his birthday), and that too became a more or less fixed system. Rampant inflation had made regular, annual payments less valuable. Although they were still made in the days of Julian the Apostate, they were probably stopped under Theodosius.

The important money payment to the troops was the one given on the accession of a new emperor and thereafter, as long as the emperor lived, on every fifth anniversary of that event. This so-called 'quinquennial donative' was a significant amount – five gold solidi and a pound of silver (equal to four solidi) on accession and five solidi on the quinquennial celebration. The amount was paid for every Augustus in the Empire and payment could therefore occur more frequently than once every five years.[125]

A special governmental bureau (called the *largitiones* or the Department of Distributions) handled pay and clothing. How often the soldiers' basic shirt (*sticharium*), tunic (*chlamys*) and cloak (*pallium*) were issued is unknown. There is some evidence that boots were made in imperial factories, but by the end of the fourth century there was a tendency to pay out cash allowances rather than actual clothing and boots.[126]

Arms were made in state factories (*fabricae*) or arsenals scattered around the Empire; around AD 400 there were fifteen such factories in the East and twenty in the West. Shields, lances, catapults, cavalry armour, arrows, bows, breastplates, swords – all were made in government shops, and some of the arsenals specialized in making only one particular commodity (arrows, for example), while others seem to have manufactured everything. There were separate factories for making the officers' armour (out of bronze, decorated with silver and gold).[127]

Woollen and linen materials were made at government mills. Although there were only two linen mills in the West in our period, there were at least fifteen woollen mills and nine dyeing houses. Operated by state slaves, these factories (along with the armouries) constituted an important part of the economy of the Roman Empire. The army was definitely big business. How supplies of wool and linen were channelled to the mills is unknown, but Egypt was almost certainly a major supplier of raw materials.[128]

Napoleon is famous for saying that an army travels on its stomach (though no one seems to know exactly when or where he said it). Roman generals, as a rule, however, showed more concern than Napoleon did for the military food supply. There were basically three ways the Roman got food – by purchase on the open market, by production on government land, and from the soldiers' own farms and gardens.[129]

It has been often noted that purchases of food (mainly grain) sometimes shaded into requisition, and requisition into taxation, particularly in the Late Empire. Normally military demands were high. In good years the army was simply a market in the regional economy, but in bad years it was a terrible drain, particularly in those areas where purchase in the open market (or requisition and taxation) was a major source of supply. In some places imperial estates were quite large, and semi-free serfs produced much of what the army needed.

In the Late Empire production by the troops themselves, or at least by those troops permanently stationed on the frontiers, probably became a significant source of military supply. Soldiers were assigned lands near their forts, which in fact became private property on condition that sons enlisted in the army on reaching legal age. It was a convenient double-edged system – frontier land produced needed food and at the same time provided recruits for the army. Some land was given to barbarians for settlement on the same terms. In this way the immobility of late-fourth-century society, the caste-like system, extended even into the army, and the structured economy found a place for military production. The soldiers' obligation was now two-fold: 'to farm and to fight.'[130]

The *limitanei*, or border troops, have not received as much attention from scholars as the mobile armies, although theoretically their role in the strategy of defence-in-depth was equally as important, if less dramatically decisive. In many respects at the end of the fourth century the *limitanei* were still militarily effective; the border forces had not yet degenerated into the 'hereditary peasant militia' that defended the western frontiers and the Danube later in the fifth century.[131] Military service was hereditary, for the central armies and the frontier forces, but the *limitanei* were something more than a peasant militia. At least down to AD 400 *limitanei* received regular rations (though they may have sold their own agricultural produce to the government for the purpose). At least they were not required to support themselves directly.

More significant is the reasonably substantial evidence that units of *limitanei* were frequently transferred for service with the *comitatenses*, and that *comitatenses* were occasionally used for frontier duty. The apparent tactical interchangeability of border troops and mobile army units suggest that the fighting quality of the frontier forces was still reasonably high at the death of Theodosius the Great.[132] Still, his settlement with the barbarians and the use of large 'federate' barbarian forces in military campaigns began almost immediately to undermine the marvellous military machine of the Roman state.

A Comparison of the Eastern and Western Armies

In the end barbarization had a much greater impact on the western than on the eastern army. That is all the more remarkable because in the fourth century the central reserve of the eastern army was simply

not as good as that of the West.[133] Constantine had won the Empire
with an army fashioned in the West, and in 361 Julian repeated the feat
(though Constantius II died before there was actual combat). Perhaps
more important, the great warrior-emperor, Valentinian I, organized
an even stronger western force. Besides, it was primarily the eastern
armies that had suffered the great defeats in Persia (363) and at
Adrianople (378). To be sure, Theodosius I beat the western army at
the Frigidus (394), but the battle was a 'near-run thing', and the
Christian emperor had been aided by a hurricane-force wind and by
twenty thousand barbarian allies who reduced the strength of the
western army in an apparent 'human-wave' attack from line of
column, while the eastern army let others do its fighting.

The simple fact is that the western army was better. It is ironic that
in the fifth century the better army lost its half of the Empire while the
weaker one preserved the East. Of course, the eastern army improved
during the fifth century, and the western one deteriorated, but for the
purposes of our story – the fall of Rome in the West – it is well to note
the differences distinguishing the two armies at the end of the fourth
century.

For one thing, despite the course of subsequent events, the eastern
army in 395 had been much more barbarized than the army of the
West. Inevitably after Adrianople and particularly after Theodosius'
settlement with the Visigoths in 382 there was a major place for
barbarian forces in the military policy of the East. The mobilization of
twenty thousand barbarians before the battle of the Frigidus was
merely a logical result of the policy decided upon by Theodosius about
a decade earlier. Ironically the élite quality of the Gallic army of
Constantine had been based on the recruitment of selected barbarian
units. Since the time of Julius Caesar in Gaul in the first century BC
Rome had employed barbarian mercenaries, and their use had been
accelerated in the third century AD, but the army had remained
essentially Roman.

'Barbarization', the use of Germans on such a large scale that the
army became German rather than the Germans becoming Roman
soldiers, begins with Theodosius the Great. The emperor won the
battle with his Gothic allies, but they began immediately to demand
great rewards for their service and to show an independence that in
drill, discipline and organization meant catastrophe. They fought
under their own native commanders, and the barbaric system of

discipline was in no way as severe as the Roman. Eventually Roman soldiers saw no reason to do what barbarian troops in Roman service were rewarded heavily for not doing. Ironically, for reasons we shall examine later, in the early fifth century the western army became more barbarized than the eastern and paid the price for barbarian settlement while the East rebelled against Theodosius' policy. Barbarization, starting in the eastern army of Theodosius, spread into the West as a plague, contributing to the fall of Rome.

There were other differences between East and West. In the eastern army, as re-organized in the last years of Theodosius, there were five great Field Marshals (each a *magister utriusque militiae*, literally 'master of both branches [infantry and cavalry] for the army'). Two were attached to the forces serving immediately at the pleasure of the emperor (the so-called *palatinae*, a branch of the mobile army), and the other three commanded the mobile armies in the dioceses of Thrace, Illyricum and the Orient. Their armies were approximately equal, and so were their rank and authority. In the West, on the other hand, two great Field Marshals (the *magister equitum* and *magister peditum*: 'master of the horse' and 'master of the foot'), shared overall authority in all military matters throughout the West. Traditionally one of them manoeuvred politically to exercise more influence than the other, and we see in the West the emergence of what have recently been called the 'generalissimos', such as Arbogast who used his pre-eminent military command to dominate even the civilian government. The western army did not depend as heavily as the eastern on the personal command of the emperor.[134] In the end, as we shall see, the rise of generals such as Stilicho and Aëtius was both a strength and a weakness of the western military system.

On balance, the role of Theodosius the Great in the defence of the Roman Empire was negative, though the problems he faced were large, and possibly only a genuinely great ruler would have done better. His policies had brought peace, momentarily, and if in them we see the seeds of later Roman military crises, it is perhaps understandable that Theodosius decided to mortgage Rome's future for peace in his own time. Only fifteen years after his death the very barbarians whom he treated so favourably put the city of Rome to the torch, and their influence on the Roman army, which they sometimes served as 'allies', did even more damage to Rome's strategic strength.

Chapter Five

The Turning Point:
AD 406–410

In the aftermath of Theodosius' death great changes reshaped the
Empire. Two new young emperors, neither of them very effective even
in their mature years, had to face the surging forces of barbarian
upheaval, particularly but not exclusively in the West. In the few short
years at the end of the first decade of the fifth century Vandals, Suebi,
Alamanni and Visigoths darted with convulsive power across Danube
and Rhine, swept through the Balkans, Gaul and Spain, and in 410 the
ancient city of Rome itself lay plundered by a barbarian assault. The
sack of Rome was merely representative of equally great destruction in
many parts of an empire that would never again look like the Empire
of old. How this occurred, and occurred so rapidly, is the subject of
this chapter.

In much happier and more optimistic times Theodosius the Great
had made preparations, unlike some of his predecessors in the purple,
for the government of the Empire after his death. Naturally, however,
he did not plan to die in 395. The grooming of his heirs, his sons
Honorius and Arcadius, was not complete by then. Since Honorius in
the West was a mere youth of ten years and Arcadius in the East only
about eighteen, both of the new emperors initially required much help
from their advisers. Arcadius had been designated for the throne in the
East since his proclamation as Augustus in 383. The murder (or
suicide) of Valentinian II, followed by the revolt of Arbogast and
Eugenius, created an opportunity for Theodosius to put the young
Honorius on the throne in Rome. He was duly proclaimed Augustus in
393, and was actually in the West, in Milan with his father, when the
latter died.

The question, then, was not who would become emperor in East
and West but rather who would be the power behind the thrones.[135] In
the West there was no doubt – Stilicho, husband of Theodosius'
beloved niece and foster daughter, Serena, had been clearly designated

by the great emperor for that role. And Stilicho was on the scene; he had served as one of the five eastern Field Marshals and was at the Frigid River. Then he remained in the West with Theodosius and Honorius after the victory and was at Milan – indeed at the emperor's bedside – when Theodosius died.

Stilicho claimed that the emperor, in a private bedside session, had urged him to assume guardianship over both new emperors, to provide direction, stability and unity in imperial policy, East and West. In short, Theodosius hoped to perpetuate his own policies, which were controversial, through one who strongly supported them and who was powerful enough to protect the dynastic line without at the same time being tempted to assume the purple for himself. Not all ancients and not all moderns have believed Stilicho's avowal that Theodosius secretly gave him a kind of regency in the East as well as the West (about which there is no doubt), but if the emperor did, and for the reasons stated above, he had picked the right man. Stilicho proved to be strict in his adherence to the Theodosian regime and policy.[136]

Perhaps no one person was more important an actor in the drama of Rome's fall than Stilicho. He is sometimes called a barbarian, or semi-barbarian, since his father was a Vandal, and a popular tradition treats him as one of the few great Germanic leaders who gave their services to Rome in defence of civilization against their own native barbarism. Such a view of Stilicho is profoundly misleading. Except for the accident of his birth Stilicho was in every sense a Roman, and not simply a Roman – he was a prominent member of the Theodosian family and a powerful general in the Roman military establishment. If barbarian blood flowed in Stilicho's veins, he was nevertheless ignorant and scarcely understanding of barbarian culture. Indeed his inability to comprehend the barbarians of his age contributed substantially to the fall of Rome. It takes more than blood (or perhaps less) to make a barbarian. Little is known about Stilicho's father except that he was a Vandal and that he commanded some Vandal units at Adrianople, fighting on the side of Valens and Rome.[137] Stilicho's mother was a Roman though we know nothing about her and would not even know that fact had not St Jerome referred to the generalissimo as a 'semibarbarus'.[138] But for these skimpy details, all that is known of Stilicho's family are his remarkable interconnections with the house of Theodosius.

How he first came to the emperor's attention we know not – perhaps simply as a reward for his father's service at Adrianople – but when Stilicho was still merely a young man (in 384) he was sent on the embassy to Persia that resulted in the settlement of the Armenian frontier. Upon his return to Constantinople he married Serena in a lavish ceremony presided over by Theodosius; and thus the young man was destined for high Roman office before he had acquired much experience in Roman government. His first major appointment after the return from Persia was as Count of the Sacred Stables (*Comes Sacri Stabuli*) from which one assumes he presided over the cavalry remount system in the emperor's mobile army. Sometime between 385 and 392 he became Count of the Domestics (*Comes Domesticorum*), the imperial bodyguard, and he must have served with Theodosius in the war against Maximus even if there is no specific evidence for that assumption. His emergence as one of a handful of major governmental officers dates from his appointment in 392(?) as Field Marshal (*Magister Utriusque Militiae*) probably for the diocese of Thrace. In the East, as we saw in the last chapter, there were five such Field Marshals altogether, exercising military commands under the immediate supervision of the emperor (and often acting quite independently when the emperor was not with them on campaign).

It was in this important capacity that Stilicho accompanied Theodosius to the Frigid River and afterwards into Italy. In the West, Stilicho became Field Marshal of the army of the West, a position which, we have seen, was even more important in the West than the roughly comparable rank in the East. In addition Theodosius made Stilicho the guardian of Honorius, which placed all the civil as well as military power of the western government in his son-in-law's hands.

One should not overlook the purely dynastic strength of Stilicho's status in the Empire. Married to the adopted daughter of Theodosius, Stilicho cemented his position in the imperial house by marrying his own daughter Maria to Honorius. His other daughter, Thermantia, also married Honorius in 408, after Maria's death. Because of these dynastic ties Stilicho could assume that someday his grandson would be emperor (though in fact Honorius and his wives never produced any children). In addition, Theodosius' daughter, who later became famous as Galla Placidia (see below), was entrusted to the care of Stilicho and Serena and was betrothed to Stilicho's son, Eucherius. The great generalissimo had no need to take the purple for himself –

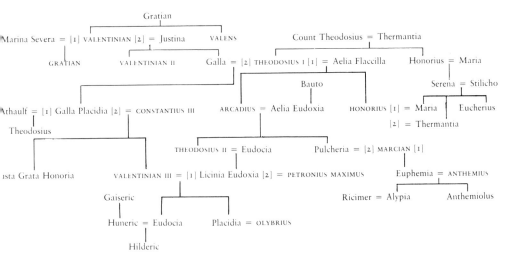

The families of Valentinian and Theodosius. Emperors' names appear in capital letters.

his bloodline was destined for it. Besides his family relationships, the basis of his own strong position was his loyalty to the house of Theodosius.[139]

One other point is critical in assessing Stilicho's predominance in the early months of AD 395. His claim to be regent of the East as well as the West may or may not have been based on the actual words of Theodosius. Those who think not have a powerful argument in suggesting that the emperor would surely have made such arrangements public had he intended them to be effective. But according to Stilicho's story, Theodosius had actually dismissed his other advisers from the room before entrusting in perfect privacy the care of Arcadius to him. Ambrose accepted the claim, as did many others who curried Stilicho's favour or sincerely supported his cause.[140] Regardless of the general's ambitions, however, or the trust that Theodosius may have had in him, in early 395 Stilicho had command of the western army, and, significantly, a large part of the eastern army that had accompanied Theodosius into Rome. The power of the battalions might, under normal circumstances, have made most Romans ready to believe whatever Stilicho said about his last meeting with the dying emperor.

Stilicho and Alaric

Unfortunately for Stilicho, the circumstances were hardly normal. The new leader of the Visigoths, Alaric, proved a formidable opponent, and the political situation at Constantinople was more complicated and confusing than Stilicho realized. Apparently Stilicho hoped that Arcadius would respond to his leadership, for family reasons if for no other, and the great general did not foresee that the influential civilian administrator, Rufinus, Praetorian Prefect of the East, left behind by Theodosius as chief adviser to Arcadius, would presume to challenge his authority and influence. Rufinus was ambitious and unscrupulous, a crafty operator in the realm of Byzantine politics. The combined opposition of Rufinus and Alaric, sometimes possibly even coordinated by the two men, confronted Stilicho with a surprising problem and one that was nearly insoluble.[141]

All three of the main actors in the events of that critical year, 395, were highly controversial at the time. Unfortunately the evidence – never good in the Late Empire – is particularly disputable for their actions and policies. As a result, modern historians have differed tremendously in their assessments of Stilicho and his contemporaries.[142] We cannot deal with the technicalities of the disputed evidence here; what follows is merely my reconstruction of events along lines that seem most consistent with the sources. Generally I follow the tradition that is 'favourable' to Stilicho insofar as his motives are concerned, but, as we shall see, morality does not guarantee sound policy.

After the battle of the Frigid River, Alaric had been angered by the unwillingness of Theodosius to reward him for his services with a regular commission as general in the Roman army. Since the Visigoths had borne the brunt of the fighting on the first day of combat and had suffered the greatest casualties, there was some suspicion that the emperor had deliberately tried to thin out the ranks of his barbarian allies. Naturally this made it easier for Alaric to inflame the Goths and lead them on a plundering foray into Thrace and Macedonia, ultimately near to Constantinople.

At the same time Huns from the Trans-Caucasus moved down through Armenia and northern Mesopotamia into Syria. From Palestine St Jerome described the 'wolves of the north' and the catastrophe they wrought:

May Jesus protect the world in future from such beasts! They were everywhere; when they were least expected, and their speed outstripped the rumour of their approach; they spared neither religion nor dignity nor age; they showed no pity to the cry of infancy.[143]

How many monasteries were captured? The waters of how many rivers were stained with human gore? Antioch was besieged and the other cities, past which the Halys, the Cydnus, the Orontes, the Euphrates flow. Herds of captives were dragged away; Arabia, Phoenicia, Palestine, Egypt were led captive by fear.[144]

Some historians, particularly those who see this period as one of transformation rather than collapse, either ignore, dismiss, or ridicule the evidence of human suffering in the age of invasions. We shall see that there is too much of it to be ignored, and only the blind or the insensitive can dismiss or ridicule it. Although a wise historian will always make allowances for rhetorical exaggeration, he also knows that effective rhetoric usually has some basis in fact.[145]

In any event, in 395 the East was hard hit otherwise by barbarian attack, and the crisis seemed greater than it might have because Stilicho continued to keep much of the eastern army under his control in Italy. In fact, Stilicho moved energetically to put down Alaric's rebellion and marched with an army of both eastern and western contingents into Thessaly where the Visigoths had moved their forces. In Constantinople, however, Rufinus hoped to retain influence over Arcadius and managed to persuade the young eastern emperor that Stilicho had designs on the Balkans, which had earlier been under the eastern emperor's control. Rufinus sowed the seeds of discord before Stilicho could defeat Alaric, though apparently the western general with superior numbers had trapped his barbarian foe in a hopeless position. The Byzantine intriguer knew that the glory of a victory over the Visigothic chieftain would yield insurmountable influence to Stilicho, and to prevent that he persuaded Arcadius to instruct Stilicho to send the eastern units on to Constantinople and take the western ones with him as he left eastern territory. Stilicho meekly obeyed.

When we look back on the situation today, with benefit of hindsight, it seems incredible that political considerations permitted Rome's implacable foe (and future destroyer) to escape certain defeat. Something in us cries out to Stilicho to smash Alaric, at least, before obeying the command of Arcadius. Yet, as is so often the case, since history sometimes unfolds with a semblance of logic, there is a 'rational' explanation of the crisis. Stilicho had earlier announced that

Illyricum was being transferred to the Western emperor in accordance with the last wishes of Theodosius. To Arcadius and his advisers this must have appeared a heavy-handed attempt on Stilicho's part to enhance his own power, which was obviously stronger in the West. His arrival in Thessaly was made to seem almost as a military invasion of the East. Indeed there is a possibility that Rufinus persuaded Alaric to move west and south in hopes of drawing Stilicho into just this kind of trap. If so, Stilicho had the last word, because the troops he sent back to Constantinople murdered the Praetorian Prefect.

Some modern scholars have suggested, on the basis of rather limited evidence, that Stilicho actually had difficulty controlling his troops, that the forces of the East and the West under his command had not yet reconciled the differences that had led to the clash at the Frigidus.[146] There is no clear evidence, however, that Stilicho lost control of his troops; there is considerable evidence, some of it admittedly highly biased, that Rufinus undermined Stilicho for his own personal political advantage, but was murdered by Stilicho's troops who realized the treachery. Stilicho had to obey Arcadius on family grounds, because his claim to empire-wide regency over both imperial brothers was based to a great extent on the hope that Arcadius would accept it. So Alaric made the first of several historic escapes. If Stilicho had been somewhat bolder, he might have crushed Alaric and still returned the eastern forces to Arcadius, but the western general was politically too cautious for this particular military crisis. Rome eventually paid a heavy price for Stilicho's 'loyalty'.

Ironically the murder of Rufinus (November 395) in Constantinople did not lead to any increase in Stilicho's influence over Arcadius. Instead, the Lord Chamberlain, a bald eunuch by the name of Eutropius, equally jealous of Stilicho, took Rufinus' place as the trusted adviser of the emperor. Although the historian Bury warns against the prejudice 'against a person with his physical disqualifications', the imperial favourite deserved most of the criticisms levelled against him.[147] Rufinus had been rapacious and greedy; Eutropius was no different, and the source of his ill-gotten gains was the use of his influence in the sale of public offices.

While Eutropius strengthened his hold over Arcadius, Stilicho inspected the Rhine frontier and promoted harmony between the courts of Milan (from where Honorius ruled) and Constantinople. Such a policy was necessary to further Stilicho's own claim, still not abandoned, of regency in East and West. In the meantime Alaric had moved south past Thebes and Athens, sacking the great centre of the Eleusinian mysteries of Demeter and Persephone, before he plunged into the Peloponnese and took Megara, Corinth, Argos and Sparta. Arcadius seemed totally incapable of dealing with the problem, and in 397 Stilicho crossed the Adriatic and met Alaric at Elis in the northwestern Peloponnese, near the site of the Greek Olympic games.

Eutropius reacted vigorously, persuading Arcadius to declare Stilicho a public enemy for his unauthorized foray into eastern territory. In the encounter on the battlefield between the two protagonists, Stilicho and Alaric, Rome's general was tactically successful, surrounding the Visigoths and cutting off their supplies. But somehow the Visigoths escaped; Zosimus claims that Stilicho's troops were too busy looting the barbarian camp to conduct a successful pursuit and that Alaric got away across the Corinthian Gulf into Epirus with all his Peloponnesian plunder.[148] Stilicho returned West and claimed victory, but he had been ordered by Arcadius to withdraw and had not destroyed the enemy's main force.

Meanwhile, the rising tension between Stilicho and Eutropius led to the revolt in 397 of Gildo, Count of Africa, who had been inspired to break with the government in Milan by the Byzantine eunuch. Africa was critically important to the western government as a source of grain for Italy and the army. Gildo had not supported Theodosius in the war with Arbogast and Eugenius, and the hostile relationship with Stilicho that followed the emperor's death created an irresistible opportunity for the eastern regime.[149] Stilicho's interference in eastern affairs was all the justification Arcadius needed to arrange the transfer of Africa to his jurisdiction.

In this crisis of 397 Stilicho secured grain from Gaul and Spain, and in the spring of 398 dispatched against Gildo an expeditionary force of five to ten thousand troops. The poet Claudian's version of the war, though charged with poetic flourishes, nevertheless makes clear the main lines of Stilicho's strategy, which were to deny Gildo whatever advantage he might have had from control of Rome's grain supply and to strike hard and fast at the African rebel with crack troops before the withdrawal of grain from the normal western markets had any long-range effect: 'Stilicho made ready for war the most famous regiments in the army, selecting therefrom special companies of picked men; he further prepared the fleet in the harbours of Etruria.'[150] In the meantime Stilicho mobilized a larger army in Italy in case it should prove necessary.

Although Gildo's force was much larger than the expeditionary army, his men were not reliable, undoubtedly restive in what was clearly an unlawful clash with Honorius' government, and in the end Gildo committed suicide without fighting Stilicho's force. The government of Arcadius had encouraged the rebellion but had made no overt contribution to its success. Eutropius, for his part, had scarcely covered himself with glory. On the other hand, Stilicho was emerging as a military hero. If he had not personally accompanied the expeditionary force to Africa, he had at least supervised the planning for the campaign, and he certainly took credit for its success. According to one (hostile but possibly truthful) version, he actually arranged the murder of his field commander so there would be no one to share the prestige of victory.[151] It was during this campaign, incidentally, that Stilicho's daughter Maria married the Emperor Honorius.

Naturally, in the aftermath of Gildo's rebellion, poor relations between East and West were further exacerbated, and in 398 when Arcadius nominated his trusted adviser Eutropius for the consulship of 399, a crisis erupted. The Lord Chamberlain had in fact won some considerable fame by defeating the Huns in the East, but no amount of military glory could compensate for the eunuch's peculiar 'physical disqualifications'. As the poet Claudian, an avowed partisan of Stilicho's cause, passionately put it: 'Every monstrosity pales before our eunuch consul; earth and heaven above are filled with shame.'[152] Arcadius and Eutropius had made a serious blunder – the scandal was probably as strongly felt in the East as in the West. During the course of his consular year the opposition (including Arcadius' wife) coalesced, and Eutropius was disgraced and banished.

Thus ended a stage in the career of Stilicho. The rest of his life was devoted to the threat of Alaric and the Visigoths, but the way he dealt with that threat had largely been shaped by the dramatic events of the first five years after Theodosius' death. Stilicho had hoped, and presumably continued to hope, that Arcadius would accept his guiding influence just as Honorius had. The great dynast undoubtedly believed that he deserved to exercise that influence because of his family relationship to the ruling brothers. Furthermore, he was deeply committed to Theodosius' policies of appeasement (or accommodation) of the Goths and Persians and the promotion of Christianity at the expense of paganism. These broad, imperial goals were often more important to the 'regent' in him than the strategic and tactical demands of the war with Alaric were to the 'general'. He was not necessarily a bad general – he was a bad politician, and political error sometimes critically compounded his military problems. Because of the breadth of his political vision, he could not settle down to the defence of Honorius and the West. In short, had he accepted the impossibility (to say nothing of the foolishness) of his eastern ambitions, he would have been a far better general in the West.

During the five years of conflict with Arcadius' advisers, Rufinus and Eutropius, Stilicho had twice met Alaric in the field. On both occasions the eastern government had ordered the western general to withdraw his army, and Alaric, saved by the tension between East and West, actually grew stronger. Before 400 the Visigothic chieftain was given the military command he had long wanted, general of the army for Illyricum (*magister militum per Illyricum*), a position that gave him and his followers access to the Roman logistical system (and specifically the arsenals) of the Balkans. Still, in the words of A. H. M. Jones: 'After five years Alaric had probably sucked the poverty-stricken Dacian and Macedonian dioceses dry, and he turned his eyes westwards for opportunities of richer booty or blackmail.'[153]

In November 401 Alaric marched the Visigoths into Italy and up to the walls of Milan. Although some historians believe that the eastern government of Arcadius encouraged Alaric to move west, there is no evidence to support that view.[154] The Visigothic leader had chosen an opportune time for invasion of the Po valley. Stilicho was tied down in the Alpine province of Raetia to the north, dealing with an attack of Suebi, Alans and Vandals, so northern Italy was undefended against attack from the east. Aquileia fell to the Visigoths as well as other cities of northeastern Italy. Fear swept the Italian peninsula, and at Milan there was talk of moving the court to Arles on the Rhône. Repairs were hastily begun on the great walls of Rome while omens and prodigies foretold dire calamities.[155]

In the face of panic Stilicho remained calm. Relying on the strength of Milan's walls, he persuaded the court to hold out while he dealt first with the crisis on the Raetian frontiers and mobilized a field army for use against Alaric. Troops from the Rhine and from Britain were assembled for the task and Vandal and Alan allies recruited.

Returning to northern Italy with his army, Stilicho hoped to attack Alaric's rear while the barbarian leader was still tied down to the siege of Milan. Hastening on in advance of the main body of his troops, Stilicho hurled himself with crack units in a surprise, night attack against Alaric's position and forced a way through into Milan. The Visigoths then raised the siege rather than allow themselves to get pinned down around the walls by an approaching Roman army.

Alaric headed south and west towards Gaul and the Maritime Alps. At Pollentia in northwestern Italy Stilicho met Alaric in a great battle on Easter Day AD 402. Stilicho hesitated to fight on such a holy day (and he was also hoping for reinforcements from Gaul), but his men, particularly his Alan allies, were eager for battle. The initial cavalry attack by the Alans was in fact repulsed, but Stilicho brought up infantry support and rallied the horsemen. After a raging battle the Goths were routed, and the Roman army took the Visigothic camp, seized booty which had been with the Goths since Adrianople, and captured Alaric's wife. Unfortunately, the poet Claudian to the contrary, Roman soldiers gave themselves up to plunder, and Alaric managed to escape with the bulk of his followers. Still, Rome had clearly triumphed over barbarism.[156]

It has been said that Stilicho, after this victory, made 'a bridge of gold' for Alaric to cross on his way out of Italy.[157] Such a statement reflects the ancient and modern frustration that the man who sacked Rome only a few years later came so close to destruction himself and yet escaped. In fact there was another battle, this second one near Verona, where again Alaric was defeated and only barely got away. The indications of indiscipline in the Roman army, which made pursuit – one of the most difficult of all military tasks – apparently impossible, merely foretold the even greater collapse that soon befell the mighty legions.

Alaric returned to Illyricum, and for a while Italy was spared the ravages of the Visigoths. Stilicho had defended the peninsula. His finest moment came in 405–6 when Radagaisus, another Gothic leader, driven possibly by Ostrogothic and Hunnic pressure, advanced across the Danube and into Italy. His followers, apparently numbering 200,000 to 400,000 in exaggerated ancient accounts, poured over the Po valley and into Tuscany. When Florence was on the verge of surrender, Stilicho arrived with an army of perhaps 20,000 *comitatenses*, drove Radagaisus into the high country of Fiesole

(*Faesulae*), and surrounded the barbarian leader. What followed, after the barbarians were weakened by thirst and hunger, was a massacre. Even Radagaisus was captured and taken to Rome for execution. Although Stilicho's glory was short-lived, it was, at this moment, immense.[158] In the years from 401 to 406 he had become the saviour of Italy.

The Vandals and the Rhine; the Fall of Stilicho

Even before the collapse of the Rhine frontier in 407, which was the chief cause of Stilicho's undoing, passionate currents in Roman politics threatened the regent's Theodosian policy of appeasement. He had several times had Alaric in his grip, or so it seemed, but always the barbarian leader got away. Possibly Stilicho simply could not control his troops firmly enough to conduct a proper pursuit, but in any event he seems to have been committed to the policy of accommodation that Theodosius had agreed to with the Visigoths in 382 and that Stilicho himself had negotiated with the Persians in 384.

As we have seen, however, from the beginning those policies had been controversial, particularly the settlement with the Visigoths, and after the death of Theodosius the Great critics of imperial strategy felt strong enough to speak out, especially following the plundering rampage of Alaric in the period 395–400. Ironically the first really strong anti-barbaric sentiment broke out in Constantinople and played a role in the fall of Arcadius' eunuch Lord Chamberlain, Eutropius, in the year 399. Many Romans felt that the German allies had become too prominent in the army, that they encouraged an unRoman indiscipline and that, when the chips were down, they could not be trusted to fight their fellow Germans in defence of the Empire. That same 'Roman party' was deeply offended by the appointment of a eunuch as consul.[159]

This 'nationalistic' anti-barbarian fervour erupted when the German general Gainas (*magister militum in praesenti*), who had commanded the eastern mobile army since Stilicho returned it to Arcadius, collaborated with an Ostrogothic chieftain, Tribigild, whose people had been settled in Asia Minor by Theodosius. As the Ostrogoths rebelled against Arcadius, the 'Roman' party led by Synesius, Bishop of Ptolemais, argued that Germans in the state had to be suppressed. This so-called 'Roman' party apparently attracted a considerable pagan following, partly because the Goths were Christians (albeit heretical Arians), but there were many Roman Christians, including Synesius, who also objected to appeasement of the barbarians.

Indeed, a popular movement of Roman peasants and slaves armed itself and hemmed in Tribigild and his forces, who managed to escape annihilation only when Gainas came to their aid. Gainas' aim was to depose the Chamberlain Eutropius, and he reported to Arcadius that Tribigild would return to his peaceful ways if the hated minister were removed. Since Arcadius' wife resented the eunuch's influence over her husband, she lent her weight to Gainas' request. When Eutropius fell, Gainas became the most influential figure in the East, after the emperor, but his pro-German policy provoked great animosity, and before the year 400 was out, the Goths had been driven out of Constantinople in a popular, 'Roman' uprising. Gainas himself, who fled to the Danube, was captured by the king of the Huns and relieved of his head, which was sent to Arcadius. The whole episode was important because the behaviour of the barbarian Roman general, Gainas, seemed to confirm the nationalistic Roman party's position, and popular sentiment had supported its cause. Stilicho, the son of a Vandal leader and the leading advocate of the Theodosian settlement with the Goths, had much to fear from this eastern, anti-barbarian movement that spread rapidly west and found fertile ground in Italy for its growth.[160]

After the defeat of Radagaisus at Fiesole in 405, Stilicho seems to have kept the forces, earlier withdrawn from Britain and the Rhine for use against Alaric, close at hand in northern Italy. This abandonment of the Rhine frontier in pursuit of a strategy that gave priority to defence of Italy proved fatal for Rome. Although it makes sense, at least superficially, that the ancient centre of the Empire should be defended at all costs, it was not in fact the wisest strategy. Nor does it require modern military science to arrive at that conclusion. Some of Stilicho's contemporaries had hit upon a better plan during Alaric's invasion of 401–2.

At that time there was discussion about the idea of moving the seat of the Western Empire to the Rhône in Gaul and resisting further barbarian aggression from that presumably stronger base. Indeed from a military point of view that is exactly what should have been done. The armies of Britain and particularly of Gaul, along with the grain of Africa, were the ultimate bases of strength in the West. Had the western government under Stilicho's direction sought to preserve them, it is possible that strategic withdrawal from Italy would have had the additional advantage of bringing irresistible pressure to bear on Arcadius and the Eastern Empire to share in the effective defence of Italy against barbarian attack, especially when Rome itself was threatened. In the end the gravest problem faced by the western government was the unwillingness of the eastern one to help in moments of military crisis.

Instead Stilicho adopted an incredibly foolish strategy. After Alaric was driven out in 402, Honorius and his court moved east to Ravenna, which became the capital of the Western Empire for much of the fifth century. It is true that Ravenna was militarily defensible, and a much stronger base for the court in northern Italy than the more exposed city of Milan. Hundreds of years earlier Ravenna had been selected by Augustus as the major Roman naval base in the northern Adriatic. Today Ravenna is some four miles from the coast and a relatively arid city, but in antiquity it was more like Venice is today, surrounded by water and marshes, and laced with canals. The water was foul, and wine was notoriously Ravenna's popular drink. Honorius and his successors beautified the city, which is even now famous for its Christian mosaics. Because of the water and the marshes, with intensive fortification Ravenna became nearly as impregnable as Constantinople, a veritable bastion for the Roman emperor of the West.[161]

This strategy proved tragic, however, because it opened the way for the sack of Rome – the western emperor was now easily bypassed in his fortress at Ravenna – but its worst consequence was to expose the Rhine frontier, so far removed from the northeastern corner of Italy where the mobile army was stationed. While two-fold catastrophes occurred in the Italian peninsula and in Gaul from 407 to 410, the ruler in Constantinople justified his own inactivity on the grounds that his brother (or uncle, after the death of Arcadius) was safe at Ravenna and was geographically based between Constantinople and the scene of the fighting. Perhaps the decision to establish court at Ravenna was made solely by Honorius – Stilicho, as general, ought nevertheless to have protested on military grounds.

While the Gallic legionaries were in Italy, on the last day of the year 406, an alliance of Vandals, Suebi and Alans crossed the frozen Rhine

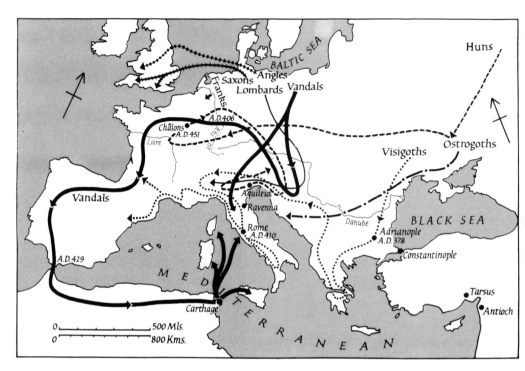

The barbarian invasions.

and swept through the undefended areas of northern Gaul.[162] Virtually overnight a major portion of Gaul was lost. Instead of taking vigorous counteraction, Stilicho concentrated on affairs in the East, because tensions between Honorius and Arcadius had recently surfaced again. A general who had one eye on Constantinople was not likely to offer much help to battered Gaul.

In the fear and turmoil of the Vandal invasion, when no help from the government in Ravenna seemed likely, a usurper, Constantine, was proclaimed emperor by his troops in Britain, and he crossed over the Channel bringing welcome relief to the plundered prefecture. Yet even so, when the dynasty was threatened by rebellion, Stilicho looked east. From Illyricum, Alaric did indeed begin to march with his Visigoths but in the direction of Noricum to the north rather than of Italy. From there the Visigothic leader demanded four thousand pounds of gold in return for an alliance and the promise of help for the western ruler against the rebel Constantine. Some senators in Rome called it blackmail, though Stilicho urged acceptance of this alliance. It was, after all, consistent with Theodosian policy, and it might mean the salvation of Honorius' regime.

While the situation in Gaul had undermined Stilicho's prestige, the deal with Alaric scandalized Romans of the anti-barbarian 'nationalist' party.[163] Rumours began to spread that Stilicho had designs on the throne – if not for himself, then for his son, Eucherius. The general's pact with Alaric was treason. When news reached the West in the spring of 408 that Arcadius had died, Stilicho made a fatal blunder. Still hoping for that regency in the East that had been his ambition since the death of Theodosius in 395, Stilicho persuaded Honorius to commission Alaric to suppress Constantine in the West while he, Stilicho, travelled to Constantinople to preside over the accession of the young Theodosius II and establish a regency, thus bringing together East and West again.

This temptation to indulge in the intrigue of Byzantium was fatal for Stilicho and, far more significantly, for the West. Everything that Stilicho's opponents had said about him seemed to be true. He was conniving with the barbarians, he had stood by silently while Germans swept through Gaul, he had allowed a usurper to challenge the Theodosian House in the West, and then, to cap it all, the death of Arcadius drew Stilicho's attention relentlessly east at the very moment when it should have been directed vigorously westwards. Palace intriguers at Ravenna buzzed with the rumours of Stilicho's treachery, and the discontent spread into the army, already confused and angered by its inactivity in the hour of crisis.

When it became apparent to Stilicho that his world was crumbling around him, he took refuge in a church in Ravenna. He was enticed to leave on the promise that his life would be spared, but immediately thereafter he was executed. The murder of his son, Eucherius, followed not much later in Rome. By the time of his fall, Stilicho had become a hated public figure and was widely blamed for the misfortunes of the West. Modern historians praise his loyalty. At the end he might have resisted, since there were certainly some German troops who would have tried to help him. But he turned aside all such overtures and went to meet his fate with a calm courage. Cowardice and treachery were, in fact, not among his many shortcomings. His errors were strategic and conceptual – the willingness to appease the

Goths, the strategy of defence around Ravenna, the lure of Constantinople (even though that was possibly consistent with the wishes of Theodosius the Great). He was, in the end, altogether too much a product of the age of Theodosius, and of the defeat at Adrianople. When the times called out for aggressive counter-measures against barbarian invaders, Stilicho hesitated. The results were as deadly for Rome as they were for the generalissimo.

The Sack of Rome

One immediate effect of the fall of Stilicho was the improvement in the relations between East and West. Equally immediate however, was the deterioration of relations with the Visigoths. An anti-barbarian witch hunt following Stilicho's execution led to the murder of some barbarians, and nearly thirty thousand allied barbarian troops marched north to join Alaric.[164] Stilicho's place in the western government had been taken by a certain Olympius, a palace politician who had masterminded the great general's fall. At this juncture Olympius had to deal with the possibility of war on two fronts: the rebellion of Constantine in Gaul and the threat of Alaric to the north in Noricum.

The more urgent problem was posed by Alaric. Although he offered to withdraw into Pannonia in exchange for money and hostages, Olympius refused to make such a major concession. The emperor's agent had no choice, given the 'nationalist' sentiment of the times, and those historians who argue that the West lost a chance to save itself from the scourge of Alaric show little understanding of the raging currents of the age. Alaric had already succeeded in extracting a large amount from Stilicho. At a certain point, it is necessary to regard the foe's demands as insatiable. In the case of Alaric that point had probably passed.

It is more reasonable to castigate Olympius and the Western emperor for failing to take steps to defend Italy. Perhaps events simply moved too quickly. Arcadius had died in the spring of 408, and his death was followed in August by the fall of Stilicho and the unrest generated by such a dramatic change in power. Stilicho, after all, had been dominant in the West for more than a decade. To compound matters Alaric acted aggressively, marching across the Julian Alps and into Italy in October 408. There was essentially no opposition. The emperor and his court took refuge in Ravenna while the Po fell to the invader. Bypassing the highly fortified cities, the Visigoths marched towards Rome, and a legend grew up that Alaric believed he was destined to take the ancient capital. *Penetrabis ad Urbem* – 'You shall enter the City' – was a voice he had heard before.[165] Although Milan and Ravenna had become the effective centres of power in the West, Rome remained the most prestigious symbol of greatness in the ageing Empire.

Down the Flaminian Way Alaric led his army, hoping probably to draw Honorius out of his fortress. Despite the legend, Alaric did not intend to sack Rome. It was well defended by strong walls that had recently been repaired, and the Visigoths lacked the techniques of siege warfare. Alaric merely hoped to extract from the Western emperor more land and more money, presumably a lot of both, as well as additional official Roman honours and offices for himself. His army marched rapidly, passed by Rome and moved west and then north again to take Rome's port of Ostia (thereby gaining control of the grain from Africa). Thus, as Romans looked towards the winter of 408–9, they found themselves cut off from their Empire and facing starvation from blockade.

Panic spread through the city in this moment of trial. Fearing that Serena, the widow of Stilicho, might open the gates to the barbarians whom her husband had so long courted, the Senate decreed her death. This did little, however, to mitigate the famine and plague that engulfed the city, as Alaric tightened his grip. Finally a legation was sent to Alaric, whose terms, according to Zosimus, were 'beyond even the insolence of a barbarian'.[166] In short, he asked for all moveable wealth in the city, specifically including but not exclusively limited to gold and silver items, and the return of all Germanic slaves. When a Roman ambassador asked what Alaric intended to leave behind, the arrogant warrior reportedly replied, 'Your lives'. As it became apparent that the government in Ravenna would do nothing to help Rome, Pope Innocent, hoping to alleviate panic, agreed to the performance of pagan rituals (which at the last moment were actually cancelled).

Finally the Senate offered a ransom of five thousand pounds of gold, thirty thousand of silver, four thousand silk tunics, three thousand scarlet hides and three thousand pounds of pepper. Alaric, however, demanded in addition a treaty of alliance with Honorius. In January 409 the emperor refused this request, and Alaric resumed the blockade. The emperor's agent, Olympius, lost much of the popularity he had gained from the overthrow of Stilicho while some Romans openly wondered whether the dead general, who had at least challenged Alaric occasionally on the field, had not in fact been better than his successor. A palace conspiracy led to the fall of the imperial favourite in February 409, and discussions with Alaric were reopened. After some Machiavellian negotiations with the Visigothic leader, Jovius, the new adviser to the emperor, urged Honorius to remain intransigent in the safety of Ravenna. Whereupon Alaric angrily broke off talks altogether and returned to the siege of Rome.

The so-called second siege of Rome, in the autumn of 409, came only after Alaric had tried to organize the Italian bishops to press Honorius to come to terms with him. His requests were 'moderate', or so he claimed – in fact reduced at this time, as a 'concession', to the two provinces of Noricum and supplies for his troops.[167] It is not surprising that many of the emperor's threatened subjects were impressed by the 'moderation' of the conqueror, that Italians were willing to give up Noricum in exchange for their own freedom. What is less explicable is the tendency of modern historians to castigate Honorius for indecision, lethargy and stubbornness. The record of history is filled with blustering conquerors speaking of peace. The victims of conquest often choose to believe the words and ignore the brutality swirling around them – their need for comfort is clear enough.

Honorius did exactly what he should have done under the circumstances – he 'stonewalled' Alaric. The emperor had no basis of strength whatsoever (except the impregnability of Ravenna) from which to negotiate, since Stilicho's army had dispersed after the fall of the general. On the other hand, Alaric's position was also weak. Rome was actually well fortified and could not be taken by direct assault. Blockades required time, and in that time it might be possible to get aid from Constantinople. Turmoil in the western provinces, resulting from the Vandal invasion and the rebellion of Constantine, made relief from the West unlikely, but delay really served the interests of the emperor while it gave him the appearance of being ineffective. The army of the Visigoths, with its primitive logistical system, lived in the long run a precarious existence in the Italian peninsula.[168]

13   A colossal marble head of Constantine the Great (306–37) in Rome. Many art historians
have seen this bust, with its frontal aspect and eternal stare, as the major aesthetic
symbol of the dawning of a new Late Imperial or Byzantine age. Constantine also laid down
new lines in grand strategy.

14 (Above left) Constantius II (337–61). He was an Arian Christian and a temperamental ruler, shown here with that eternal stare that characterizes fourth-century sculpture. Constantius died before he could face his rebellious cousin, Julian the Apostate, who then secured the throne.

15 (Above) This miniature bust of Julian the Apostate (361–63), made of chalcedony, is now in Leningrad. Julian's generalship was at least as important as his religious policy in the history of the Late Roman Empire. He defended the Rhine in Gaul, but fell mortally wounded in his abortive invasion of Persia (363).

16 (Left) A sculptural relief portrait, in silver, of Theodosius the Great (379–95). After the Roman defeat at Adrianople Theodosius emerged as the shaper of Roman grand strategy. His decision to allow the Goths to remain within the Empire, under arms as federates or allies, may have been a serious error.

17 (Right) This colossal bronze statue is probably Valentinian I (364–75). It stands before the Church of the Holy Sepulchre in Barletta. Valentinian was the best emperor-general of the late fourth century and was particularly active in restoring the defences of the Rhine frontier.

IN NOMINE XPI VINCAS SEMPER
D N HONORIO SEMP AVG
D N HONORIO SEMPER AVG
PROBVS FAMVLVS V C CONS ORD
PROBVS FAMVLVS V C CONS ORD

18 Two portraits of the Emperor Honorius (395–423) given to him on his assumption of the consulship in 406. When Honorius pursued a strategy of exhaustion against Alaric in 408–10, he appeared to his contemporaries to be incompetent. In fact his strategy may have been wise, but it failed when someone inside Rome opened the Salarian Gate in August 410. Later, Honorius' government made a reasonably effective recovery.

20 (Below) The Notitia Dignitatum, a list of military and civilian offices in the Eastern and Western Roman Empires after 395, was illustrated. This shows the insignia of the Count of the Saxon Shore in Britain, from a manuscript in the Bodleian Library, Oxford.

19 (Above) Stilicho, from one panel of an ivory diptych, c.400. The general had served Theodosius the Great and was regent to Honorius in the West. Several times Stilicho defeated but did not destroy Alaric and the Visigoths. Normally he pursued the Theodosian policy of accommodating the barbarians. His desire to extend his influence to Constantinople led to his execution in 408.

21 (Above) A cameo showing the Emperor
Honorius (395–423) and the Empress Maria. Maria
was the daughter of the general Stilicho, whose
various connections with the house of Theodosius
kept him in the forefront of military and political
activity until Honorius finally had him executed in
408. By that time Maria had died.

22 (Left) A seal of Alaric, King of the Visigoths.
In 410 Alaric sacked the city of Rome, the first time
in 800 years that it had been taken by a foreign
army. Alaric died afterwards in Italy, where he was
buried in a secret grave, and the Visigoths then
moved into Gaul and Spain.

23 (Above) A marble bust of the Eastern Emperor Arcadius (395–408), the son of Theodosius the Great. In the late fourth and early fifth centuries Arcadius turned the Visigothic invaders towards the West. Jealousy between Stilicho and the advisers of Arcadius prevented cooperation between East and West.

24 (Above right) A portrait of Galla Placidia. Her amazing career has often intrigued modern students. She was the daughter of Theodosius the Great, the wife of the Visigothic King Ataulf, the wife of the Roman Emperor Constantius III, and the mother of the Emperor Valentinian III.

25 (Right) The Emperor Valentinian III (425–55) in military dress. In fact he did not personally command his own armies. He killed his general Aëtius in a coup, but was himself then murdered.

26 *The so-called* currus drepanus, *designed by Anonymus for his military treatise,* De Rebus Bellicis. *He actually proposed three different versions of scythed chariots. The one above, drawn by two horses and riders, is similar to the others in that all have hinged scythes attached to the axles that can be raised or lowered as needed. The chariot had not been an efficient war machine since Assyrian times and was certainly not the answer to Rome's military problems in the fourth and fifth centuries.*

27 *One of the dubious inventions of the anonymous author of* De Rebus Bellicis *was this Liburna, a warship powered by oxen-driven gears attached to paddle wheels. The manuscripts of* De Rebus Bellicis *were illustrated with drawings, presumably based on ancient ones.*

Such considerations were little consolation to the inhabitants of Rome, who rebelled rather than submit to the suffering of starvation. In collusion with Alaric, the Senate recognized a new emperor, Attalus, and renounced the rule of Honorius. In this new imperial government Alaric became Field Marshal of the West (*magister utriusque militum*), but Attalus refused to attempt the conquest of Africa with Gothic troops. The loyalty of Africa to the regime in Ravenna was a critical element of Honorius' strength in the face of this rebellion.

Events moved rapidly in the crisis. Constantine invaded Italy from the West, publicly to help Honorius against Alaric, but with uncertain secret objectives. Then came the long-awaited aid from Constantinople – only four thousand troops, but well trained, and symbolizing a deep commitment. Constantine, however, unwilling to be trapped in Italy by a resurgent Ravenna, returned to Gaul. As Honorius' government became more stable with the support of the East, Alaric deposed Attalus (summer 410), who had become an obstacle to settlement with the western regime. By this time Alaric had taken custody of Honorius' sister, Galla Placidia, the daughter of Theodosius the Great, granddaughter of Valentinian I. She had been raised by Stilicho and Serena and was in Rome at the time of the first and second sieges.[169]

When the dethronement of Attalus brought no conciliation from Honorius at Ravenna, Alaric moved for a third time against the walls of Rome in early August 410. For some days Romans lived again with starvation, and there are even indications of possible cannibalism. Then came the inevitable. On 24 August 410 someone on the inside opened the Salarian Gate (one of the twelve gates of the city) and a foreign army marched on the streets of Rome for the first time in eight hundred years.

The sack of Rome shook the world. St Jerome felt its effects in Bethlehem, and Augustine thundered from North Africa in his *City of God* against those pagans who blamed the fall on Christianity. To the pagans, of course, it was clear that the ancestral gods and goddesses had protected the city in the past and were punishing Romans for deserting them in favour of Christ. Naturally there were many versions of what actually happened. According to one story an aristocratic Roman lady, Faltonia Proba, shocked by the suffering of the Romans, opened the gate to bring an end to the misery.[170] There is no controversy, however, about the fact of treachery – someone, for whatever reason, opened the gate.

For three days Rome was plundered. How much damage was done no one knows, but it was probably considerable. To argue that 'not too much harm could be wrought' in only three days is to miscalculate rather gravely the force of human violence.[171] A disorganized mob can leave desolation in its wake; an army, entering a besieged city in victory, can do whatever it pleases. There is no doubt that it pleased Alaric to plunder Rome. Palaces and temples were stripped of every moveable decoration and idol. Romans were wantonly killed, women were raped, buildings were burnt. To be sure, had the city not been barren of food, because of the blockade, the harm might have been even greater, since the Goths with their inadequate logistical system moved out quickly and down to Campania around the Bay of Naples to find food. This incidentally suggests that they could not have maintained a long blockade outside Rome, as they looked towards the autumn of 410, and that treachery in the city undermined what might otherwise have been a reasonably successful strategy by the government at Ravenna.

Alaric took with him Honorius' sister, Galla Placidia, who was about sixteen years old at the time, and with the valuable hostage he and his army streamed through southern Italy, a region of great untapped wealth, which had not seen such a force since the days of Hannibal. The destination of this horde was Africa, the breadbasket of Italy, itself a centre of many wealthy cities, ripe for the taking. To deny Honorius the advantage of Africa would be to deliver a deadly blow to Ravenna. The barbarian chieftain finally reached the tip of the toe of the boot of Italy and stood gazing across the strait at Sicily. As preparations were made for the crossing, the miracle Sicilians had prayed for seemed to happen. A storm scattered the Gothic fleet, and Alaric decided to march north, back up the peninsula. Then, without the warning of a lingering illness, the sacker of Rome died.

His manner of burial has contributed mightily to his myth. We are told that the river Busento in Southern Italy was diverted from its course by captive labour and that Alaric was laid to rest in the river-bed while the water then resumed its normal course. If the idea was to conceal the king's final resting place – and it must have been, since the labourers were killed – the method has so far at least been successful. The tomb defies discovery.

Alaric was immediately succeeded by his brother-in-law, Ataulf, who marched with the Visigoths, and with Galla Placidia, northwards, slowly out of Italy. Again Italians suffered, but late in 411 the Visigoths arrived on the Po, and early in 412 they crossed the Alps and moved into Gaul. Thus came to an end a grisly chapter in the story of the Roman people. It is for the most part a story of strategy gone wrong, sometimes because it was conceptually flawed, sometimes because luck was on the other side. It is not a story of lethargy. Honorius, who liked to tend chickens, was said at the time to have been more interested in them than in Rome, but such is the criticism that the strategy of delay inevitably entails. Antoninus Pius also liked chickens, and he was one of the Five Good Emperors. The great historian Bury did Honorius a disservice by describing him as an emperor 'whose mind did not travel far beyond his family and his poultry-yard'.[172]

The greatest mistake, attributable presumably to both Stilicho and Honorius, was the decision to shift the court from Milan to Ravenna in the Visigothic invasion of 401–2. Milan, which had been a reasonable base for the defence of the Rhine and Danube frontiers, was less good for the defence of Italy – a major military problem of the early fifth century. As we have seen, a decision to centre the western Roman government on the Rhône, at Arles or elsewhere, was actually considered and would have been far wiser than the decision taken, to move to Ravenna. From the Rhône it is quite possible that the barbarian invasion of Gaul, starting on the last day of the year 406, might have been forestalled as well as the rebellion of Constantine that followed. To be sure, a government centred at Arles could not have prevented the invasion of Italy, except to the extent that it was determined by the earlier invasion of Gaul. If Honorius had ruled from Arles, however, while Alaric sacked Rome, the pressure on Constantinople to share in the defence of Italy would have been much greater. The nearness of Ravenna to Rome and its location between Rome and Constantinople placed the responsibility for Rome's defence squarely and irretrievably on Honorius.

Once the strategic mistake of falling back on Ravenna was made, however, it is not clear that Honorius actually mismanaged the campaign against Alaric in 408–10. The western government was in no position to challenge Alaric on the field. Stilicho had relied heavily on barbarian allies, and the effectiveness of the western army had been destroyed or seriously weakened by the fall of the general, when the friendly barbarian units on which he had relied so strongly, in accordance with Theodosian policy, defected to Alaric in the face of a strong, 'nationalist', anti-barbarian policy at the court. Unable to strike at the enemy's main force, Honorius took advantage of the few strengths he had – an impregnable capital in Ravenna, an impenetrable system of walls around Rome, Visigothic incompetence in logistics and siege warfare, and the heavy moral claim on help from Constantinople, made possible by the welcome overthrow of Stilicho, who was looked upon with suspicion on the Bosporus. Honorius could not negotiate without making major damaging concessions to Alaric. His only chance in the long run was to wait and hope for the best – either withdrawal of the invaders because of problems of supply or the arrival of strong reinforcements from the East. There are indications that this strategy was working, on both scores, when on 24 August 410 someone opened the Salarian Gate, and the Visigoths sacked Rome. Honorius, understandably enough, was not given credit by his contemporaries for a wise strategy. His plan had been undermined, and he seemed simply a do-nothing emperor at a critical moment in Roman history when almost any 'active' mistake would have been better received.

The sack of Rome had revealed the military impotence of the Western emperor, a remarkable fact considering the apparent military strength of the Roman Empire just a few years earlier in AD 395. The great army of the West had degenerated to such an extent that it could not challenge Alaric in the field, even with the help of units from the Rhine. To what extent the army under Stilicho's command had been weakened in the several clashes with the Visigoths earlier, in the Balkans and in northern Italy, is uncertain. It is likely however, that Stilicho relied more and more on the use of allied barbarian troops and that he allowed recruitment of regular Roman forces to decline. The decisive act in the military enfeeblement of the West seems to have come when thirty thousand of Stilicho's barbarian allies defected to Alaric in 408, after the general's execution and when the remaining forces of Britain and Gaul gave their support to a rebel. The road to military recovery for the government of Honorius would be a long one, and the recovery was never fully complete.

Chapter Six

The Grand Strategy of the Western Roman Empire in the Early Fifth Century

It is easy to believe in the 'inevitability' of the fall of Rome particularly after the sack of the city in 410. Yet the fate of the western government had not been fully shaped even in the decisive, though not determinative, years 406–10. Africa remained loyal. Britain, Gaul and Spain were in rebellion but might yet be restored to Ravenna's control. The fateful decision to establish the western court at Ravenna permanently put priority on the military defence of Italy, a mistake in the end impossible to rectify, but the terrible consequences of that flaw in the grand strategy of the Western Roman Empire had not yet incapacitated Honorius and his associates. Resurgence of imperial influence and military power in the West was still possible. It would be a serious mistake to let our knowledge of Rome's destiny blind us to the fact that even after Adrianople and the sack of Rome, the emperor in the West had some scope for military planning. Most of the Western Roman Empire still remained Roman and vigorous military action might stave off the impending collapse.

Constantius III and the Crisis in the West

In the last chapter we noted the crisis in Gaul after the invasion of 31 December 406, and the revolt of Constantine in Britain in 407. From 408–10 the court at Ravenna was more deeply concerned with Alaric and the Visigoths in the Italian peninsula than with the agony of Gaul. The Vandals, Suebi and Alans crossed the Rhine originally near Mainz, and after advancing generally westwards to Trier, which they sacked and fired, and to Boulogne, the barbarians swung southwards towards Aquitaine and the Pyrenees. Most of the towns of northern and western Gaul were sacked and plundered, and one writer said: 'All Gaul went up in a single pyre.'[173]

Some of the cities of northeastern Gaul, such as Strasbourg and Worms, seem to have fallen at this time to the Burgundians and the

Alamanni. While Gaul waited in vain for help from Italy, rebellion in Britain led ultimately to the elevation there of the soldier Constantine to the purple by Roman troops. When he moved into Gaul at Boulogne, he dealt a heavy blow to the barbarians and restored the Rhine frontier. Unfortunately, the majority of Rome's enemies were already inside the Empire. This Constantine ruled in Gaul for four years and was a major player in the drama of Rome's fall, but he is sometimes overlooked. As the historian Hodgkin put it, Constantine's career distracts 'attention from the far more important events which were passing at the same time in Italy'.[174]

Ironically Constantine did what Honorius should have done – he headed for the Rhône and established his court at Arles. From the Rhône Constantine's army drove back the forces of Honorius sent out to oppose him. By 408 the usurper controlled all Gaul, from the Channel to the Alps, if one excepts from consideration that territory in the hands of barbarian invaders, particularly in southwestern and northeastern Gaul. He then sent his son Constans as Caesar into Spain and added the vast extent of that land to his dominion. In 409, when Honorius was severely pressed in Italy by Alaric, the court at Ravenna actually briefly recognized Constantine as an Augustus, hoping to gain his help in Italy, but Honorius soon repudiated that, and the government of the Eastern Empire in Constantinople never joined in the recognition.

Then, in the autumn of 409, Vandals, Suebi and Alans crossed the Pyrenees from Gaul into Spain, the first of several blows that led to the fall of Constantine and the restoration of the Honorian regime throughout the West.[175] Imperial troops in Spain, restless because they believed the defence of the Pyrenees had been mishandled by Constantine's government, rebelled from his authority and proclaimed their own emperor, an otherwise unknown Maximus.[176] So at the beginning of that eventful year, 410, there were six emperors or pretenders in the Empire: Honorius, Theodosius II in the East, Constantine and his son Constans (who had been raised to the emperorship as colleague of his father), Attalus in Rome, and Maximus in Spain.

By 411 the rebel government in Spain had defeated and killed Constantine's son and put the ruler of Gaul under siege in Arles. By this time Alaric was dead, and Honorius sent his new military adviser, Constantius, west. Even though Ataulf and the Visigoths were still in

Italy, that was a wise strategic decision on the part of the emperor in Ravenna. Since Constantius will emerge as the military mainstay of the emperor in the West, the successor to the power and influence of Stilicho, we should briefly examine his connections and character. His appearance was decidedly peculiar – with big eyes that darted right and left, set in a broad head on a long neck, he seemed strong and suspicious in public although he apparently relaxed with his friends over wine and food. If he became greedy in the course of time, he could not, in his early career, be bribed, a rare virtue in a corrupt age. As time went by, he developed a passion for Galla Placidia, the emperor's sister, a captive of the Visigoths. An Illyrian, Constantius had fought under Theodosius I and may have been a partisan of Stilicho.[177]

For Honorius, Constantius was the right man at the right time. As the imperial general marched west with his army, Spanish troops renewed their allegiance to the central government, and Maximus went into exile among the barbarians of Spain. Then Constantius took Arles, captured Constantine and sent him in chains to Italy, after the usurper from Britain had been ordained a priest when he fled for refuge to a church. The rebel emperor was not saved by his newly acquired priesthood – on the road to Ravenna he was beheaded, and his head was displayed on a pole for all to see.[178] Thus at the end of 411, just as Ataulf was about to leave Italy and enter Gaul with the Visigoths, there had been a significant change for the better throughout the West for Honorius. The Roman government was relatively stable, but barbarians had seized large stretches of territory.

The Settlement of Barbarian Nations

In the fourth century, after the battle of Adrianople, Theodosius the Great had established a policy for dealing with Visigoths in Roman territory. As we have seen, he had assigned them definite lands along the Danube and allowed them to retain their armies under their own leaders in return for a promise to support the emperor in war. This 'federate' status actually permitted a more or less autonomous state within the confines of the Empire. From 382 to 395 the policy had worked reasonably well. After the chaos of Adrianople, barbarians had generally settled down in the Empire, and Theodosius used their military support to great effect in his victory over Arbogast and Eugenius at the Frigidus in 394.

From 395 to 410, however, the Theodosian policy of barbarian settlement, as pursued by Stilicho, had been a miserable failure. The inability of the East to cooperate with the West had created a situation that Alaric used much to his advantage, until finally, in 410, smoke rose from the ashes of a battered Rome. The Visigoths were adrift in the Roman Empire. No longer tied to their lands along the Danube, they seemed to move at will throughout the Balkans and Italy, though Ravenna remained safe behind its intricate and strong defences. In the meantime Vandals, Suebi, Alans and Burgundians had crossed the Rhine, and parts of Gaul and Spain witnessed the violence of their depredations.

Under the circumstances, the government of Honorius had only limited alternatives. Ideally it could smash the barbarian nations, subject the barbarians to Roman law and dissolve their political autonomy, or, more practically, it could try to accommodate them within the Roman system as Theodosius the Great had done. Stated simply, the emperor in the West had to destroy them or let them keep their arms, and he could not destroy them. The Visigoths surely would never accept, willingly, less than what they had received under Theodosius, and, if they retained their autonomy, the Vandals and other tribes would naturally expect to do the same. Unfortunately for Honorius, the breach in Roman defences had been too big. Had the Rhine frontier not collapsed in 406–7, had Honorius retained control over a strong Britain, Gaul, Spain and Africa, with the cooperation of the East that came after the deaths of Arcadius and Stilicho in 408, there might have been a military solution to the problem of the Visigoths.

Still there was some hope in the years after 411 that the barbarians might exhaust themselves in mutual conflict and that Rome would be able to maintain a dominant position as the referee of barbarian disputes. After Constantius returned to Italy, a new rebel, Jovinus, elevated by Burgundians and Alans at Mainz, threatened the tranquility of Gaul. When Ataulf crossed the Alps into Gaul early in 412, Jovinus was hostile to his intrusion, and it was not long before the Visigothic king found himself fighting a pretender who was hated as much by Honorius as by himself. Accordingly Honorius accepted his old foe Ataulf as an ally in the war against Jovinus, who was captured and executed in the autumn of 413, and whose head also eventually decorated the streets of Ravenna.[179]

In the meantime Constantius had turned his attention towards Africa where Count Heraclian, formerly a strong supporter of Honorius, yielded to the temptation of power and rebelled in his own name.[180] After interdicting commerce between Africa and Rome, Heraclian attacked Italy with a fleet of 3,700 ships, presumably most of them transports. At a battle on the Tiber, near Rome, he was defeated and fled with only one ship back to Carthage where he yielded his head to the executioner (March 413). Honorius rewarded Constantius, who had supervised the campaign, with Heraclian's considerable private fortune.

While Africa was made secure, the new alliance with the Visigoths was complicated by the captivity of Galla Placidia, who remained in Ataulf's custody. Honorius requested his sister's return, and Ataulf agreed to it on condition that the Visigoths received grain and 'federate' territory in Gaul. The emperor at Ravenna acquiesced in terms imposed by the barbarian leader, but Heraclian's revolt in Africa had interfered with the flow of grain, and Honorius was unable to live up to the bargain. As a result, in January 414, Ataulf married Galla Placidia (apparently not against her wishes) and simply seized territory in southern Gaul for his Visigoths. The marriage was conducted according to Roman ceremony, and the Visigothic chieftain, in Roman dress, poured upon the new queen of his people the gold and gems taken as spoil from Rome. The former emperor Attalus, who had served briefly in Rome under Alaric's tutelage in 410, was present at the festivities.[181]

According to the Christian historian Orosius, Ataulf soon showed how deeply he had been influenced by his Roman bride:

At first, he said, I ardently desired that the Roman name should be obliterated, and that all Roman soil should be converted into an empire of the Goths; I longed that Romania should become Gothia and Ataulf be what Caesar Augustus was. But I have been taught by much experience that the unbridled licence of the Goths will never admit of their obeying *laws*, and without laws a republic is not a republic. I have therefore chosen the safer course of aspiring to the glory of restoring and increasing the Roman name by Gothic vigour; and hope to be handed down to posterity as the initiator of a Roman restoration; as it is impossible for me to change the form of the empire.[182]

Some Christians of the time believed that their God had brought Ataulf and Galla Placidia together for the benefit of mankind. Naturally, this view was not popular at the court of Ravenna.

There is no particular reason to see in the statement quoted above any genuine barbarian compromise with 'Romania' – the civilization of the ancient Romans. Admiration of certain features of Roman life was not sufficient to turn a barbarian into a civilized man. Just as Romans of the fifth century bore a long tradition of culture on their shoulders, so too the Visigoth found it difficult to escape 'Gothia' for some of the obvious advantages of Mediterranean civilization (a fact that Ataulf actually claimed to recognize). When Orosius, himself a Spaniard, says in passing that some Roman subjects preferred barbarian simplicity to the corruption of Roman government, we need not attach undue significance to the statement.[183] Every nation has its malcontents and its oppressed (and the two groups are not always the same). It is not surprising that there were some non-barbarians in the vast extent of the Roman Empire who applauded the fall of the central government. Rather, the continuing loyalty to Rome of the bulk of the population throughout the West, even when its military power seemed inadequate to the task of defence, is more impressive.[184]

The inevitable tension generated between Honorius and Ataulf by the barbarian leader's marriage with Galla Placidia led finally to the re-emergence of Attalus, who was prepared once again to serve as the Goths' puppet. Attalus' renewed claim to the purple could not be ignored in Ravenna, and Constantius moved out towards Gaul with an army, not so much to deal with Attalus as with Ataulf. Making use of the naval power that was one of the distinguishing characteristics of the western ruler's arsenal, Constantius blockaded the Mediterranean coast of Gaul, cutting off Ataulf's supplies. Whereupon, early in 415, leaving Attalus behind to be captured, the Visigoths moved to Barcelona in Spain. Later the two-time pretender graced an imperial triumph in Rome before he was mutilated and banished to Lipara, on an island north of Sicily. (Mutilation was a common punishment in this period, but pretenders normally lost their heads; Attalus sacrificed only a thumb and finger.) Ataulf died in Barcelona, killed by a rebellious stable-groom, and after a chaotic interval of seven days was succeeded by Vallia (415–18).[185] One result of the migration of the Visigoths into Spain was the liberation of Gaul from barbarian rulers, except for the Burgundian kingdom around Worms on the Rhine, which had been given 'federate' status by Honorius.

Britain's connection with Ravenna was somewhat more tenuous. The troops withdrawn in 407 left the diocese a prey to attack from

Picts and Scots in the north and Saxons across the channel. Although the Count of the Saxon Shore and the Duke of Britain, supporters undoubtedly of the rebel Constantine, defended the two regions as best they could and represented Roman government on the island, a massive Saxon invasion in 408 led to rebellion and the formation of a citizen militia. Taking defence of the province into their own hands, the Britons must have been disappointed when in 410 Honorius gave them his blessing and encouraged their efforts but was unable to make a material contribution to their cause. Although the Romano-British natives held out on a gradually declining basis for two or three decades after the withdrawal of 407, the island was never again an integral part of the Western Roman Empire. As late as 446 there was an appeal to the Western Empire for help, but by that time Roman civilization in Britain had been virtually destroyed. By the end of the century, perhaps by mid-century, urbanization, the Latin language, and Christianity were swamped by brutal Saxons.[186] Elsewhere in the West the collapse of Roman government was less complete, but the example of Britain serves as a reminder of the powerful, destructive forces unleashed by the barbarian invasions.

After the departure of the Visigoths from Gaul in 415 Honorius and Constantius did reassert imperial control over most of the region. To be sure the Burgundians had carved out a niche for themselves, and in some areas of Gaul, particularly in the Alps and in the west in Armorica (later to be known as Brittany since so many Britons fled across the Channel to escape the Saxons), a lawless brigandage became endemic, making it difficult for Romans or barbarians to exercise effective control. The so-called Bagaudae, robber chiefs (the word means simply 'rebels'), who gained control of parts of Gaul, were essentially separatists recognizing no authority but their own.[187]

In Spain the situation was much more complicated. Honorius' government had a foothold in Tarraconensis, and from there Constantius used the fleet to shut off supplies to northeastern Spain, a policy that may have alienated Rome's subjects even though it worked. Vallia, the new leader of the Visigoths, did not share any of Ataulf's pro-Roman sentiments. Indeed, he responded to the blockade by leading his people down to the Strait of Gibraltar, hoping to cross over into Africa and seize possession of Rome's granary (416), but storms prevented the crossing.

At this point Vallia decided to give up Galla Placidia in return for food for his people and an alliance with Honorius that authorized him to fight the other barbarian tribes in Spain. Constantius clearly understood the strategic use of supplies and of the fleet, and employed Rome's vastly superior logistical organization to good effect in negotiations with his enemies.[188] The Roman general satisfied another dream by securing from Honorius Galla Placidia's hand in marriage, despite her own reluctance.

From the time of the alliance with Vallia in 416, Honorius and Constantius pursued a consistent grand strategy in the West. They made no effort to deploy their limited military strength in the reassertion of imperial control in Britain. Instead they concentrated on holding Gaul and Italy and on regaining control over Spain, not with their own army but with the federate Visigoths. The imperial grip on Africa and naval strength in the western Mediterranean gave Honorius a stable base of power, especially after Constantius triumphed over Ataulf in southern Gaul. It was, under the circumstances, not a bad plan. Since there was no immediate military threat to Italy, there was less need in 416 than there had been in, say, 406 to move the capital to southern Gaul. In the new world that emerged after the sack of Rome, Ravenna proved a convenient base. If the Visigoths had done their part in Spain just a little better and not left the Vandals strong enough to cross into Africa, as they did in 429, the grand strategy of Honorius and Constantius might have saved a weaker and more restricted Roman Empire in the West. Both Roman leaders died natural deaths, however, before the loss of Africa, and the last decade of their lives witnessed a reawakening of the Roman spirit in the West.

In Spain from 416 to 418, Vallia went about the conquest of some of the barbarians with a vengeance. The result was a devastation of the countryside, which was plundered by armies on both sides. In two years of alternatively desultory and vicious fighting the Alans settled in Lusitania (modern Portugal), and the Suebi and some Vandals in northwestern Spain. Central and eastern Spain continued under direct rule from Ravenna. Following an ancient Roman policy of divide and conquer, Honorius agreed to accept the Suebi as federates, but except for the Vandals and Alans who fled into Suebian territory Vallia destroyed the rest of the barbarians in Spain. Later the surviving Vandals marched across Spain to Andalusia, but at the time the Visigoths seemed to have dealt effectively with them.

In 418 the Visigoths were rewarded for their service in Spain by the gift of Aquitaine in southwestern Gaul, which they settled under their new king Theodoric I after the death in the same year of Vallia. Theodoric, a grandson of Alaric, became a strong ally of the Roman emperor in the West, yet the Visigoths had done terrible damage to Roman power on their way to ultimate friendship with their ancient foe. In many ways this new settlement with the Visigoths, however, was better than the one Theodosius the Great had negotiated with their grandfathers after Adrianople. Their new kingdom did not intersect Ravenna's line of communication overland from Italy to Spain and provided no outlet for a naval base in the Mediterranean. Although Bordeaux and Toulouse came under Visigothic control, Roman provincials in Aquitaine remained subject to Rome. Some fraction of the land and other property in the region was probably ceded to the Visigoths, although one recent author has suggested that the cession was only a third of the taxes previously paid to the Roman government.[189]

The great migrations of the Visigoths finally came to an end – as much to the relief of Rome as to the descendants of Fritigern. Ironically their ultimate homeland was selected purely as a matter of policy by the government of Honorius and was not acquired by act of conquest. In alliance with Burgundians and Visigoths the Roman emperor in the West held Gaul, though the imperial prefect of Gaul now worked from a centre in Arles, not Trier, as in the fourth century. Roman power in the West had diminished, and the Rhine was not as important as the Rhône. In Spain, conditions were so unsettled that war broke out again shortly after 418 when the Vandals and Alans, who had joined the Suebi in northwestern Spain, separated and moved south into what became Andalusia (by 422). Still, when Constantius died in 421, only several months after having been made an imperial colleague of Honorius, and when Honorius followed him in 423, the two Romans had done as well as any one could to save the Empire in the West from the mistakes of Stilicho and the tragedy of those eventful years, 406–10. Bury's judgment, that Honorius' 'name would be forgotten among the obscurest occupants of the Imperial throne were it not that his reign coincided with the fatal period in which it was decided that western Europe was to pass from the Roman to the Teuton', is too harsh.[190] Gibbon was no more favourably disposed to the unfortunate Honorius who, according to the great historian, enjoyed 'a long and disgraceful reign of twenty-eight years'.[191] Yet Honorius laboured under many handicaps not of his own making and had the resilience to bounce back from a disaster that might have daunted many another man. His policy throughout Rome's troubles in the early fifth century was tough and tenacious, and he held to it, and to his throne, at a time when many would have added his head to those frequently on display in Ravenna. He had made mistakes – but he and the Empire had survived them.

The Western Army after the Sack of Rome

In the roughly fifty years from Julian's abortive invasion of Persia to the sack of Rome, the Roman army had suffered one humiliating loss after another. Stilicho had some limited success against Alaric and an even clearer victory over Radagaisus, but on balance the Roman army had not lived up to its tradition of greatness. Furthermore, after 410 at least, the western half of the army was sufficiently demoralized and weakened that it would never recover its former status.

Ironically, as we have seen, from Constantine to Theodosius the Great the western army had been better than the eastern one. Within a generation after Theodosius' death that was no longer the case. The invasions of Italy, Gaul, Spain and Britain had caused major modifications in the command system of the western army, so many that they are in fact difficult to reconstruct.[192] By the death of Honorius there was again a Field Marshal for Gaul (*magister equitum per Galliae*), though throughout much of his reign after 408 there had not been such a post. There was also a Count of Spain (*Comes Hispaniarum*), of Africa and of Illyricum. For a while there had actually been a Count of Italy, but that position was suppressed after the military threat to Italy passed. The vagaries of high command merely illustrate the unsettled conditions of the Roman Empire in the West.

Numbers in fifth-century campaigns are difficult to specify. The major benchmark, the one certain figure, comes from a source who tells us that in 428–9 the Vandal king, Gaiseric, took a census and counted some 80,000 people ready to cross over to Africa under his leadership. That figure probably includes men, women, children and slaves, but unfortunately even that is not certain. Still, if the assumption is correct, there were perhaps 25,000 fighting men in the

Vandal army.[193] Jerome says that there were 80,000 Burgundians, though that was presumably not based on an actual census, and there were supposed to be 200,000 Goths on the Danube in 376. We have seen that there were 20,000 Visigoths on the Frigid River in 394.

On the other hand relatively decisive military action in this period sometimes involved only 5,000 to 20,000 men. That should perhaps not be surprising. Throughout the history of warfare armies have been smaller than we in the twentieth century tend to believe.[194] According to evidence in the *Notitia Dignitatum* the western army of about 425 contained somewhat fewer than 250,000 men altogether, but more than half of them were frontier troops and could not easily be brought together into a field army. The mobile armies, scattered around the Western Empire in Spain, Gaul, Illyricum and Africa numbered about 115,000 men. When we realize that the mobile army in Spain was only about 10,000 strong, it is easier to understand why the Roman government needed the help of Vallia and the Visigoths to deal with the Vandals, Suebi and Alans.

Numbers, however, tell only a small part of the story. From the days of the Republic, strategists had taken it for granted that Roman armies might easily be outnumbered by barbarian tribes. Discipline and training, sophisticated logistics, the techniques of siege warfare, military engineering, a professional system of command, and high morale based upon justifiable confidence had given Roman armies an edge no barbarian horde could hope to match. The Visigothic victory at Adrianople, however, had robbed the Romans of their advantage in morale, and as time went by Roman armies, particularly in the West, lost some of their other distinguishing features.

We are fortunate to have available a remarkable work on warfare, written by a Roman, Flavius Vegetius Renatus, sometime between 383 and 450, that explains many of the reasons for the decline of Roman military power.[195] Vegetius' *De Re Militari*, as it is called, has sometimes been dismissed in the twentieth century as a second-rate hodge podge, an unsophisticated discussion of military matters, but in the Middle Ages and in early modern Europe it was widely read, and even today much can be learned from careful study of it. One modern analyst has called the *De Re Militari* 'the most influential military work written in the western world', probably an exaggeration, though he had in mind its extraordinary popularity before the nineteenth century.[196] Among the many interesting points that Vegetius makes is the fact that Roman cavalry was competitive with barbarian cavalry. Ironically, it was in infantry, for which the Romans had been so famous, that the Late Roman army needed improvement.[197]

The manual is a description of the earlier Roman system of military conscription, training, strategy and tactics (as well as siege and naval warfare) that, Vegetius said, had been forgotten in his own day – so much so that it was necessary to relearn it all from the study of books. There was no one alive who had experienced the old system. Naturally in Vegetius' discussion of the 'ancient' legion we learn much about the western army of the fifth century, since Vegetius was apparently a westerner, writing for a Western emperor and concerned primarily with problems of the western army.[198] Partly because the author's literary style is unsophisticated and unadorned, partly because Vegetius' knowledge of the early imperial army has been proved faulty on some points, and partly because his solution to Rome's military problems – a return to the better institutions of the distant past – seems unreasonably antiquarian, modern authors have been contemptuous of him. But as a military analyst he deserves much better, especially as a source for the fifth century. As for his style, a prominent figure of the Napoleonic age, Marshal de Ligne, made a comment about it that bears repeating: 'I don't know why his Latin is not liked; I myself like it very much, because I understand it.'[199] Vegetius did at least write clearly.

Certain other features mark the pronounced Late Roman flavour of the military treatise. First, Vegetius was a professed Christian who nevertheless believed that military victory came from training and discipline – not from faith.[200] Further, the analyst was concerned with the urgent military problem of his day – how to preserve rather than expand the Empire. As one modern commentator says, 'weakness is the recurrent theme', but optimism, the belief that 'beaten armies can be restored to efficiency', permeates Vegetius' approach to Roman military problems.[201] Where Vegetius rises far above his modern military critics is in his recognition that effective fighting required an *integrated* army, one that deployed skirmishers, heavy and light cavalry and heavy and light infantry in balanced coordination.[202]

And his main point, that Rome's chief military problem was its weak infantry, was undoubtedly sound. Vegetius says that down to the death of the Emperor Gratian, footsoldiers wore breastplates and helmets. But when, because of negligence and laziness, parade ground drills were abandoned, the customary armour began to seem heavy since the soldiers rarely ever wore it. Therefore, they first asked the emperor to set aside the breastplates and mail and then the helmets. So our soldiers fought the Goths without any protection for chest and head and were often beaten by archers. Although there were many disasters, which led to the loss of great cities, no one tried to restore breastplates and helmets to the infantry. Thus it happens that troops in battle, exposed to wounds because they have no armour, think about running and not about fighting.[203]

If there is some exaggeration in this passage, as perhaps there is, what we know about actual combat in the early fifth century nevertheless confirms the general picture. In the last half of the fourth century, in Persia, at Adrianople, and at the Frigid River, Roman legionaries fought with the old discipline and held their ground or died trying. In Stilicho's campaigns against Alaric in the Balkans and later in Italy, the Roman army often could not be held together for effective pursuit – admittedly a difficult task. By the great crisis of 406-10 Roman infantry was simply no longer able to stand up to the barbarian forces.

The cause of this deterioration in Roman arms is almost certainly the 'barbarization' of the army resulting from the use of 'federate' troops by Theodosius the Great and his successors.[204] Federate troops fought under their own commanders and were not subjected to Roman training and discipline. They were used extensively and in large numbers, as we have seen, and it would have been extraordinarily difficult for Roman commanders to have imposed the rigorous ancient discipline on Roman conscripts while a large part of the army made up of 'federates' enjoyed presumably a much easier life. Vegetius nowhere specifically attributes the collapse of infantry morale and discipline to the influence of the 'federate' barbarians – perhaps the topic was too sensitive politically – but by emphasizing how much Rome had learned from barbarian cavalry he does indirectly call attention to the cause of Rome's inadequate infantry.

To restore Roman greatness in infantry Vegetius recommends that recruits be selected for their likely good qualities as soldiers. Pragmatically recognizing that the old standards of height were no longer feasible, he argues that strength is more important than height.[205] More than anything else, though, Vegetius emphasized drill, drill, and more drill – in every weapon including sword, javelin, sling and bow, and in every militarily useful activity such as digging, marching with heavy pack, swimming, and precision parade-ground exercises.

His work is filled with common-sense maxims or aphorisms: a good army is no more expensive to maintain than a bad one; one who hopes for peace should plan for war; bravery is superior to numbers; men are not born brave but become so through training and discipline. Some modern commentators find them banal, but they are less so when they actually address genuine problems, as in the fifth century. It probably does no harm to repeat them even in better days – thus Napoleon's maxims have always been popular reading for students of warfare. Vegetius' proposal for the reintroduction of ancient discipline and training was not implemented by the imperial government. Perhaps it could not have been. Lax troops in a lax age are the most difficult to reform, and there are political costs of various kinds connected with the effort, not the least of which is the possibility of open rebellion. Vegetius' work at least illustrates and documents a profound deterioration in Roman military power whether his solution was practical or not. In the sections on siege and naval warfare, because Roman advantages over the barbarians were immeasurably greater, the tone is different.

It would be unfair to leave the impression that Vegetius' *De Re Militari* is a supremely sophisticated treatise on military affairs. In some respects it is not as good as those produced earlier in antiquity by Aeneas Tacticus, Frontinus and Arrian. On such matters as the effective use of reserves, however, it is a real improvement over its Graeco-Roman predecessors.[206] In the Latin West it became a kind of Bible of battle, but in the Eastern Roman Empire, beginning in the sixth century, some outstanding studies of warfare were written, most notably the *Strategikon* of the Emperor Maurice (582–602).[207] The point here has been not to determine Vegetius' place in the honour roll of military writers but to examine the light he sheds on the fall of Rome. On that score his importance is substantial.

The same could be said of another work, somewhat earlier, probably written in the fourth century between 337 and 378, the *De Rebus Bellicis*, by that prolific author Anonymus, about whom absolutely nothing is known.[208] For reasons difficult to explain Anonymus is fashionable today, rating much higher in scholarly esteem than the wiser if somewhat less imaginative Vegetius. The *De Rebus Bellicis* was included in the cluster of manuscripts at Speyer that

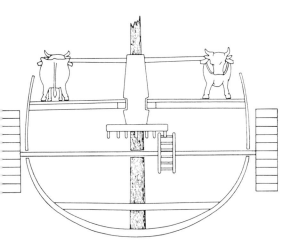

The gearing system for the rotary motion of the central capstan in the Liburna invented by Anonymus. This drive system was in fact not new in the late ancient world and had been used in the Vitruvian watermill. The gears, powered by oxen, could not have achieved speeds high enough for naval warfare.

also contained the *Notitia Dignitatum*. Like the *Notitia*, it was illustrated, and scholars generally believe that the medieval copies faithfully represent the ancient depictions.

For the most part Anonymus saw a need to restore or at least increase imperial military power, but his solution to Rome's problems differs dramatically from that of Vegetius. After urging some unrealistic proposals for reducing military expenditure Anonymus moves to his main point – the invention of superweapons that will save the Empire. Perhaps the twentieth-century fascination with super-weapons has led to a renewed interest in the *De Rebus Bellicis*, and it is true that the Roman Empire's technological superiority over the barbarian invaders might have been used to better effect. In any event the weird weapons proposed by Anonymus are certainly more romantic than the discipline and drill advocated by Vegetius.

One of the weapons Anonymus designed was a horse-drawn, arrow-firing catapult that could be swivelled around in a complete circle on a four-wheeled cart. It could be mechanically raised or lowered to determine trajectory of fire. Another device was a movable armoured shield under which attackers could advance against a wall or fortification. One sees genuine antiquarianism in the so-called *Currodrepanus*, a two-wheeled axle, studded with knives and with scythes extending from the axle, which can be raised or lowered by ropes, pulled by two armoured horses and riders, or in another version by only one. The *pièce de résistance*, perhaps, is a warship (*Liburna*) powered by yoked oxen driving turn-wheels on the sides of the ship.

Historians have carefully debated whether these inventions were foolish or ingenious, realistic or irrational. They are certainly interesting, and for the history of science may have some fascinating implications, but as solutions to Rome's military problems in the Late Empire, they are utterly absurd. Improvements in weapons can result in tactical advantages and some of the proposals by Anonymus may have done that. It is one of the worst-kept secrets of warfare, however, that the morale and training of the men who use the weapons are infinitely more important than the technology of weaponry (especially in an age, such as the Late Empire, when the technology, even if used effectively, offered only rather modest tactical advantages). Men – not gadgets – win wars. Vegetius had a much better grasp of Rome's military problems than Anonymus, and his solution, a return to rigorous training and discipline, though rooted in the past and lacking the inventive genius of Anonymus, was also better.

Ironically, one brief paragraph in Anonymus, normally ignored because it involves no invention, contains a much sounder proposal for the security of the Roman Empire. It is every bit as antiquarian as anything in Vegetius, but it reflects judicious disagreement with the grand strategy of Constantine the Great, based on defence-in-depth, and urges a return to preclusive security:

Among the measures taken by the State for its own advantage there is also the effective care of the frontier-works which surround all the borders of the Empire. Their safety will be better provided for by a continuous line of forts constructed at intervals of one mile with firm walls and very powerful towers . . . with watches and pickets kept in them so that the peaceful provinces may be surrounded by a belt of defences, and so remain unimpaired and at peace.[209]

As we have seen, in the early fifth century, especially after the sack of Rome in 410, the Emperor Honorius found his military flexibility drastically reduced. The great army he had inherited from his father in 395 had not even been strong enough to take the field in 410. Yet, partly through the use of Visigoths as his allies in Spain and Gaul, and partly through a resurgence of military strength engineered by his sister's husband, Constantius, the emperor presided over a modest recovery of Roman might. Honorius had been wise enough not to attempt too much, and Britain remained beyond imperial control. Africa, however, and at least parts of Gaul and Spain were still ruled directly by Ravenna, and the western Mediterranean remained a Roman lake. Military analysts such as Vegetius and Anonymus reveal an awareness of Roman weakness, but the end had not yet come.

Chapter Seven

Aëtius, the Vandals, and the Huns

After the deaths of Constantius (421) and Honorius (423) power shifted eventually to Galla Placidia, mother of the child-emperor, Valentinian III (425–55). When that six-year-old boy became emperor of the West, he could not rule in his own right, and his fascinating mother tried to control the politics of the court. For quite some time she succeeded in at least exercising very strong influence, and her connections have always titillated modern students of ancient history: she was the granddaughter of Valentinian I, daughter of Theodosius the Great, half-sister of the Emperor Honorius, wife of Ataulf and queen of the Visigoths, wife of the Roman Emperor Constantius III, mother of the Emperor Valentinian III – and during his youth she was effectively empress of Rome, in her own right an official Augusta.[210]

Strangely, however, it was not to be the age of Galla Placidia, despite her dramatic lineage. Virtually from the beginning she had a rival for power and influence, the general Aëtius, and in the end it was he who came to be known as 'the last of the Romans'.[211] At the battle of Châlons (451), Aëtius saved the Western Roman Empire from the Huns, the scourge of God, and he stood out as a popular, active champion of Roman civilization at a time when the dynasty of Theodosius seemed lethargic, incompetent and degenerate. Possibly the great general did not deserve the high repute he achieved – we shall see that his military strategy was sometimes flawed – but in the tragic drama of Rome's fall, history assigned him one of the leading, heroic roles.

To understand Aëtius' rise in the mid-fifth century, we must return momentarily to the court at Ravenna after the death of Constantius in 421. For a short time Galla Placidia and Honorius got along famously, and their obvious affection for one another spawned undoubtedly baseless rumours of incest.[212] It was not long, however, before they had a serious falling out – probably caused by some of Honorius' advisers who resented the sister's influence and hoped to prevent the accession of her young son should the childless emperor die. The situation was exacerbated by the Visigothic followers of Galla Placidia, who still admired her from her days as Ataulf's wife and who served her as a kind of bodyguard. This close contact with the Visigoths apparently led to a charge of treason after Placidia's followers scuffled with regular Roman troops during riots in Ravenna. Honorius banished her, and she fled with the young Valentinian and his sister to Constantinople, where she laid claims to the protection of her nephew, the Eastern emperor Theodosius II, and other members of the family. If the truth be known, the Byzantine ruler was surely not pleased to have to find a place for this western Augusta in the eastern court. In fact, Theodosius II had never recognized Placidia's late husband Constantius III as Augustus, but he did offer sanctuary, in reduced circumstances, to Placidia in the spring of 423.

In the meantime Honorius relied upon a general, Castinus by name, the emperor's leading adviser and by virtue of that fact Placidia's open foe.[213] When Honorius died in August 423, Theodosius II briefly served as emperor of a united Empire and ruled through Castinus in the West.[214] For some reason, however, before the end of 423 the general engineered a rebellion and raised to the purple in Rome a man named John, who had been a ranking figure in the civil government of the Western Empire and who, except for this rebellion, was a man of high character and competence.[215] This threat to the Theodosian dynasty led Theodosius II to recognize posthumously the imperial status of Constantius III and to send an army west, probably in summer 424, in support of Constantius' son Valentinian, who was accompanied by his mother, the Augusta, Galla Placidia.

In Gaul John's regime was shaky, and his Praetorian Prefect was murdered by mutinous troops at Arles. This resulted in a Visigothic attack on the Rhône which had the incidental effect of supporting the cause of the former queen, Galla Placidia.[216] The Count of Africa, Boniface, remained loyal to Theodosius II in the East and the new regime of Valentinian III in the West. He became Placidia's staunchest ally, and forced John to dissipate his strength by sending troops on an unsuccessful mission to Africa to lift the grain blockade imposed on Rome.

It was in the midst of this crisis that Aëtius made his debut in the grand saga of the Roman people. As a partisan of John, Aëtius was sent on an important mission to the Huns to seek military support in the war against Constantinople. John's hope was to bring an army of Huns (about whom we shall learn a great deal more, later in this chapter) down on the rear of the eastern army as it approached Ravenna. Aëtius, who was probably in his mid-thirties at the time, was ideally suited for this sensitive task since he had once been a hostage, as the son of a leading Roman general, among the Goths and the Huns, and had made many friends, particularly among the latter. Until the end of his life this special relationship with the Huns gave Aëtius a unique advantage in Roman affairs.[217]

Unfortunately for the pretender, John, before the Huns arrived, the eastern army took Ravenna in 425 with the help of partisans on the inside of the city. John was captured and killed (not without public abuse and molestation), and his head was added to the reasonably large collection in Ravenna. Only three days later Aëtius arrived in Italy with a force of Huns. To save Italy from the menace of the barbarians, Placidia gave them money and hostages and agreed to appoint Aëtius to a major military command as Field Marshal in Gaul against the Visigoths who had put Arles under siege.

The affinity with the Huns had saved the Roman's life and produced for him a ranking post in the new government. Placidia could scarcely have liked him. Her favourite general was without doubt the loyal Boniface in Africa. Castinus, the general who had launched John's rebellion, fled into banishment; to that extent at least he was luckier than his imperial protégé. Inevitably one can sense, from the outset of the new reign, a developing tension between Boniface and Aëtius, one supported by the empress-regent, the other by his influence with the barbarians. In the end, Aëtius triumphed, but far more important than the political rivalry was its strategic implication. To strengthen his own base Aëtius placed priority on Gaul, where he became the chief representative of the Roman government. His ultimate victory over Boniface led as well to the weakening of Roman rule in Africa and eventually to the loss of Carthage, a bastion of Roman strength in the area.[218]

The Loss of Africa

After the accession of Valentinian III, Aëtius moved on to victory against the Goths at Arles, forcing them to retire again to Aquitaine. In the next several years he strengthened the Rhine frontier and defended Noricum against barbarian attack. On the other hand, Boniface in Africa fell into disfavour, possibly because of differences with Placidia on matters of religion – differences exacerbated by the political intrigues of other Roman generals, probably including Aëtius.[219] In 427 the African general actually went into rebellion against Ravenna and over the next two years defeated a force sent from Italy against him. Finally, however, in 429 Boniface restored relations with Placidia.

In the early 430s Aëtius and Boniface held equally high military rank, but in 432 when Placidia favoured Boniface by giving him the lofty title of *patricius* (a title formerly held by Stilicho and Constantius), Aëtius realized that Placidia had finally decided to destroy him.[220] Boniface crossed to Italy with his army, and Aëtius marched against him to fight a great battle near Rimini, a battle that Boniface won tactically but to no avail since he suffered a mortal wound and died some three months later. In the words of a recent authority: 'For the first time, a civil war was fought not over who should be emperor, but over who should be the emperor's generalissimo.'[221] Aëtius escaped first to Dalmatia and then to his old friends, the Huns. With their help he was restored to power by Placidia (in 433), and from then to the end of his life (454) he was Rome's dominant general.

This struggle between the two military dynasts had grave repercussions in Africa. In the last chapter we saw how the Vandals had gained control of southern Spain. In 422, after the death of Constantius, they defeated a force sent out from Italy against them and thereafter seized the Balearic Islands and raided into North Africa. No doubt because of the civil war in Africa in 427–8 between Boniface and Placidia's government, Gaiseric, King of the Vandals, decided in June 429 to lead his people, eighty thousand altogether, across the Strait of Gibraltar into the wealthy, grain-producing region. From Roman Mauretania – not, in fact, a land of milk and honey – the Vandals headed east towards the more luxurious region of Carthage. Near Hippo, the home of St Augustine, Boniface was defeated in the field and forced to take refuge in the city. Although the Vandals eventually had to abandon the siege after about a year – Augustine died during the course of it – Boniface later retreated to Carthage, and Hippo eventually fell to the barbarians.

Thus by the summer of 431 a large part of Africa had been lost, and Roman control of the sea was no longer uncontested.[222] In these extraordinary circumstances Placidia appealed to Constantinople, and Theodosius II, anxious to avoid encroachment in North Africa that threatened Egypt, sent an eastern army under the general Aspar to help Boniface.[223] In 432, however, Gaiseric actually defeated the combined forces of Aspar and Boniface. It was at this critical point that Placidia recalled her general to Italy in the hope of suppressing Aëtius.

Aspar stayed in Carthage while Boniface rushed to his destiny at Rimini, but in 434 the eastern general returned home. Aëtius was by then in full control of the Western Empire's grand strategy, and he was more concerned with threats to Gaul than to Africa. As a result, in 435 Ravenna accepted the Vandals as 'federates' in Africa, controlling territory up to but not including Carthage. One recent author, reflecting a modern tendency, has suggested 'that in some ways the Vandals must have looked like liberators'. Rather than seeing an invasion, this author says merely: 'The Vandals trickled across in the general direction of Carthage.'[224] Unfortunately it has become a common mistake to let sympathy for twentieth-century oppressed minorities blind us to the savagery of ancient barbarians. The Vandals were brutal, and the toll in human suffering is as much a part of their story as the impact they had on the strategic security of the Roman Empire in the West. The difference between Vandal and Roman Africa, in Carthage at least (which soon fell to the barbarians), has been revealed in recent archaeological excavations which show public buildings falling rapidly into disrepair under the Vandals. As we shall see below, there is also evidence of blind, gruesome bloodshed.

The treaty of 435, however, brought a few years of peace to Africa. The Vandals, though everywhere victorious, needed some time to consolidate their extensive territorial gains and to recover the loss in strength that accompanies a too-rapid expansion. But since Aëtius in the late 430s was inextricably involved in the affairs of Gaul, Gaiseric was able to recuperate without challenge and to strike successfully at Carthage in 439. The fall of that great city caused nearly as much consternation as the sack of Rome twenty years earlier – the difference is that in 410 barbarians held Rome for only three days; Carthage was lost forever. The defences of Carthage had been strengthened sometime around 425 by the construction of a great wall, the so-called

Theodosian Wall named after Theodosius II. Whether it was built because of the upheavals connected with the usurpation of the Emperor John or because of fear of barbarian attack remains unknown.[225] But for whatever reason (perhaps treachery) the great wall did not stop the Vandals. According to the sole surviving contemporary source, when Gaiseric and his troops entered Carthage on 19 October 439 they left 'a trail of corpses as they proceeded', and 'snatched babies from the arms of nurses or mothers who were powerless to retrieve their bodies from scavenging birds or dogs'.[226] Sicily and Rome were now dangerously close to the barbarian spear and fleet, while the grain of Africa would never again feed the mouths of Romans, at least not as tribute.

Indeed Gaiseric did attack Sicily. Theodosius II sent the eastern fleet, now much more powerful than the western, into the area, and in 442 Gaiseric negotiated a new treaty with Ravenna. The Western Empire reacquired the poorer western parts of North Africa and recognized the Vandals in the richer central region around Carthage. In addition Valentinian III agreed to permit his daughter Eudocia (who was only five years old) to marry at some future time Gaiseric's son, Huneric. The betrothal effectively symbolized the Vandal victory in Africa, and for many years Gaiseric kept the peace of 442.

It is difficult to calculate the effect of Africa's loss on the Roman Empire in the West. Strategically it meant the near abandonment of naval action in the western Mediterranean, since the Vandals now had control of the sea, and Aëtius in any event never showed Constantius' appreciation of the proper use of naval power. The naval balance of power actually shifted to the emperor in Constantinople. The loss of African grain and revenue severely damaged the strength of Valentinian III, and made the position of the Western Roman emperor weaker in other parts of his rapidly diminishing Empire. Although Egypt was prosperous, its resources were controlled by the Eastern emperor, not by the West.

When the peace was negotiated with Gaiseric and the Vandals in 442, it had been only about fifty years since the death of Theodosius the Great. One emperor had ruled over all the civilized world (if we may allow the Romans their somewhat boastful claim to monopoly in the arts of civilized man). But in slightly less than fifty years the successors to Theodosius in the West, his son and grandson, had lost Britain, parts of Gaul and Spain, and the most productive part of

North Africa under western rule. What caused this tremendous decline in Roman power?

Some historians have seen the political bickering and open rebellion among the great generals as the decisive cause of Rome's fall. It is true that Honorius and Valentinian never took the field in command of their own armies, that their generals were therefore relatively more powerful than Roman generals had been in the past, and that the strife of those generals, as we saw in the case of Boniface and Aëtius, contributed to Ravenna's problems.[227] The generalissimos of the Western Roman Empire, however, were themselves relatively weak in military power, at least by earlier standards. Boniface, with 10,000 to 20,000 men, had not been able to stop Gaiseric's 25,000 in North Africa, not even with the help of the eastern general Aspar.

The fact is that after the death of Theodosius there was a dramatic reduction, at least in the West, of the emperor's capacity to project military force to his frontiers, a capacity vitally necessary in the grand strategy of defence-in-depth. This diminished military capacity is only partly explained by contention among the generals. Since the days of the Republic, of Marius and Sulla, of Caesar and Pompey, Roman generals had fought for power, yet the explosive military potential of the Roman state remained strong. Why did it shrink so rapidly in the first half of the fifth century AD?

One explanation can be examined briefly and set aside. Although many historians emphasize the civilizing effect of Rome on the barbarian nations, and can point among other things to the adoption of writing and of Christianity by the Goths and others, it does not necessarily follow that the barbarians of the fifth century had become militarily much stronger than their ancestors. The decline of Roman power is not simply the result of facing a stronger and militarily more sophisticated foe. On the contrary, evidence suggests that the barbarian armies of the period were much as they had always been, and were still grossly deficient in the art of siege warfare and weapons technology as well as in tactical organization and command.[228] Why then had Roman armies, even though outnumbered, not dealt more effectively with Vandals, Suebi, Visigoths and Alans?

Let me merely reaffirm at this point in the narrative a possible explanation – one that we will consider again later. Many historians have paid lip service to it, though it has in fact not been much in vogue in the twentieth century, which has a much too idealized view of the barbarians. If there had been no significant improvement in barbarian military science (using the word loosely), there had been a demonstrable deterioration in the Roman army, especially in the West, largely because of the process of barbarization that had begun in the reign of Theodosius the Great. When Vegetius urged a return to the ancient training, he indirectly recognized the root of Rome's problem. Too long and too close an association with barbarian warriors, as allies in the Roman army, had ruined the qualities that made Roman armies great. No wonder the army of Boniface had not destroyed Gaiseric in Africa. The Roman army of AD 440, in the West, had become little more than a barbarian army itself, and no longer had the great tactical advantages of the past. The Romans had even adopted the German *baritus*, or war cry. Obviously some Roman strengths continued at a slightly reduced level – siege warfare, weapons production, and logistical support among others – but the actual fighting ability on the field, the drive to control that no-man's zone between two hostile armies facing one another in combat, was gone.[229]

A Russian archduke once said: 'I hate wars, they spoil the armies.'[230] His point was that during wartime armies ballooned in size, compromises in recruitment and training were required, officers were advanced too rapidly through the ranks, and the dictates of military science were sacrificed to diplomacy or to the vagaries of unpredictable battlefield conditions. 'Real soldiering' is a peacetime occupation, when the benefits of parade-ground drill and all that goes with it can be confidently reasserted. There is a sense in which the wars from 360 to 410 had 'spoiled' the Roman army. The stagnating effect of defeat and the disturbing influx of barbarian laxness in matters of drill and discipline destroyed the greatest fighting force the world had yet seen or would know again until the age of Napoleon. Although politics made a difference, the decisive development was mainly military.

The Army of the Huns

We must now turn to the role of the Huns, direct and indirect, in the fall of Rome.[231] During the fourth century, in the reign of Valens, these nomadic, Asiatic horse-people subjugated the Ostrogoths on the other side of the Roman frontier and forced the Visigoths to cross the Danube in 376 on the way to the battle of Adrianople (378). In the earliest period of the Hunnic relationship with Rome and Rome's neighbours in the late fourth century, the plains-fed horse was synonymous with the Hun. Later, as we shall see, after the Huns settled down in the Great Hungarian Plain, they developed a more sedentary existence and turned to infantry rather than cavalry, but Romans usually associated the Huns with the horse.[232]

Ammianus Marcellinus, writing at the end of the fourth century, makes the main features of the tactics of the Huns clear; as does a briefer passage from the poems of Claudian:

> Not e'en the Centaurs – offspring of the Cloud
> Were horsed more firmly than this savage crowd.
> Brisk, lithe, in loose array they first come on,
> Fly, turn, attack the foe who deems them gone.[233]

This poetic description reminds one of the tactics of the later Mongols – Asiatic horse-people too – and requires the further elaboration of Ammianus:

The nation of the Huns . . . surpasses all other barbarians in wildness of life. . . . And though [the Huns] do just bear the likeness of men (of a very ugly pattern), they are so little advanced in civilization that they make no use of fire, nor of any kind of relish, in the preparation of their food, but feed upon the roots which they find in the fields, and the half-raw flesh of any sort of animal. I say half-raw, because they give it a kind of cooking by placing it between their own thighs and the backs of their horses. . . .

When attacked, they will sometimes engage in regular battle. Then, going into the fight in order of columns, they fill the air with varied and discordant cries. More often, however, they fight in no regular order of battle, but by being extremely swift and sudden in their movements, they disperse, and then rapidly come together again in loose array, spread havoc over vast plains, and flying over the rampart, they pillage the camp of their enemy almost before he has become aware of their approach. It must be owned that they are the most terrible of warriors because they fight at a distance with missile weapons having sharpened bones admirably fastened to the shaft. When in close combat with swords, they fight without regard to their own safety, and while their enemy is intent upon parrying the thrusts of the swords, they throw a net over him and so entangle his limbs that he loses all power of walking or riding.[234]

After the rather dramatic arrival of the Huns on the Danube, for almost fifty years they made only limited and infrequent inroads into the Empire (such as the one in Armenia, Syria and Mesopotamia in 395). Indeed they seem to have served the Romans more often as allies than attacked them as enemies. In the 420s the Eastern emperor, Theodosius II, paid them an annual subsidy and Galla Placidia recognized their right to a part of Pannonia. Sometime after 435 however, Attila became king of the Huns, and with his accession the course of Roman history was changed.

Gibbon's description of Attila, based on an ancient account, reveals the wonder of the writer as much as the personality and appearance of the Hun:

His features, according to the observation of a Gothic historian, bore the stamp of his national origin . . . a large head, a swarthy complexion, small, deep-seated eyes, a flat nose, a few hairs in the place of a beard, broad shoulders, and a short square body, of a nervous strength, though of a disproportioned form. The haughty step and demeanour of the king of the Huns expressed the consciousness of his superiority above the rest of mankind; and he had a custom of fiercely rolling his eyes, as if he wished to enjoy the terror which he inspired. . . . He delighted in war; but, after he had ascended the throne in a mature age, his head, rather than his hand, achieved the conquest of the North; and the fame of an adventurous soldier was usefully exchanged for that of a prudent and successful general.[235]

At the beginning of his reign Theodosius II agreed to double the annual subsidy (and to send back fugitives who had fled from the Empire of the Huns to that of the Romans). Up to this time, except for Aëtius' attempt to involve the Huns in the affairs of the West in the abortive reign of John in 425, and in their support of the western general after his defeat by Boniface, the terror of the Huns had been directed towards the Balkans and the emperor in Constantinople. In the early 440s, however, Attila turned his attentions westward and was for a decade and a half the most powerful foreign force in the affairs of the Western Roman Empire.

The army with which he terrorized Europe was in fact quite different from those Hunnic horsemen who had struck fear into Roman and barbarian alike in the late fourth century. Several decades of sedentary life in the Great Hungarian Plain led to important changes in the way Huns fought in war.[236] To a very great extent they had been forced by circumstance to abandon their earlier cavalry tactics in favour of infantry, and their infantry was probably very little different from that of the Germanic barbarians.

The reason for this transformation in the tactics of the Huns is that nomadic horse nations require enormous stretches of suitable territory for the support of their horses. To get the speed, mobility and range necessary for effective raiding, nomads needed many remounts for every cavalryman. Marco Polo noted that on the Asian steppe as many as eighteen horses might be used in a string by a single horseman, while

The Huns of the late fourth century were fearsome warriors mounted on peculiar, fat-headed plains horses. Everywhere Romans and barbarians alike were terrified by the Asiatic people. Later, especially in the fifth century, the Huns usually fought on foot.

in the nineteenth century the American pony express used a minimum of seven mounts and frequently ten or more per rider per day.[237] If one assumes that the Huns used ten horses per cavalryman for large-scale horse campaigns and that the Great Hungarian Plain (with some 42,400 square kilometres of pasture) could have supported only about 150,000 grazing horses, then there were enough for approximately 15,000 cavalry.[238] Roman cavalry resources, based upon stable-fed horses, were actually greater. When the Huns crossed the Carpathians and moved out of the much larger Asian steppe into the Great Hungarian Plain, they lost the logistical base of their horse-mounted military power. As a recent authority concludes, 'When the Huns first appeared on the steppe north of the Black Sea, they were nomads and most of them may have been mounted warriors. In Europe, however, they could graze only a fraction of their former horse-power, and their chiefs soon fielded armies which resembled the sedentary forces of Rome.'[239]

As I have suggested above, the army of the Huns probably resembled the Germanic barbarian forces more than they resembled

(Above left) Ostrogothic leaders of the mid-fourth century fought on horseback with helmet and chain armour, but most Ostrogoths fought on foot without armour.

(Above right) The Visigothic soldier of the early fifth century was an infantryman fighting without armour except for a shield which could take many unusual shapes. Frequently he carried equipment that had been plundered from dead Roman soldiers.

the Roman ones, but the Roman army itself had been greatly barbarized.

Perhaps a brief review of the barbarian armies of the fifth century would be helpful in understanding the final demise of the Roman Empire in the West. We have already noted some of the most important features of barbarian warfare. Despite a view still popular in some circles, barbarian armies relied mainly on infantry. Although they usually included some cavalry, Roman cavalry was at least equal to that of the barbarians. Military discipline and training were neither sophisticated nor rigorous among the barbarians, but Vegetius demonstrates conclusively that Roman infantry had declined sadly in those respects. In 357 at the battle of Strasbourg Julian had defeated an army of 35,000 Alamanni with a Roman army of only 13,000, and Roman infantry had saved the day. In the fifth century Roman infantry could save nothing.

Barbarian infantrymen normally wore no armour, at least no breastplate or helmet – a practice adopted in the fifth century, as we have seen, by the Romans.[240] Germanic and Hun nobles probably wore helmets of one sort or another but the common soldiers of the line fought bare-headed.²⁴¹ Some Huns and some Germans wore mail armour, but this was also uncommon. For the most part barbarian infantry was light and mobile.²⁴²

The barbarian shield, normally a light wooden or wicker one, sometimes had an iron boss projecting outward to a point, thus making the shield a thrusting weapon for offence as well as defence. Again, Romans eventually adopted this shield themselves. If the Germans lagged far behind the Romans in the manufacture of weapons, and they surely did, they were aware of their disadvantage and compensated for it, not by developing their own arsenals, but by stripping defeated Roman forces or, perhaps even more important, by securing official commands in the Roman army, usually as 'federates', that gave access to Roman armouries.

In cavalry Romans and Huns relied heavily on mounted archers and the mobility and firepower of their force could be devastating against light infantry. The Germanic barbarians normally did not employ mounted archers, and were often routed by Huns and Romans as a result. Goths and Vandals deployed infantry armed with bows and spears, but the Franks along the Rhine used the sword and double-headed battle-axe, forming a heavy infantry (though still without much body armour). In siege warfare, as we have seen, barbarians (except for the Huns) had none of the Roman skills and relied on blockade or on treachery behind the walls. Considering their limitations they were amazingly successful. When Roman generals could no longer field infantry forces greatly superior to the barbarian armies, they lost by far their greatest military advantage, and many of their other assets (such as their logistical system) became prey to Germanic and Hunnic leaders.

The Battle of Châlons and the Invasion of Italy

Ultimately the great power of Attila and the Huns was brought to bear against Aëtius in Gaul and Italy. In the mid and late 430s the Roman general, strengthened by the death of Boniface and the renewal of relations with Galla Placidia, devoted his attentions to Gaul while the Vandals completed their conquest of North Africa. In 436 the Burgundians, 'federates' on the middle Rhine, tried to take advantage of disturbances caused by lawless Bagaudae and moved into the lower

Rhine. Aëtius persuaded the Huns to intervene and twenty thousand Burgundians were wiped out, the basis of the legends that form the *Nibelungenlied*, a German epic.

In the same year the Visigoths under Theodoric attacked the city of Narbo in southern Gaul, and after three years of fighting Roman troops drove them back to Toulouse (though the Roman general, Litorius, was taken prisoner in battle). Aëtius became virtually the monarch of Gaul. In 432 the Romans in Spain had appealed to him for help (rather than to Valentinian or Galla Placidia in Ravenna), and in 446 the remnants of the Romans in Britain sought his aid against their many foes. There is little doubt that Aëtius deliberately tried to strengthen his ties with the aristocracy in Gaul in furtherance of his political aspirations.[243]

In the early 440s Aëtius gave land to the Alans around Valence and Orléans to control unrest in Brittany, while Burgundians who had survived the invasion of the Huns were settled in Savoy, south of Lake Geneva.[244] Throughout the rest of the 440s difficulties in Gaul, particularly with the Bagaudae, and in Spain with Bagaudae and the Suebi, kept Aëtius occupied. The success of Gaiseric in North Africa from 435 to 442 must be seen partly against this background. In the meantime Attila had been able to increase the tribute paid to the Huns by the Eastern emperor in 441, after fattening his revenues with the Burgundian campaign in Gaul.[245]

So much for prelude; the decisive intervention of the Huns in the history of the Western Roman Empire came in the early 450s, when – presumably – Aëtius' earlier influence with them had waned. To give some indication of what horrors resulted from an invasion of the Huns, we should examine a contemporary description of a city in the Danubian provinces, Naissus, roughly a hundred miles south of the Danube on the Nischava River, devastated in the late 440s during one of Attila's attacks against the East in the Balkans. Roman ambassadors passing through the region to a meeting with Attila were forced to camp overnight, outside the city on the nearby river. Because the site had been so completely ravaged, and the stench of human death was so great, it would have been unsafe to enter the city: 'Upon arrival at Naissus we found the place abandoned since it had been ravaged. There were a few sick people in the churches. We stopped near the river but not on its banks since they were filled with human bones of those killed in fighting.'[246]

It was this kind of devastation that Attila threatened in the West. The story is that Gaiseric, king of the Vandals, urged Attila to attack the West hoping that the Huns would destroy the Visigoths in Gaul. At one time Gaiseric's son, Huneric, married the daughter of Theodoric I, king of the Visigoths, but when Valentinian III agreed to the betrothal of his daughter to the son of the Vandal king in 442, the Visigothic princess was returned to her father with her nose and ears brutally mutilated. Thus hostility between Vandal and Visigoth was enormous. There is some reason to believe that Attila may have initiated the discussions in a diplomatic attempt to keep the Vandals out of his western war. Whatever happened, the Vandals did not join the great coalition of powers that Aëtius organized to resist this Hunnic attack on Gaul.[247]

Nor did Attila limit his own diplomacy to the Vandals. In his attack upon the Rhine the immediate target was the Franks. Attila tried to persuade the Visigoths to join his cause, to break their federate status with the Romans. Aëtius, however, responded to the crisis with great energy and was able to cement a grand alliance among Goths, Burgundians, Alans and Romans in defence of Gaul. The battle that followed, known to history as the battle of Châlons (or, alternatively, the battle of the Catalaunian Plains, AD 451) was one of the decisive encounters in the history of the western world.[248]

Part of the complicated interrelationship of events leading to this important clash was the death in 450 of the Eastern emperor, Theodosius II, who was thrown by his horse. The new emperor in Constantinople, Marcian (450–7), took a hard line on barbarian encroachment in the Balkans and refused to pay Attila the regular subsidy. Although the leader of the Huns was furious, he took out his anger on the West, partly because the West was obviously weaker and partly because scandal had created an immediate pretext to justify war with Ravenna. In 449 Valentinian's sister, Honoria, was discovered in an illicit affair with her steward, who was executed, while the princess was kept in seclusion (probably pregnant).[249] In a rage Honoria smuggled a ring and a message to Attila, asking him to become her champion. The barbarian took up her cause, considered her his bride-to-be, and demanded as dowry half of Valentinian's Empire! Thus he could claim that the invasion of Gaul was merely to secure what was rightfully his by virtue of his betrothal to Honoria.

Early in 451 Attila invaded the Rhine supported by a large army of

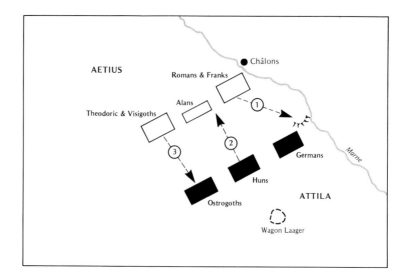

The Battle of Châlons, AD 451. *1 Romans seize high ground on Attila's right. 2 Attila attacks and drives back Alans in the centre. 3 As Attila wheels to hit the Visigoths in their flank, Theodoric leads a counterattack while the Romans threaten Attila's right. Theodoric was killed, but Attila withdrew, and Aëtius had won a decisive battle though the losses on both sides were heavy.*

Huns and associated allies such as the Ostrogoths and some Burgundians and Alans (though not those permanently settled as federates in Gaul). Some of the Franks joined the cause of the invaders while others remained loyal to Rome. By April Attila had taken Metz. His army was huge even if we reject as exaggerations the figures of 300,000 to 700,000 given by some sources. Paris clung tenaciously to the defence of its walls, but Rheims, Mainz, Strasbourg, Cologne, Worms and Trier fell to the Huns and were sacked and put to the torch.

After securing the Rhine Attila turned towards Orléans from where he could threaten the Visigoths in Aquitaine. When the Alans of the region seemed ready to defect to Attila, Aëtius and Theodoric moved up with their combined forces to relieve the besieged city. Unwilling to be trapped around the walls of Orléans, the Huns abandoned the siege and retreated to the open country, the Champagne district of France, where on the Catalaunian Plains (some believe closer to Troyes than to Châlons) a great battle developed.[250] In the confusion of retreat, pressed hard by Aëtius and the Visigoths, Attila was uncertain of victory. On the day of the battle he stayed with his forces behind his lines in the laager until afternoon (presumably to delay battle so that retreat in the darkness of night would be possible if he lost the engagement), but finally the Hun sent out his troops to form battle-array.

In what was to be primarily an infantry rather than a cavalry battle, the barbarian king took up position in the centre of his line with his best troops and placed the Ostrogoths on his left while his other German allies held the right. Aëtius decided to let his least reliable troops, the Alans, take whatever attack Attila might launch in the centre and to use the Visigoths on his right and the Romans on his left to execute a double envelopment on the flanks of the enemy. An initial skirmish centred around some high ground on Attila's right, ground that the Romans seized, which gave them an advantage for their planned flanking attack.[251] Attila tried to encourage his troops after this tactical loss, and both sides prepared for the main engagement. In the fighting that followed all sources agree that the slaughter was horrible: *cadavera vero innumera* ('truly countless bodies'), is merely one example from numerous ancient (or early medieval) notices.[252]

What apparently happened is that Attila struck hard against the Alans in the centre of Aëtius' line and drove them back. The Alans seem to have held their rough formation even though they yielded ground. When the Huns had made some progress against the Alans, Attila then wheeled to hit the Visigoths in the flank. In heavy fighting Theodoric was killed, but the Visigoths rallied and counterattacked. In the meantime Romans and Franks from the high ground threatened Attila's other flank, and the barbarian leader decided, as night fell, to retreat to the safety of his laager where the Hunnic archers kept the Romans and their allies at bay. It proved, nevertheless, a great triumph for Aëtius. Attila was subsequently forced to retreat beyond the Rhine. In the words of Gibbon, Attila's withdrawal 'confessed the last victory which was achieved in the name of the Western empire.'[253]

Historians have long debated the wisdom of Aëtius in letting Attila retreat with his army intact. The Roman general urged his new Visigothic ally, Thorismund, the son of Theodoric, to return with his forces to Aquitaine and secure his position on the throne. Some ancients and moderns believe Aëtius wanted to ensure the loyalty of the Visigoths by keeping the Huns as a threat and that the Roman general lost a splendid opportunity to annihilate his foes. Militarily, however, Aëtius probably took the proper course.[254] The battle had been a bloody, near-run thing. It is a truism in military theory that one should allow a beaten enemy a line of retreat when he retains enough strength after battle to do potential harm. Although Italy paid dearly in the following year because Attila's Huns survived to fight again, western Europe would have paid a far greater price had Attila been forced into a successful counterattack in Gaul.

In that sense the battle of Châlons was genuinely one of the great decisive battles in western history. Twentieth-century 'scientific' historians have tended to denigrate the concept of 'decisive battles' in the belief that human events are rarely determined on the battlefield, and perhaps no battle has suffered so much from this approach as the battle of Châlons. Delbrück omitted it entirely from his classic *History of the Art of War Within the Framework of Political History* (1920–21), and Bury tried to strip it altogether of its significance:

The battle of Maurica [Châlons] was a battle of nations, but its significance has been enormously exaggerated in conventional history. It cannot in any reasonable sense be designated as one of the critical battles of the world. . . . The danger did not mean so much as has been commonly assumed. If Attila had been victorious . . . there is no reason to suppose that the course of history would have been seriously altered.[255]

Such was the view of the learned historian who even refused to call the battle by its traditional name! In fact, Gibbon and the historians of the nineteenth century were much sounder in their approach to the significance of the battle. It is true that the victory did not save the Roman Empire and that the Empire of the Huns might have collapsed on Attila's death anyway, since it was held together largely by the force of his personality. Yet, as a conflict between Christians and heathens, as an engagement that seemed to confirm Christian power in western Europe, indeed as a formidable, real blow to the power of the Huns in their relations with Rome, it was one of the world's most important battles.

For the Romans and Aëtius, however, the trial had not ended. In 452 Attila moved over the Alps and into Italy.[256] The savagery of this invasion exceeded even that of his descent into Gaul. Aquileia was besieged, burnt, obliterated. Scarcely a trace of its existence could be found in the generation after Attila. Milan, Verona and Pavia were left standing but bankrupt and in some cases depopulated. The Po was in the grip of the Hun. Naturally the Visigoths and other federate nations were less disposed to meet Attila in Italy than they had been to do so in Gaul, and Aëtius was in a dangerous position. He urged Valentinian to abandon Ravenna and establish a base in southern Gaul, showing to that extent far more strategic insight than Stilicho had shown against Alaric.

In the end Rome was saved. Tradition holds that Pope Leo met Attila and persuaded him to withdraw from Italy, and there may be substantial truth in the story. There were, however, other pressing considerations, and Attila probably allowed himself to be dissuaded from an attack on Rome because his power had waned. There had been a famine in Italy in 450–1, and Attila had grave logistical problems, while at the same time plague swept through his army. Possibly even more important, the eastern emperor Marcian dispatched an army across the Danube to strike at the Hun's home base. Coupled with the losses he had earlier suffered at Châlons these considerations must have driven Attila to see merit in the humanitarian arguments of Pope Leo.

For whatever reason Attila did withdraw, and Rome was saved. In the following year the great king took a young new bride, and on the wedding day he celebrated with excessive drink. During the night he was afflicted with a nosebleed and drowned in his own blood as he lay on his back. With his death the Empire of the Huns passed from the pages of history. In 454 Ostrogoths and then other Germans rebelled against the disunited sons of Attila, and, in the words of Bury, the Huns were 'scattered to the winds'.[257] Aëtius, 'the last of the Romans', although he was blamed by some for not destroying Attila in Gaul, could look upon his work with satisfaction – at least briefly.

During the ascendancy of Aëtius in the 430s, 40s and early 50s, the Western Roman Empire had suffered a terrible loss in Africa where the Vandals not only seized important, economically productive territory but also a base for naval operations. After 439 the emperor of the West never again controlled Carthage. Yet in Gaul and Spain, through the skilful use of barbarian allies, Aëtius managed to maintain Roman authority with a dwindling Roman army, and in 451 at Châlons he saved the West from the Huns. Rome's military position was precarious, but Roman leaders could still mobilize some military resources.

Chapter Eight

The Fall of Rome

There is a sense in which Aëtius' success in the defence of Gaul and Italy was also his undoing. The death of Attila and the dissolution of the Hunnic Empire removed the major immediate threat to the northern frontier. In Africa Gaiseric the Vandal remained content with the peace of 442. In 453 Thorismund, the new Visigothic king, was assassinated, and his successor, Theodoric II, was cooperative with Rome. One recent historian has observed that this combination of circumstances and events 'rendered Aëtius positively super-fluous'.[258] Valentinian III had been dominated for so long both by his mother, who died in 450, and by Aëtius, that when he saw an opportunity to rid himself of the general, he personally murdered him with the imperial sword (September 454). One of Valentinian's advisers said, 'You have cut off your right hand with your left', but the consequences were even greater than that: in the spring of 455 two of Aëtius' barbarian retainers avenged their former master by killing the emperor. The slaying of Valentinian III threw the Western Roman Empire into its own death agonies – in about twenty years, less than a generation, Rome had fallen.

The Roman Army after Châlons

Before the outbreak of serious fighting at the battle of Châlons, Attila tried to rally his troops by telling them, among other things, that the Roman forces facing them were beneath contempt. 'The dust of battle overwhelms them while they fight in close formation under a screen of protective shields.' He ordered his Huns to ignore them and to attack the formidable Alans and Visigoths instead.[259]

How the mighty had fallen! One hundred years earlier the Roman army had been the most efficient fighting force on the face of the earth.

By the time of Attila it was so contemptible it could be ignored in actual combat. In fact, of course, Roman troops contributed to the victory at Châlons, mainly by seizing high ground at the outset of battle, but the passages quoted above offer a fascinating commentary on the fate of the Roman army in the fifth century. Despite the impact of barbarization, Roman forces continued to fight according to traditional Roman tactics, yet those tactics, previously so superior, seemed absurd to the barbarians of the fifth century.

What must have happened is reasonably clear. To fight effectively in close order, troops require intensive drill and rigorous discipline. Romans of the fifth century apparently maintained the old formations but abandoned the necessary training. As a result they combined the worst features of the Roman and barbarian styles of fighting. Close formation and indiscipline make a very sad conjunction. Troops not drilled to fight in formation should not try to do so. Without intensive training the looser formations of the barbarians (who did not try to maintain a rigid line) are actually a better use of manpower. In the East, Byzantine emperors – less influenced by federate barbarian units – maintained a firmer discipline and drill, resulting in the superb army of Belisarius in the sixth century under Justinian.[260] As the emperors and generalissimos of the West relied more and more heavily on federates, the traditional Roman army of the West simply disintegrated.

The actual process of this military collapse is unclear. Western emperors lacked the revenues (which were gradually and relentlessly reduced, compounding the problem) to maintain large Roman forces. They also had difficulty imposing a system of conscription. The *comitatenses* deteriorated in quality. A. H. M. Jones believed that by the end of the Roman Empire in the West 'there was probably little difference between the surviving regular units of the field army and the federates', but the words of Attila, quoted above, indicate otherwise.[261] Jones is probably right, however, in suggesting that the *limitanei*, under Valentinian III and his successors, simply withered away, 'disbanded for lack of pay'.

The Sack of Rome by the Vandals

In the examination of the immediate causes of Rome's fall, there is no need to find a villain or a scapegoat. Aëtius did some things very well and other things badly. He faced far greater challenges than most grand strategists have done, though the military fate of the Western Empire had not been completely determined when he gained control of Roman policy in the early 430s. A military genius (and history has produced some) might have saved the day. Aëtius was no genius, yet that is scarcely a cause for shame. We have no reason to believe that his ascendancy stifled a wave of military brilliance that might otherwise have cast its light over the Roman Empire in the West.

The deaths of Aëtius and of Valentinian III created a grave crisis in Italy. No provision had been made for the succession, and there were riots in the streets of Rome as a political enemy of Aëtius, the wealthy senatorial aristocrat, Petronius Maximus – who had also arranged the murder of Valentinian III – purchased the support of the nearby troops and assumed the purple.[262] Maximus forced Valentinian's widow to marry him, although she hated him, and he gave the former emperor's daughter, Eudocia, to his son. This Eudocia, about seventeen years old at the time, is the same girl who had been promised, as a child of about five, to Huneric, the son of the Vandal Gaiseric.[263]

Maximus was merely the first of a series of Rome's most obscure emperors, the men who ruled what was left of the Empire in the few years between the death of Valentinian in 455 and the overthrow of Romulus Augustulus in 476. The story of their reigns is a dreary tale, and as much as possible we shall avoid the telling of it. If the truth be known, after Valentinian III, the emperor in Italy was no longer the most important figure in the West. That honour indubitably went to Gaiseric, king of the Vandals.

According to a tradition that is possibly reliable, the abused widow of Valentinian asked Gaiseric to overthrow Maximus.[264] Whether inspired by the damsel's call for aid, driven by anger at the treatment of his promised daughter-in-law, or impelled by the opportunity created by political crisis, Gaiseric prepared an armada for an attack on Rome. As it approached the city, Maximus tried to ride away, but someone in a riotous crowd hit him on the head with a stone, and the mob mutilated his body (31 May 455). Early in June the Vandals entered Rome. There was no attempt to defend the city militarily. Pope Leo met the invaders at the gate, but his spiritual power could not stay the Vandals, who devoted fourteen days to the systematic plunder of Rome, promising the pope merely that there would be no burning and no bloodshed. The Vandals took everything they could get their hands on, including the gilded bronze tiles from the roof of the temple of Jupiter Capitolinus and the booty Titus had brought to Rome from Jerusalem. When they finally turned their heavy-laden ships back towards Africa, they took with them Valentinian's former wife and two daughters. Upon their arrival in Africa Huneric married Eudocia.

Ricimer and the Defence of Italy

Rome, the mistress of the world, had been violated once again, this time without protest or resistance. Government had nearly collapsed. There was no emperor, no established authority. Avitus, the Field Marshal of Gaul, established himself as emperor in Arles with the support of the Visigoths, and by the end of 455 he crossed the Alps to take Italy. The Eastern emperor Marcian recognized him as an Augustus.[265]

By this time, unfortunately, the hostility between Gaul and Italy that was the natural result of Aëtius' policies made Avitus unacceptable to Italian Romans. Many Italians believed that Attila's invasion of Italy came because Aëtius sacrificed the peninsula to save Gaul. He had even urged Valentinian to abandon Italy, and he had courted the favour of Romano-Gallic aristocrats who saw relations with the Visigoths as infinitely more important than defence of Italy against Huns or Vandals. Avitus seemed to offer more of the same, and senators in Rome feared that Italy would become an appendage of Gaul. Before the end of 456 he was deposed by one of his own generals, a full-blooded barbarian, Ricimer, who ruled through puppet-emperors over what was left of the Western Roman Empire for the next fifteen or so years.

In fact, not much was left, and Ricimer saw the defence of Italy as his primary strategic objective. The new generalissimo was an Arian Christian, the grandson through his mother of the Visigothic king, Vallia, and his father was a Suebian. He was also uncle of the Burgundian king, Gundobad. Little is known of his early career in the Roman army, but he had served under Aëtius. He owed his rapid rise as a general to the favour of Avitus, the emperor he overthrew. When the Vandals attacked Sicily in 456, Ricimer met them at Agrigento, blunted their attack, and pursued them to Corsica where he defeated them at sea. Later that year, as Field Marshal (*magister militum*), he deposed Avitus and in 457 supported Majorian (457–61), a fellow soldier who had been a favourite both of Aëtius and of Valentinian. In that same year Marcian, the emperor in Constantinople, died and was replaced by Leo I (457–74), who recognized Majorian as Augustus in the West.[266]

Since the defence of Italy required, as much as possible, the retention of Roman authority in Gaul, and since the death of the Gallic Avitus was naturally disturbing to Gallic aristocrats, as well as to the Visigoths and Burgundians, Ricimer and Majorian decided to reassert Roman rule forcefully. Ricimer remained in Italy while in 458–9 Majorian marched to Gaul where the Burgundians had taken Lyons with the cooperation of its inhabitants. Majorian regained it, and his forces then drove back the Visigoths who were besieging Arles. Although the Burgundians had in fact increased the extent of territory they controlled along the Rhône, Roman Gaul had been saved.

Gaiseric and the Vandals remained the most serious threat to Roman rule in the West, and in 460 Majorian mobilized an expeditionary force of some three hundred ships on the coast of Spain, but Gaiseric decided on a pre-emptive strike and destroyed the Roman fleet. When Majorian returned to Italy in 461, defeated and without an army, Ricimer arrested and executed him. Gaiseric's power had grown, and the Vandal king had every reason to despise Rome's Visigothic defender, the power behind the throne, the patrician Ricimer, simply because he was a hated Visigoth.

Ricimer appointed a new emperor, Libius Severus (461–5), an Italian who was never recognized by Leo I in the East.[267] The new emperor was so obscure and so overshadowed by Ricimer that almost nothing is known of him.[268] Again, it was Gaiseric, and not the emperor of the West, who dominated the 460s. After the Vandal king destroyed the Roman fleet off the coast of Spain in 460, he attacked Sicily in the following year. Ricimer was unable to bring Gaiseric to terms, but in 462 Leo I from Constantinople persuaded the Vandal king to release Valentinian's widow and his daughter, Placidia, both of whom journeyed not to Rome but to Constantinople. The other daughter Eudocia, wife of Gaiseric's son Huneric, naturally remained with her husband, while Leo undoubtedly recognized Vandal control over western North Africa, the Balearic Isles, Corsica and Sardinia.

This relationship with the emperor of the East raised Gaiseric's prestige and emboldened him to interfere in the dynastic politics of the

Roman Empire in the West. He championed the cause of a certain Olybrius, the husband of the freed Placidia, for the throne in Italy. Because of Huneric's marriage to Placidia's sister Eudocia, Olybrius had a family connection with the Vandal king. Since Leo had never recognized Severus in the West, this attack on Ricimer's puppet was a serious threat. Gaiseric used his support of Olybrius' cause to justify renewed attacks on Sicily and Italy.[269] It was probably fortunate that Severus died, apparently of natural causes, in 465, for Ricimer then referred the matter of the succession to Leo and made the emperor of the East, in the meantime at least, partly responsible for the defence of Italy.

Indeed, for almost two years Leo ruled over a united Empire, using Ricimer as his agent in the West, but in 467 Gaiseric actually raided the Peloponnese. Leo decided to smash Vandal power in Africa, and, to guarantee the support of the West, he appointed as emperor the distinguished patrician Anthemius (467–72), son-in-law of the former Eastern emperor Marcian. To cement the bond among the potentates of East and West, Anthemius, perhaps reluctantly, allowed his daughter to marry the barbarian Arian, Ricimer.

Fortunately for Gaiseric this Roman alliance was shaky from the outset. Leo poured tremendous resources into the war against the Vandals. Over 1000 ships sailed from the Bosporus in 468 with some 100,000 men, but they were commanded by the emperor's brother-in-law, Basiliscus, an unreliable incompetent. In the West Anthemius gave command of his contingent to the general Marcellinus, and in doing so the new emperor alienated Ricimer, who hated Marcellinus. Incompetence, jealousy, lack of cooperation, even treachery are not the ingredients of a successful military campaign.

The plan was to subject Gaiseric to a three-pronged attack.[270] Basiliscus was to move the fleet immediately against Carthage itself while another eastern general, Heraclius, advanced westwards across North Africa from Byzantine Egypt. The western forces under Marcellinus were to protect their Italian base by striking at Vandal Sardinia and then join forces with their eastern allies at Carthage. The strategy of this campaign, which might have restored Africa to Rome, was sound. As is so often the case in warfare, however, execution – not strategic conception – was the difficulty. On the tactical level Basiliscus made a stupid blunder. All three arms of the united attack on Carthage made initial progress. Orthodox Catholics in Africa were prepared to help in expelling their Arian conquerors; Gaiseric despaired. Then, instead of striking immediately at Carthage after first dispersing the Vandal fleet, Basiliscus established headquarters elsewhere on the coast. This gave Gaiseric a chance to rally his forces, and Vandal fireships caught the Roman fleet by surprise. Basiliscus retreated to Sicily with only about half his fleet to join with Marcellinus, but the western general was murdered there under mysterious circumstances. (Some historians have seen the hand of Ricimer in the assassination.) Heraclius countermarched his forces back to Egypt.

The Loss of Gaul and Spain

The Vandals had withstood the combined assault of the Eastern and Western Roman Empires. The cost to Rome and Constantinople in money and manpower was enormous, but in the West the effect on morale was more important. The German nations of Gaul did not fail to note the weakness of Rome. In 466 Euric had become king of the Visigoths, and that able ruler pursued an expansionist policy, putting 'an end forever', in the words of E. A. Thompson, 'to the treaty of 418'.[271] In Italy strained relations between Ricimer and Anthemius made it virtually impossible to offer Gallo-Romans effective protection, though probably little could have been done for them in any event. The only option seemed to be to give the Burgundians more control in Gaul as a means of restricting Visigothic power, but that policy did little to protect Roman interests directly.

Finally, in 472, Ricimer besieged Rome from his base in Milan in order to overthrow Anthemius and to replace him with Olybrius, a candidate who also had Gaiseric's support. Clearly Ricimer's interests were primarily in Italy, and the effect of his policies had been to weaken Rome outside the peninsula. The general died from natural causes shortly after he had executed Anthemius, and his new puppet, Olybrius, died soon thereafter, in November 472, also from natural causes.

In the meantime Roman control in Gaul had virtually evaporated. The wily Euric, a fanatical Arian, extended Visigothic power to the Loire, then seized Arles and raided along the Rhône. When Euric died in 484, he ruled over a kingdom that included most of Spain and southern Provence as well as the traditional Gothic stronghold of

Aquitaine. Burgundians, Bretons and Franks controlled the rest of Gaul. In 475 Euric had proclaimed his Visigothic kingdom fully independent of Rome, but the wave of the future did not roll from Aquitaine. In 481 Clovis became king of the Franks, and after his conversion to Catholic (rather than Arian) Christianity, he led his people to domination in Gaul. In 486 at the battle of Soissons Clovis defeated Syagrius, the heroic defender of an autonomous Gallo-Roman enclave between the Bretons and the Franks. In effect the Roman government in Italy had exercised no power in Spain or Gaul since 475. The Roman Empire in the West consisted only of Italy and parts of the two provinces to the north, Raetia and Noricum.[272]

Odovacer and the Overthrow of Romulus Augustulus

After the deaths of Ricimer and Olybrius in 472, there had been some months of chaos in Italy. Ricimer's nephew, the Burgundian Gundobad, had taken his uncle's place as *de facto* military ruler of Italy, and he secured the purple for a puppet, Glycerius. The Emperor Leo at Constantinople would not recognize Glycerius, however, and he sent one of his relatives, Julius Nepos (474–5), to be emperor in the West. Gundobad returned to Burgundy where he later became a Burgundian king, and Glycerius obliged Julius Nepos by giving up his throne for the bishopric of Salona.[273]

In this age of weak emperors Julius Nepos was reasonably strong. He had been a successful general in Dalmatia, but he found it necessary to cater to Rome's now almost exclusively barbarian army by appointing a generalissimo acceptable to the barbarian troops. Eventually, in 475, the choice fell on Orestes, a man who, like Aëtius, had spent time at the court of the Huns, as Attila's secretary. Although he was Roman by birth, his long association with barbarians made him acceptable. Before the year was out, however, Orestes rebelled against Nepos, and the emperor fled to the East (Dalmatia) while the general elevated his own son, Romulus (475–6), to the throne.[274]

The emperor at Constantinople still recognized Nepos, but for the next year Orestes ruled in Italy under the banner of his young son who took the title Augustus but was generally called Augustulus (or 'little Augustus') because of his age. In the end not even Orestes was able to control the Germanic troops who served the Roman emperor in the West. They wanted a settlement in Italy, just as the Visigoths and others had been settled in Gaul. Whether that involved a third of the land or merely of the tax revenues remains uncertain, but it was a large concession in either case. Orestes refused, and in a meeting the Germans elected one of their own officers, Odovacer, as king. The new ruler deposed and executed Orestes and sent Romulus Augustulus off to retirement on a public pension.

The Roman Empire in the West was finished. Rome had joined the company of Nineveh and other fallen empires. Odovacer was a German, the son of a Thuringian father and a Skirian mother.[275] He ruled in Italy as king (*rex*), and the Roman Senate returned the imperial regalia to Constantinople, sending a legation to the Eastern emperor Zeno (474–91) saying that there was no longer any need for an emperor in the West. Zeno did not acquiesce; he ordered the Roman Senate to take back Julius Nepos, but Odovacer ignored those instructions, and Nepos died four years later (480).

Historians have forever quarreled about the year 476 and presumably will always do so. Is it a reasonable date for the fall of Rome? The deposition of Romulus Augustulus lacks the earth-shaking, cataclysmic drama of Julius Caesar's assassination. Contemporaries had become accustomed to the rapid rise and fall of emperors since the death of Valentinian III in 455. They could not be certain that there would never be another emperor in the West. Yet there was not, and the fall of Rome may confidently be dated to the 'age of 476' even if we fall short of dogmatically insisting on the exact year.

To some the qualification above may seem wishy-washy, a professor's attempt to avoid coming to grips with the question. Yet brief reflection will confirm that history often acts in this evasive way, allowing great events to unfold relatively rapidly but nevertheless in stages over a few years or a generation. So it was, earlier in Roman history, with the failure of the Roman Republic and the beginning of the Roman Empire. Is the critical date for that great change in Roman history the Ides of March, 44 BC, or the deaths of Brutus and Cassius at Philippi in 42, or the victory of Octavian over Antony and Cleopatra at Actium in 31 or Octavian's political settlement with the Senate in 27 and his assumption of the name Augustus? Actually any attempt to be too precise about it can be misleading. Suffice it to say that the great transformation occurred over a period of nearly twenty years and that even then contemporaries were not altogether certain what had happened. The writing and teaching of history, however, often require somewhat greater precision than that. A book on the failure of the Roman Republic has to end somewhere, and authors have traditionally been granted some freedom in the choice of decisive dates between 44 and 27 BC.[276]

So it is with the fall of Rome. If one prefers the date 481 when Clovis became king of the Franks, or 488 when Theodoric and the Ostrogoths invaded Italy, or the death of the great Gaiseric in 477 or the defeat of Syagrius at Soissons in Gaul in 486, there is little reason to quibble. In the early sixth century, writers in Byzantium began to date the fall of Rome to 476.[277] In the last half of the fifth century the Roman Empire in the West ceased to be, forevermore; 476 is the traditional date, and it has reasonably just claim to be honoured by historians whenever it is necessary to give an exact year.

The Fall of Rome

When the adherents of the 'Late Antique' school use the word 'transformation' in describing the fall of Rome, they mean it as an explanation as well as a description. The transformation they see from Rome to the Middle Ages developed over centuries, not years. Yet the fall of Rome in the West was more than a process – it was also an event, one that occurred rather suddenly, in the same sense at least in which the fall of the British Empire after World War II required about a generation but can nevertheless be said to have been sudden.[278]

If one takes 476 as the date of the fall, and looks back merely a hundred years to 376, one can see an empire still strong, still as large as the Empire of Augustus, still respected by its foes across the imperial frontiers. Furthermore, it was defended by an army that continued to fight effectively despite the catastrophe in Persia under Julian, a strategic blow that cannot be laid at the feet of the legions.

On the other hand, 376 was itself an important year in Roman history. It was then that the Visigoths, driven by the pressure of the Huns and the Ostrogoths, crossed the Danube with the emperor's permission to settle permanently in Roman territory. Thus began a series of invasions (for the crossing of the Danube soon turned into an invasion) that led in a hundred years to the fall of the Western Roman Empire. It is easy with hindsight to regard that fall as inevitable, to emphasize the vulnerability and fragility of the Roman Empire, to see

Europe in AD 476. *The Western Roman Empire no longer existed. The Byzantine Empire survived until the fifteenth century.*

Finns

Balts

Finns

Slavs

ium

Danube

goths

Black   Sea

Constantinople

•*Nicomedia*

Kingdom
of Iberia

Persian
Empire

E a s t e r n

°

•Athens

•*Antioch*

Arabs

Sea

Roman Empire

Nile

in the fall of Rome what has been called, in another context, 'the weary Titan syndrome'.[279] One cannot argue, as in the case of modern Britain, that the loss of empire 'cushioned' Rome's fall in the world. The Empire had been so inextricably identified with Rome itself that the fall of the Empire *was* the fall of Rome.

To see Roman history from Marcus Aurelius on, as the story of a troubled giant, as so many historians do, a decaying empire, the victim of 'cultural and world-political Angst',[280] is to miss the point. Some historians, recognizing the common fallacy, turn the problem around and ask why the Empire survived so long. Both tendencies, however, have the same effect – to direct attention away from a consideration of the factors that led to the disappearance of the Western Roman Empire in the last half of the fifth century; one by seeking the causes in the much too distant past and the other by accepting the fact as inevitable.

The Roman Empire on the eve of Adrianople was not obviously on a downhill course. Nor had Roman citizens lost faith in their destiny to rule the world. The Empire was strong, despite a recent defeat in Persia, and it continued to show remarkable strength in the devastating thirty or so years between the defeat at Adrianople and the sack of Rome by Alaric. Since the days of the Punic Wars the strategic strength of Rome had consisted to a certain extent in the ability of the Empire to suffer tactical defeats in the field and yet mobilize new forces to continue the fighting.

Even after AD 410 some of that resilience remained, but there was one difference, particularly in the West. Rome had almost stopped producing its own soldiers, and those it did draw into military service were no longer trained in the ancient tactics of close-order formation though they tried to fight that way. Many historians have argued, either directly or more often by emphasizing other causes, that the fall of Rome was not primarily a military phenomenon. In fact, it was exactly that. After 410 the emperor in the West could no longer project military power to the ancient frontiers. That weakness led immediately to the loss of Britain and within a generation to the loss of Africa. One need not produce a string of decisive battles in order to demonstrate a military collapse. The shrinkage of the imperial frontiers from 410 to 440 was directly the result of military conquests by barbarian forces. To be sure, the loss of strategic resources in money, material and manpower compounded the mere loss of territory and made military defence of the remainder of the Empire even more difficult. It is simply perverse, however, to argue that Rome's strategic problems in the 440s, 50s and 60s were primarily the result of financial and political difficulties or of long-term trends such as gradual depopulation.

The modern historian must keep in mind the fact that Rome in the East did not fall, and any explanation of the fall of Rome must also account for its survival in Byzantium. Why was the East to marshal its military resources, to survive the barbarian invasions and to emerge under Justinian in the sixth century with a burst of military power, sufficient to reconquer, at least temporarily, parts of the West? Some specifically military explanations can be set aside. Recruitment in the Late Empire was difficult, but too much has been made of imperial legislation on that score. Even in the great days of the Roman Empire, for example in the last years of Augustus, recruitment could be a problem during military crises. In the fourth and fifth centuries it was no greater a problem in the West than in the East, at least not until western difficulties were highly exacerbated by military and territorial losses. The strategic strength of the East behind the impenetrable walls of Constantinople is often emphasized as a factor in the survival of the Byzantine Empire, but one must look also at the elements of weakness in the West.

In fact, of course, the sack of Rome, the loss of Britain and of Africa, and parts of Gaul and Spain, dealt heavy blows to the military capacity of the Western emperor. If one begins the story of Rome's fall with the year 440, the collapse of the West and not of the East is easy enough to explain. By 440 western forces were much weaker than those of the East. That was not true, however, on the last day of the year 406, the day Vandals, Suebi and Alamanni crossed the frozen Rhine and moved into Gaul. In 406, on paper, western power was as great as eastern. Stilicho had driven Alaric and Radagaisus out of Italy. Indeed on behalf of the West he had dealt more effectively with Alaric than eastern generals had done. Yet in the short period, 407–10, the West received an ultimately fatal blow. After 410 it was never again militarily as strong as the East. Barbarians were permanently established in Gaul and Spain, and Britain had been lost.

One could argue, as I am inclined to do, that even after 410 the emperor of the West had not lost all military options, that he might yet have restored Roman military power, if not in Britain, at least in the rest of the Western Empire. But military losses in 407–10 were sufficient to make a major difference between the strategic, projective military power of the Eastern and Western emperors. Those few years constitute a turning point after which it is no longer necessary to explain why the West fell and the East survived.

Why, then, did the West do so badly in 407–10? To a certain extent, as we have seen, the strategic strength of the East contributed to the fall of the West. Constantinople was heavily defended. No barbarian tribe could possibly hope to storm those walls. Furthermore, the emperor in the East was better able to afford the heavy subsidies barbarian leaders demanded in the years after Adrianople, though in fact the West also paid a heavy monetary price for peace.

Perhaps the most popular approach to the explanation of Rome's fall, if we can set aside the examination of those long-term causes such as depopulation, race mixture, political and economic deterioration, lead poisoning and other fashionable theories, has been to find a scapegoat, to see in an error or errors of human judgment the fatal mistake that caused the tragedy. Although this approach has often been ridiculed in recent times, it is not without merit. Leaders do matter. Strategic decisions produce successful or unsuccessful results. The weight of history, in the form of long-term trends, may impose limitations on the military mind, but a good general or political leader will bear the burden and solve his strategic problems one way or another.

The Emperor Honorius has been asked by ancient and modern historians alike to take far too much of the blame for Rome's fall. Partly that is because Rome suffered its great humiliation in 407–10 under his rule, and since he did not prevent it, he must undoubtedly be held responsible for it. As citizens we apply this kind of standard to our present leaders, and it is perhaps not unreasonable to do the same for leaders of the past. On the other hand, if it is possible to be right and still lose, Honorius may have done just that. He does not deserve the criticism he uniformly gets for doing nothing, since doing nothing was almost certainly, for him, an 'active' or conscious strategy, not simply negligence, a strategy that might in fact have worked if someone had not opened a gate to Rome for Alaric's Visigoths in August 410.

Stilicho's role in the fall of the West is harder to assess, and he has had vigorous attackers and defenders. That he was much too interested in affairs in Constantinople rather than in Italy is certain. Whether he can also be accused of having let Alaric escape on several occasions when the barbarian leader might have been crushed is impossible to determine on the basis of the inadequate surviving evidence. To those who see the fall of Rome as a matter of trends, Stilicho's efforts are of no concern. Presumably if he had not left Alaric free to sack Rome, someone else would have sacked it. How can even Rome fight trends? But in fact the fate of the Western Roman Empire might have been very different had events in 407–10 taken another course. Insofar as human agency might have prevented them, the failure of Stilicho is significant. His inability to shape a better future for the Western Roman Empire was much more the result of actual mistaken judgment (leading to his execution in 408) than was the failure of Honorius. Stilicho was wrong; Honorius was unlucky.

It is also true, however, that the army itself underwent significant deterioration between 378 and 410, more so in the West than in the East. In the fourth century the western army had been the better one. It was the eastern army that had been defeated in Persia and at Adrianople, but at the Frigid River in 394 Theodosius had beaten the western army with the help of twenty thousand Visigoths, who attacked Arbogast and Eugenius in line of column suffering extraordinarily heavy losses (50 per cent). The loss at the Frigidus undoubtedly demoralized the western army to a certain extent, but it must have been much more humiliated by its treatment at the hands of Stilicho, who commanded it from 395 to 408.

At that time there was a reaction in the East against the use of Germans in the Roman army, but in the West Stilicho imposed the Theodosian policy of barbarization. First, with the western army in the Balkans he failed to crush Alaric on at least two occasions, and then, during the successful campaigns in Italy from 401 to 405 against Alaric (who got away again, twice) and Radagaisus, Stilicho relied heavily on barbarian troops. His use of barbarians became a matter of controversy and contributed to his downfall in 408. For that reason 'barbarization' in this period is often treated as a political problem (which it was), and little consideration has been given to the probable effect the policy had on the proud army of the West.

There is no way of knowing, unfortunately, to what extent the central, mobile army in Italy, by 408, was a traditional Roman army and to what extent it had become overwhelmed by barbarian influences. Possibly, if the resources of Britain and Gaul had been united with the army of Italy in the crisis of 408–10, it might have been possible to have defeated Alaric again, but the revolt of Constantine prevented that kind of cooperation, and Honorius decided to pursue a strategy of exhaustion rather than to bring Alaric to battle. Such a policy was extremely humiliating for the army. General Sir John Hackett has said: 'An army's good qualities are best shown when it is losing.'[281] To fight on in the face of certain defeat requires much more than courage. But the army of the West in the crisis of 408–10 was not allowed to fight at all, and after what it had suffered earlier at the hands of Stilicho, this was the crushing blow. Never again was the emperor of the West the military equal of his eastern counterpart.

In the aftermath of 410 Constantius and Aëtius had done the best they could to maintain Rome's reduced position in the West. Constantius was the better strategist of the two, and his skilful use of naval power did give the regime, now in Ravenna, a new lease of life. Aëtius was unfortunately too interested in Gaul at the expense of Italy, Spain and particularly Africa. The loss of Carthage was a double blow to Rome since the emperor in the West had relied heavily on African grain and because the resources of the African city now strengthened the Vandal kingdom. Declining revenues and territory made recruitment difficult, and the true Roman contingent of the army that fought Attila at Châlons was the object of ridicule. In the last twenty years of the Western Empire, after the death of Valentinian III, the central government in Italy relied exclusively on barbarians until the latter finally, in 476, put one of their own officers in as king and abolished the emperorship in the West.

It is clear that after 410 the Roman army no longer had any special advantage, tactically, over barbarian armies – simply because the Roman army had been barbarized. Hans Delbrück has argued that Roman strength had always been strategic rather than tactical, that man for man Roman armies were no better than Germanic ones:

Vis-a-vis civilized peoples, barbarians have the advantage of having at their disposal the warlike power of unbridled animal instincts, of basic toughness. Civilization refines the human being, makes him more sensitive, and in doing so it decreases his military worth, not only his bodily strength but also his physical courage.[282]

Delbrück goes on to say that Roman tactical organization and training merely 'equalized the situation'.

This is stuff and nonsense, as careful reading of du Picq might have revealed.[283] Rome's army had always been small, relative to the population of the Empire, because Roman training and discipline gave it an unparalleled advantage in tactically effective, close-order formation. By 451, to judge from the speech Attila gave to the Huns at the battle of Châlons, the feeble remnant of the once-proud legions still fought in the ancient formation, but apparently without the training and discipline. Without them, close order was worse than no order at all. Romans could be expected to huddle behind their screen of shields; Visigoths and Alans would do the fighting. As the western army became barbarized, it lost its tactical superiority, and Rome fell to the onrush of barbarism.

Sixth-century Germanic medallion showing cavalryman.

Table of Emperors

Augustus	27BC–AD14	Macrinus	217–18
Tiberius	AD14–37	Elagabalus	218–22
Caligula	37–41	Alexander Severus	222–35
Claudius	41–54	Maximinus	235–38
Nero	54–68	Gordian I & II (in Africa)	238
Galba	68–69	Balbinus & Pupineus	238
Otho	69	Gordian III	238–44
Vitellius	69	Philip the Arab	244–49
Vespasian	69–79	Decius	249–51
Titus	79–81	Gallus	251–53
Domitian	81–96	Aemilianus	253
Nerva	96–98	Valerian	253–60
Trajan	98–117	Gallienus	253–68
Hadrian	117–38	Claudius Gothicus	268–70
Antoninus Pius	138–61	Quintillus	270
Lucius Verus	161–69	Aurelian	270–75
Marcus Aurelius	161–80	Tacitus	275–76
Commodus	180–92	Florianus	276
Pertinax	193	Probus	276–82
Didius Julianus	193	Carus	282–83
Septimus Severus	193–211	Numerian	283–84
Caracalla	211–17	Carinus	283–85
Geta	211–12		

West		East	
Maximian	286–305	Diocletian	284–305
Constantius	305–06	Galerius	305–11
Severus	306–07	Maximinus Daia	310–13
Constantine the Great	306–24	Licinius	308–24
(West and East) Constantine the Great		324–37	
Constantine II	337–40	Constantius II	337–53
Constans	337–50		
Magnentius	350–53		

West		East	
West		**East**	
(West and East) {	Constantius II	353–61	
	Julian	361–63	
	Jovian	363–64	
Valentinian	364–75	Valens	364–78
Gratian	367–83	Theodosius	379–95
Valentinian II	383–92		
Eugenius	392–94		
Theodosius	394–95		
Honorius	395–423	Arcadius	395–408
Valentinian III	425–55	Theodosius II	408–50
Maximus	455–57	Marcian	450–57
Majorian	457–61	Leo	457–74
Severus	461–65		
Anthemius	467–72		
Olybrius	472–73		
Glycerius	473–74	Leo II	474
Julius Nepos	474–75		
Romulus Augustulus	475–76	Zeno	474–91

Notes

Except in rare instances references are to modern discussions only. Ancient sources are fully cited in Jones 1964 and in numerous other modern works referred to in these notes. Books are usually cited in a shortened form (e.g. Starr 1982) and the full bibliographical information may be found in the Select Bibliography. Articles are usually cited in full in the notes and will not be found in the bibliography.

Chapter One

1 For recent, good surveys of the history of the Roman Empire in English see books by Starr 1982, Baldwin 1980, Wells 1984, and Millar 1967.

2 Starr 1982, p. 3.

3 There are several so-called 'problems' books on the fall of Rome. See esp. Kagan 1972 and Chambers 1963. The book in German, which arrived too late for use in research on this book, is Demandt 1984.

4 For the quotation from Twain see Gavin de Beer's review of D. Proctor, *Hannibal's March in History*, Oxford 1971, in *Journal of Roman Studies*, 62 (1972), 180.

5 Gibbon, Bury ed., 1909–14, I, p. ix.

6 Gibbon, Bury ed., 1909–14, I, pp. 85–6. See a similar statement by Theodor Mommsen, quoted in Wells 1984, p. 2.

7 Gibbon, Bury ed., 1909–14, I, p. 104. For a recent treatment of Commodus see Birley 1972, pp. 97–143.

8 Gibbon, Bury ed. 1909–14, I, p. 137. Starr 1983, p. 132, calls the Severan dynasty 'a massive turning point in the political, economic, and military history of the Empire. . . .'

9 On literature see Duff 1964, pp. 521–7, and for all cultural and intellectual aspects of Roman life in this period see esp. Starr 1954. See also Barry Baldwin, 'Literature and Society in the Later Roman Empire', in Gold 1982, pp. 67–83. For the second century see his 'A Bibliographical Survey: The Second Century from Secular Sources 1969–80', *Second Century*, 1, (1981), 173–89.

10 For a good, recent survey of this period see MacMullen 1976, and Frèzouls 1983. See also King and Henig 1981.

11 Gibbon, Bury ed. 1909–14, I, p. 378.

12 Quoted in Walbank 1969, p. 14.

13 Gibbon, Bury ed. 1909–14, III, p. 507; see also G. W. Bowersock, 'Gibbon on Civil War and Rebellion in the Decline of the Roman Empire', in Bowersock, Clive and Graubard 1977, pp. 27–35.

14 For the quotes above see Gibbon, Bury ed. 1909–14, IV, pp. 174–5.

15 There are many books on Gibbon. See Jordan 1971, Gossman 1981, and Ducrey 1977.

16 Starr 1982, p. 3, and Birley 1972, p. 1.

17 See also Brown 1982 and his essay, 'The Rise and Function of the Holy Man in Late Antiquity', *Journal of Roman Studies*, 61 (1971), 80–101, and a review article on Patlagean 1977 by A. Cameron, 'Late Antiquity – The Total View', *Past and Present*, 88 (1980), 129–35. Haywood 1958 is another important spokesman of the continuity theory. See also Goffart 1980 and Matthews 1975. For a recent Marxist view see Ste. Croix 1981 and Chris Wickham, 'The Other Transition: From the Ancient World to Feudalism', *Past and Present* 103 (May 1984), 3–36. There is an excellent discussion of recent work by Barry Baldwin, 'Late Antiquity: A Review Article', *Classical Views*, 3 (1984), 57–67.

18 Papyrologists have produced some important sources. See, for example, Alan K. Bowman, '*Papyri* and Roman Imperial History, 1960–75', *Journal of Roman Studies* 66 (1976), 151–73. See also J. D. Thomas and R. W. Davies, 'A New Military Strength Report on Papyrus', *Journal of Roman Studies* 67 (1977), 50–61, and Bell, Martin, Turner, and van Berchem 1962. In epigraphy, the discovery of virtually the complete text of Diocletian's Edict on Prices is one instance of advance. Wells 1984, pp. 43–52, offers a

judicious summary of the importance of epigraphy, papyrology and archaeology in the study of the Roman Empire.

19 T. Frank, 'Race Mixture in the Roman Empire', *American Historical Review*, 21 (1915–16), 689–708. He is most respected for the multivolume *An Economic Survey of Ancient Rome* (Baltimore, 2nd ed., 1940), which he edited and partially wrote.

20 Bowersock (n. 13, above), p. 27.

21 Climate: Ellsworth Huntington, 'Climatic Change and Agricultural Exhaustion as Elements in the Fall of Rome', *Quarterly Journal of Economics*, (1917), 108. Population: Book 1955. Lead Poisoning: S. Colum Gilfillan, 'Roman Culture and Dysgenic Lead Poisoning', *The Mankind Quarterly*, 5 (Jan–March 1965), 3–20. See also Jerome Niragu, 'Saturnine Gout Among Roman Aristocrats. Did Lead Poisoning Contribute to the Fall of the Empire?', *The New England Journal of Medicine*, 308, no. 11 (March 17, 1983), pp. 660–3. For a criticism see C. R. Phillips III, 'Old Wine in Old Lead Bottles: Niragu on the Fall of Rome', *Classical World*, 78 (1984), 29–33.

22 Walbank 1969, p. 13.

23 p. 466 (translation mine). The best known statement of the continuity theory in French is by Lot 1931. For a recent discussion see Mathias Springer, 'Haben die Germanen das weströmische Reich erobert?' *Klio*, 64 (1982), 179–87.

24 But note the philosopher Herder, whose views are quoted in the quotation from Piganiol, above. For the *Völkerwanderung* in German scholarship see Goffart 1980, pp. 3–39, and Diesner 1982.

25 See Hermann Aubin, 'Zur Frage der historischen Kontinuität im Allgemein', in Aubin 1949, p. 70, and Vogt 1967, pp. 223–46.

26 In addition to the work mentioned in the text above see also Jones' somewhat more popular book on the decline of Rome, 1966.

27 Jones 1964, II, p. 1027.

28 Ibid.

29 Ibid., p. 1038. For a recent discussion of usurpation see A. E. Wardman, 'Usurpers and Internal Conflicts in the 4th Century AD', *Historia*, 33 (1984), 220–37.

30 Jones 1964, II, p. 1045. See also MacMullen 1976, p. 183. On taxation and corruption see the outstanding article by R. I. Frank, 'Ammianus on Roman Taxation', *American Journal of Philology*, 93 (1972), 69–86. See also Starr 1982, p. 165.

Chapter Two

31 Gibbon, Bury ed. 1909–14, I, p. 1.

32 'Das römische Militärwesen seit Diocletian', *Hermes*, 24 (1889), 195–275 (reprinted in Mommsen 1910, pp. 206–83).

33 See esp. Grosse 1920.

34 So, van Berchem 1952, Jones 1964, and Hoffmann 1969. The first serious attack on Mommsen's dating came with E. Nischer, 'The Army Reforms of Diocletian and Constantine and Their Modifications up to the Time of the *Notitia Dignitatum*', *Journal of Roman Studies*, 13 (1923), 1–55. H. M. D. Parker, 'The Legions of Diocletian and Constantine', *Journal of Roman Studies*, 23 (1933), 175–89, defended Mommsen. See also N. H. Baynes, 'Three Notes on the Reforms of Diocletian and Constantine', *Journal of Roman Studies*, 15 (1925), 195–208, who said 'I still remain an unrepentant disciple of Mommsen' (p. 204).

35 Zosimus (translation Buchanan and Davis), II, 34.

36 For recent discussions see Luttwak 1976, pp. 51–126, and F. Millar, 'Emperors, Frontiers and Foreign Relations, 31 BC–AD 378', *Britannia*, 13 (1982), 1–23, and J. C. Mann, 'The Frontiers of the Principate', in Temporini, ANRW, II, 1, pp. 508–33. On the African frontier see Brent D. Shaw, 'Fear and Loathing: The Nomad Menace and Roman Africa', in Wells 1982, pp. 29–50. For the frontier generally see the many essays in Haupt and Horn 1977. See also Aricescu 1980.

37 E. A. Thompson, 'Early Germanic Warfare', *Past and Present*, 14 (1958), 18. On Roman logistics see Adams 1976.

38 Starr 1982, pp. 87–8. K. Hopkins, 'Taxes and Trade in the Roman Empire (200 BC–AD 400)', *Journal of Roman Studies*, 70 (1980), 116, estimates that an army of 300,000 cost 'over 400 million sesterces per year'. See also R. MacMullen, The Roman Emperors' Army Costs', *Latomus*, 43 (1984), 571–80.

39 Arther Ferrill, 'The Wealth of Crassus and the Origins of the First Triumvirate', *Ancient World*, (1978), 169–77, and 'Caesar's Private Fortune: Wealth and Politics in the Late Roman Republic', *Indiana Social Studies Quarterly*, 30 (1977), 101–11.

40 In some ways the strategy actually begins with Augustus, who by the end of his reign had begun to organize Rome's basic frontiers. I do not believe that one can readily accept the rather sharp distinction Luttwak 1976 makes between the policies of Augustus and Hadrian. See the opening remarks of van Berchem in Haupt and Horn 1977, p. 541. By the end of the reign of Augustus a general policy against imperial expansion had been adopted (despite the ingenious arguments of Josiah Ober, 'Tiberius and the Political Testament of Augustus', *Historia*, 31 (1982), 306–28). See Wells 1972. Luttwak places too much emphasis on client kings and impermanent legionary camps in the Early Empire. The difference between Augustus and Hadrian was more tactical than strategic. Both generally thought in terms of defending the frontiers (though for much of his reign Augustus was also creating them). Obviously there were important modifications in Roman grand strategy between Augustus and Hadrian, but there is also a continuity that requires some emphasis.

41 Dio Cassius, LXXVII, 15, 2. On Septimius see E. Birley, 'Septimius Severus and the Roman Army', *Epigraphische Studies*, 8 (1969), 63–82, and R. E. Smith, 'The Army Reforms of Septimius Severus', *Historia*, 12 (1972), 481–500. See also Campbell 1984, pp. 401–14.

42 Domaszewski 1967, p. 123, believed that the Severans turned the army over to Asiatics, Africans and Illyrians, but Birley (n. 41, above), 70–8, shows that 'Italians and other westerners' continued to dominate.

43 See Luttwak 1976, pp. 82–3, for travel time (or 'strategic mobility' as he calls it) of armies in the Roman Empire. See also Millar (n. 36, above).

44 For a discussion see Jozef Wolski, 'Le rôle et l'importance des guerres de deux fronts dans la dècadence de l'Empire romain', *Klio*, 62 (1980), 411–23.

45 Luttwak 1976, p. 61.

46 See above, n. 43. See also Starr 1982, pp. 126–30.

47 For discussion of the way in which Hadrian's Wall was used as a base for forward tactical forays see E. Birley 1961, and Breeze 1982.

48 See esp. the works of Parker 1928, Cheesman 1914, Webster 1969, Watson 1969, Grant 1974, Robinson 1975, Humble 1980, Connolly 1981, Maxwell 1981, Campbell 1984, Speidel 1984, and Keppie 1984.

49 Du Picq 1921 (originally published in the 1860s), pp. 109–11. For a discussion of du Picq see Stefan T. Possony and Etienne Mantoux, 'Du Picq and Foch: The French School', in Earle, ed., 1943, pp. 206–33; Keegan 1976, pp. 70–1; and Ferrill 1985, *passim*. See also Snyder 1984, pp. 57–60.

50 Josephus, *The Jewish War* (translated by Whiston, 1867), III, 10, 2.

51 For a fascinating discussion of the various formations the Romans did use, including even occasionally the phalanx, see Everett S. Wheeler, 'The Legion as Phalanx', *Chiron*, 9 (1979), 303–18.

52 On Germanic tactics see Delbrück 1980, II, pp. 39–56. For Frankish 'warbands' of the late fifth century see Bachrach 1972, pp. 13–17.

53 The best treatment of this period is Demougeot 1969. See also Grant 1968, Brauer 1975, MacMullen 1976, and King and Henig 1981.

54 Luttwak 1976, p. 129.

55 Luttwak 1976, pp. 130–45.

56 See the reasonable discussion in De Blois 1976, pp. 29–30. On cavalry at the accession of Diocletian see Seston 1946, pp. 298–300, and p. 305. On the history of Roman cavalry see the excellent article by John Eadie, 'The Development of Roman Mailed Cavalry', *Journal of Roman Studies*, 57 (1967), 161–73. A full book on Roman cavalry would be useful. See also Speidel 1984, pp. 391–6.

57 See Hoffmann 1969, I, pp. 247–8, and Grosse 1920, p. 15. The main source for Gallienus' cavalry is a Byzantine one (Georgius Cedrenus) dating from about AD 1100.

58 Finally there is a book in English solely devoted to Diocletian: Williams 1985. In French see Seston 1946. There is much in Jones 1964 and MacMullen 1976. See also Barnes 1982. The best discussion of Diocletian's army and frontier policy is Demougeot 1979, pp. 39–56, and Williams 1985, pp. 91–101, who relies heavily on Luttwak 1976.

59 See T. D. Barnes, 'Imperial Campaigns, AD 284–311', *Phoenix*, 30 (1976), 174–93, and Jerzy Kolendo, 'La chronologie des guerres contres les Germains au cours des dernières années de la tétrarchie', *Klio*, 52 (1970), pp. 197–203. See also Peter Brennan, 'Diocletian and the Goths', *Phoenix*, 38 (1984), 142–6.

60 For the date see Barnes 1982, p. 225. For one aspect of governmental reorganization see Clauss 1980, which must be read in conjunction with the review by R. I. Frank, *Gnomen*, 54 (1982), 755–63.

61 For various estimates see R. MacMullen, 'How Big Was the Roman Army?', *Klio*, 62 (1980), 451–60; R. P. Duncan-Jones, 'Pay and Numbers in Diocletian's Army', *Chiron*, 8 (1978), 541–60; and the table in Luttwak 1976, p. 189. See also Demougeot 1979, p. 40.

62 Jones, 1964, I, p. 54.

63 Luttwak 1976, p. 176, is not persuasive in his argument that Diocletian followed a strategy of *shallow* defence-in-depth rather than one of preclusive security though it is possible that the distinctions between the two systems are so fine that very little is at stake in the argument other than the name. Demougeot 1979, pp. 42–53, offers a more realistic analysis.

64 The views of Mommsen and Grosse (n. 32 and 33, above) that the new grand strategy was the joint work of Diocletian and Constantine are now almost unanimously rejected. The best argument for attributing the change to Constantine is Hoffman 1969, I, p. 2 and *passim*, esp. p. 231. See also van Berchem 1952, p. 99; Jones 1964, I, p. 608; and Demougeot 1979, pp. 72–7. D. van Berchem, 'Armée de frontière et armée de manoeuvre: alternative strategique ou politique?' in Haupt and Horn 1977, pp. 541–3.

65 The exact size of Constantine's mobile army is unknown, but Hoffmann 1969, I, p. 304, estimates the size in the mid-fourth century at 110,000 to 120,000 (not including Africa).

66 Gibbon, Bury ed., 1909–14, II, pp. 188–9.

67 The best discussion of defence-in-depth is in Luttwak 1976, pp. 127–94, who tends to see Roman military history from the third century on, including the reign of Diocletian, as a drift towards the new strategy.

68 On reserves in ancient warfare see Adcock 1957, pp. 77 and 89.

69 MacMullen 1976, p. 185.

70 On barbarization see Jones 1964, I, p. 98 and Waas 1965. See also Demougeot 1979, p. 73.

71 For the Late Roman army, in addition to items listed above, see the essay by Roger Tomlin, 'The Mobile Army', in Connolly 1981, pp. 249–59. On the *Scholae Palatinae* see Frank 1969.

Chapter Three

72 For chronology in this complicated period see T. D. Barnes, 'Imperial Chronology, AD 337–350', *Phoenix*, 34 (1980), 160–6. On Julian there are many books. See esp. Browning 1975, Head 1976, and Bowersock 1978, who represent well the different approaches to that perplexing figure. See also Demougeot 1979, pp. 86–105.

73 Browning 1975, pp. 187–218, Head 1976, pp. 158–79, and Bowersock 1978, pp. 106–19, offer narrative accounts. Browning and Head are richer in detail and in strategic understanding. Head and Bowersock cite the major ancient evidence for the campaign. See also Walter Emil Kaegi, 'Domestic Military Problems of Julian the Apostate', *Byzantinische Forschungen*, 2 (1967), 247–64 (reprinted in Kaegi 1982, Chap. II); R. T. Ridley, 'Notes on Julian's Persian Expedition (363)', *Historia*, 22 (1973), 317–30; Walter Emil Kaegi, 'Constantine's and Julian's Strategies of Strategic Surprise Against the Persians', *Athenaeum*, N.S. 59 (1981), 209–13 (reprinted in Kaegi 1982, Chap. IV); and Gerhard Wirth, 'Julian's Perserkrieg: Kriterien einer Katastrophe', in Klein 1978, pp. 455–507. See also Paschoud 1979, pp. xix–xxiv, and A. Marcone, 'Il significato della spedizione di Giuliano contro la Persia', *Athenaeum*, 57 (1979), 334–56.

74 Ammianus, XIII, 2, 8.

75 Kaegi in *Athenaeum* (n. 73, above).

76 The story that Julian was deceived by Persian treachery into destroying his fleet is absurd. No matter where Julian decided to go after abandoning Ctesiphon, the fleet had to be destroyed.

77 For a contrary view see Ridley (n. 73, above). On Alexander as inspiration for Julian see Baynes, 'Julian the Apostate and Alexander the Great', in Baynes 1955, pp. 346–7.

78 See Robert Turcan, 'L'abandon de Nisibe

et l'opinion publique (363 ap. J.-C.)', in Chevallier 1966, II, pp. 875–90.

79 On Valentinian and Valens generally see Jones 1964, I, pp. 138–54, and Demougeot 1979, pp. 105–21. The best ancient sources are Ammianus Marcellinus and Zosimus.

80 See esp. Ammianus, XXXI, 11–16, and Zosimus, IV, 20–4. For recent modern discussions see Thomas S. Burns, 'The Battle of Adrianople: A Reconsideration', *Historia*, 22 (1973), 336–45; Crump 1975, p. 95, and M. Pavan, 'La battaglia di Adrianopoli (378) e il problema gotico nell'impero romano', *Studi Romani*, 27 (1979), 153–65. See also Delbrück 1921, II, pp. 269–84, and Demougeot 1979, pp. 140–6.

81 On the Huns see Thompson 1948 and Maenchen-Helfen 1973. For the Visigoths in this period see Thompson 1966, and Demougeot 1979, pp. 134–40.

82 For the number see Burns (n. 80, above), 337, n. 10.

83 Ammianus, XXXI, 6, 4: 'pacem sibi esse cum parietibus memorans.'

84 Burns (n. 80, above), 344. The myth, however, dies hard. See Pavan (n. 80, above), 164.

85 See Thompson (n. 37, above) and Burns (n. 80, above), 341.

86 For additional details see Runkel 1903.

87 On the Alans see Bachrach 1973, pp. 27–9, and on the Ostrogoths see Burns 1980, pp. 35–56.

88 Ammianus, XXXI, 12, 16, identifies them as 'sagitarii' and 'scutarii', units normally associated with the *Scholae Palatinae*. See Frank 1969, p. 53.

89 Du Picq believed that skirmisher fire was the *only* effective fire in battle. The rest was merely confusion and noise. In ancient battles involving genuine shock (hand to hand combat), however, the sword and the spear could also, at least at times, be effective.

90 Ammianus, XXXI, 12, 17: 'ut fulmen prope montes.'

91 Ammianus, XXXI, 13, 18: 'Constatque vix tertiam evasisse exercitus partem.'

92 Ammianus, XXXI, 14, 5.

93 Julian's body was recovered and transported for burial to Tarsus.

94 Senger und Etterlin 1964.

95 Hackett 1983.

96 See Jones 1964, II, p. 1425, who estimates that one-seventh of the *comitatus* was replaced after 378. See also Burns (n. 80, above), 344.

97 See the excellent article by Gary Crump, 'Ammianus and the Late Roman Army', *Historia*, 22 (1973), 91–103, in addition to his book (1975). See also Bitter 1976, and Austin 1979.

98 Ammianus, XV, 8, 1–18; XVI, 2, 8.

99 See Crump (n. 97, above), 100.

Notes

Chapter Four

100 On the Elder Theodosius see Hodgkin 1892, I, pt. 1, pp. 287–92, and Jones, Martindale, and Morris, *PLRE*, I, pp. 902–4. See also A. Demandt, 'Der Tod des älteren Theodosius', *Historia*, 18 (1969), 598–626.

101 Jones 1964, I, p. 156, and Hoffmann 1969, I, pp. 458–68.

102 Jones 1964, I, p. 157. See also Thompson, 'The Visigoths from Fritigern to Euric', in Thompson 1982, pp. 38–57, who emphasizes (p. 42) the continued hostility of the Visigoths towards Rome in the years immediately after the settlement. The major study is Pavan 1964. See also Cameron 1970, pp. 370–7, and O'Flynn 1983, pp. 57–8.

103 Themistius, *Orat.*, XVI (quoted in Hodgkin 1892, I, pt. 1, pp. 316–19). On Themistius see Jones, Martindale, and Morris, *PLRE*, I, pp. 889–94. See also G. Dagron, 'L'Empire romain d'Orient dans IVe siècle et les traditions politique de l'hellénisme. Le témoignage de Thémistos', *Travaux et memoires*, 3 (1968), 1–242, and L. J. Daly, 'The Mandarin and the Barbarian: the Response of Themistius to the Gothic Challenge', *Historia*, 21 (1972), 351–79.

104 On Synesius see Martindale, *PLRE*, II, pp. 1048–50, and Jones, 1964, II, p. 1099, n. 46. See also Bregman 1982.

105 See N. H. Baynes, 'Rome and Armenia in the Fourth Century', in Baynes 1955, pp. 186–208; and in *Cambridge Medieval History*, I, p. 240. See also Stark 1966, pp. 354–5.

106 The story of the famous clashes between Ambrose and Theodosius may be found in many books, including Dudden 1935.

107 Otto Seeck and George Veith, 'Die Schlacht am Frigidus', *Klio*, 13 (1913), 451–67 (with a map at the end). See p. 463 for the size of the armies. See also Herbert Block, 'A New Document of the Last Pagan Revival in the West, 393–394 AD', *Harvard Theological Review*, 38 (1945), 199–244, whose account is fascinating but not particularly concerned with military matters. See also Paschoud 1979, app. C, pp. 474–500. The account by Dudden 1935, pp. 428–32, is somewhat sketchy. On the death of Valentinian II, a much debated problem, see Brian Croke, 'Arbogast and the Death of Valentinian II', *Historia*, 25 (1976), 235–44, who provides full citations.

108 For a recent study of the generals of the Late Empire see O'Flynn 1983, who is, however, much more interested in their political than in their military significance. His book is a balanced, thoughtful assessment of the period.

109 Zosimus, IV, 53 (translation mine). On Arbogast see Jones, Martindale, and Morris, *PLRE* 1971, pp. 95–7. On Eugenius see Brian Croke, 'Jordanes' Understanding of the Usurpation of Eugenius', *Antichthon*, 9

(1975), 81–83, and Barry Baldwin, 'Jordanes on Eugenius: Some Further Possibilities', *Antichthon*, 11 (1977), 103–4.

110 For the indirect approach see esp. Hart 1954, p. 161. For direct attack in ancient warfare see Ferrill 1985, *passim*. On the Gothic losses Seeck and Veith (n. 107, above), 461, are sceptical.

111 See the latest edition of *Encyclopaedia Britannica* under 'Bora'.

112 On Claudian see Cameron 1970. The poem quoted is *De Consulatu Honorii*, 93–101 (translation Hodgkin 1892, I pt. 2, 577, slightly modified by me).

113 Zosimus, IV, 59 (translation Hodgkin 1892, I, pt. 2, 580–1).

114 Gibbon, Bury ed., 1909–14, III, p. 197.

115 The bibliography is enormous. See esp. Seeck 1876; Clemente 1968; Jones 1964, App. II, pp. 1417–50; John H. Ward, 'The *Notitia Dignitatum*', *Latomus*, 33 (1974), 397–434; E. Demougeot, 'La *Notitia Dignitatum* et l'histoire de l'empire', *Latomus*, 34 (1975), 1079–1134; Hoffmann 1969; and Goodburn and Bartholomew 1976.

116 On the size see items cited above in n. 61 and n. 65.

117 By far the most important description of the mobile armies, based on the *Notitia*, is Hoffmann 1969. On the importance of Gallic units see Hoffmann, I, pp. 131–208. On the fourth century army in Britain see Holder 1982, pp. 97–103. See also Aricescu 1980 and Welsby 1982.

118 Some of the units can be traced back into the second century AD, but only on a limited scale. See, for example, Eadie's article on Roman cavalry (n. 56, above). For a good survey of the special units see L. Vrady, 'New Evidence on Some Problems of the Late Roman Military Organization', *Acta Antiqua*, 9 (1961), 333–96, esp. 381–5.

119 On logistics in ancient and Napoleonic warfare see Ferrill 1985, *passim*. The most important work for ancient warfare, some of which is valid even for the Late Empire, is Engels 1978. See also Adams 1976.

120 For horse recruitment I have relied heavily on R. W. Davies, 'The Supply of Animals to the Roman Army and the Remount System', *Latomus*, 28 (1969), 429–59, who cites the evidence for much that follows. For comparison see my discussion of horse recruitment in the Assyrian Empire in Ferrill 1985, pp. 71–4. On a related topic see Colin Wells, 'Where Did They Put the Horses? Cavalry Stables in the Early Empire', in Fitz 1977, pp. 659–65.

121 Tacitus, *Ann.*, I, 71; II, 5.

122 Davies (n. 120, above), 435.

123 Ammianus, XXIX, 3, 5.

124 Jones 1964, I, pp. 625–6.

125 On pay see Jones 1964, I, pp. 623–4 and

the items cited above, n. 38 and n. 61.

126 Jones 1964, I, pp. 624–5.

127 Jones 1964, II, pp. 834–6; MacMullen 1967, pp. 24–6.

128 Jones 1964, II, pp. 836–7.

129 MacMullen 1967, p. 1. For the food supply of the Late Roman army generally see pp. 1–22.

130 MacMullen 1967, p. 17.

131 Jones 1964, I, pp. 649–54.

132 Hoffmann 1969, in a major work on the mobile army, has much to say about the interrelationship of *limitanei* and *comitatenses*.

133 See Hoffmann 1969, I, pp. 199–208, 387–96, and 458–68.

134 See the judicious comments of O'Flynn 1983, who relies on Hoffmann 1969. See also Ward (n. 11, above), p. 422.

Chapter Five

135 The best discussion of this period is Demougeot 1951, but readers will find thoughtful studies by O'Flynn 1983, Matthews 1975, and Cameron 1970. Bury 1923 remains a basic work. See also Demougeot 1979, pp. 421–72. For works that emphasize the Eastern rather than the Western Empire see Kaegi 1968, 1981, and 1982.

136 There is a good, recent discussion of the bedside promise and Stilicho's position in O'Flynn 1983. See also Demougeot 1951, pp. 129–39, and A. Cameron, 'Theodosius the Great and the Regency of Stilicho', *Harvard Studies in Classical Philology*, 73 (1969), 247–80.

137 Claudian, *On Stilicho's Consulship*, I, 35–40, and Orosius, VII, 38.

138 Jerome, *Letters*, 123, 16. See also Jones, Martindale and Morris, *PLRE*, I, p. 853.

139 See O'Flynn 1983.

140 Zosimus, V, 4, 3; Claudian, *Against Rufinus*, II, 4–6; and Ambrose, *On the Death of Theodosius*, 5. For other evidence see Jones, Martindale and Morris, *PLRE*, I, pp. 855–6.

141 On Rufinus see Jones, Martindale and Morris, *PLRE*, I, pp. 778–81.

142 See, for example, the quite different views of Hodgkin 1892, I, pt. 2, pp. 756–60; Bury 1923, I, pp. 172–3; O'Flynn 1983, pp. 14–62; and Cameron 1970, *passim*.

143 Jerome, *Letters*, 77, 8 (translation Bury 1923, I, p. 114).

144 Jerome, *Letters*, 60, 16 (translation Bury 1923, I, p. 115).

145 To a certain extent the impressive and highly valuable study by Cameron 1970 fails to distinguish adequately between ancient and modern techniques of propaganda. See the review of Cameron by Christian Gnilka in *Gnomon*, 49 (1977), 26–51.

146 O'Flynn 1983, p. 31. Hoffmann 1969, I, p.

31, argues that Stilicho's primary goal in 395 was to take Constantinople and the campaign against Alaric was a pretext.

147 Bury 1923, I, p. 115.

148 Zosimus, V, 7, 2–3. See also Cameron 1970, App. C, and O'Flynn 1983, pp. 33–6, for a somewhat different interpretation.

149 On the affair of Gildo see Bury 1923, I, pp. 121–6; Demougeot 1951, pp. 173–82; O'Flynn 1983, pp. 36–8; S. I. Oost, 'Count Gildo and Theodosius the Great', *Classical Philology*, 57 (1962), 27–30; Hans-Joachim Diesner, 'Gildos Herrschaft und die Niederlage bei Theueste (Tebessa)', *Klio*, 40 (1962), 178–86.

150 Claudian, *The War Against Gildo*, I, 415–17 (translation M. Platnauer, 1922).

151 Zosimus, V, 11.

152 Claudian, *Against Eutropius*, I, 8–9 (translation mine). On Eutropius and the Huns see Maenchen-Helfen 1973, pp. 51–9, and Gerhard Albert, 'Stilicho und der Hunnenfeldzug des Eutropius', *Chiron*, 9 (1979), 621–45.

153 Jones 1964, I, p. 184.

154 See William N. Bayless, 'The Visigothic Invasion of Italy in 401', *Classical Journal*, 72 (1976), 65–7. On the invasion generally see Pastorino 1975.

155 Demougeot 1951, pp. 270–1, and Richmond 1971, p. 258. See also Hodgkin 1892, I, pt. 2, p. 713, and Wolfram 1979, pp. 178–82.

156 On Pollentia see Demougeot 1951, pp. 275–6.

157 Hodgkin 1892, I, pt. 2, p. 724.

158 On Radagaisus see Martindale, *PLRE*, II, p. 934, and Bury 1923, I, p. 168.

159 On the struggle of Eutropius and Gaïnus see Bury 1923, I, pp. 126–37.

160 On Stilicho's commitment to the Theodosian policy of accommodation see O'Flynn 1983, pp. 53–6, and Cameron 1970, pp. 370–7.

161 For a description of Ravenna see Hodgkin 1892, I, pt. 2, pp. 851–62, and Oost 1968, pp. 271–8. On the fleet see Starr 1941, and Kienast 1966.

162 For further details on the Vandal invasion and the rebellion of Constantine see the next chapter.

163 There is a good, recent discussion of the fall of Stilicho in O'Flynn 1983, pp. 56–62; see also Matthews 1975, pp. 264, 275–9, on the meeting with the Senate; Oost 1968, p. 75; and Bury 1923, I, pp. 166–73. See also Mazzarino 1942, p. 250.

164 Zosimus, V, 35.

165 Claudian, *The Gothic War*, 547. For this invasion see Bury 1923, I, pp. 174–85; Hodgkin 1892, I, pt. 2, pp. 766–816; and Demougeot 1951, pp. 431–85, who describes Alaric's demands in this crisis as 'plus modestes' (p. 433).

166 Quoted in Hodgkin 1892, I, pt. 2, p. 770.

167 Zosimus, V, 50. Earlier he had asked for Venetia as well as Noricum and for an official appointment as a general in the West.
168 On the logistical inadequacies of barbarian armies see E. A. Thompson, 'Early Germanic Warfare', *Past and Present*, 14 (1958), 2–29. See also D. Jones, 'The Sack of Rome', *History Today*, 20 (1970), 603–9.
169 On Galla Placidia see esp. Oost 1968.
170 See Oost 1968, pp. 96–7, n. 32. For Augustine see T. D. Barnes, 'Aspects of the Background of the *City of God*', in Wells 1982, pp. 69–85.
171 Oost 1968, p. 97.
172 Bury 1923, I, p. 196.

Chapter Six

173 See Bury 1923, I, pp. 185–94; Demougeot 1951, pp. 376–96; and Oost 1968, pp. 108–35. Matthews 1975, pp. 307–8. For the quotation in the text above see Bury 1923, I, p. 187. On Constantine see C. E. Stevens, 'Marcus, Gratian, Constantine', *Athenaeum*, 25 (1957), 316–47. On the importance of Gaul in imperial strategy see J. R. Moss, 'The Effects of the Policies of Aetius on the History of Western Europe', *Historia*, 22 (1973), 711–31. See also Wightman 1970, pp. 68–70.
174 Hodgkin 1892, I, pt. 2, p. 741.
175 On the Vandals in Spain see Belda 1969 and Courtois 1955; on the Alans see Bachrach 1973. On both see Demougeot 1979, pp. 310–17; 430–49; 497–502; and 508–13.
176 On Maximus see Martindale, *PLRE*, II, p. 745. Maximus' capital was Tarragona.
177 Martindale, *PLRE*, II, pp. 321–5; Bury 1923, I, pp. 192–3; and O'Flynn 1983, pp. 63–73. For the problems in describing Late Roman emperors see Constance Head, 'Physical Descriptions of the Emperors in Byzantine Historical Writing', *Byzantion*, 50 (1980), 226–40, and Barry Baldwin, 'Physical Descriptions of Byzantine Emperors', *Byzantion*, 51 (1981), 8–21.
178 Martindale, *PLRE*, II, pp. 316–17.
179 On Jovinus see Martindale, *PLRE*, II, pp. 621–2.
180 On Heraclian see Martindale, *PLRE*, II, pp. 539–40. See also S. I. Oost, 'The Revolt of Heraclian', *Classical Philology*, 61 (1966), 236–42.
181 On the marriage of Galla Placidia with Ataulf see Oost 1968, pp. 120–30, and Sirago 1961.
182 Orosius, VII, 42 (quoted in Bury 1923, I, p. 197). See also S. I. Oost, 'Galla Placidia and the Law', *Classical Philology* 63 (1968), 114–21.
183 Orosius, VII, 41, 7. See Oost 1968, p. 109.
184 For an examination of the problem see MacMullen 1967 and Minor 1971. Paschoud 1967 was unavailable to me. For a contrary view see Frank's interesting discussion of the

evidence of Salvian (n. 30, above), pp. 81–6.
185 For Vallia see Martindale, *PLRE*, II, pp. 1147–8.
186 For recent discussions of the end of Roman Britain, a complicated problem, see Arnold 1984; Welsby 1982; Morris 1973, pp. 10–28; Scullard 1979, pp. 176–7; Johnson 1976, pp. 151–4; and Birley 1980, pp. 151–61. See also Starr 1982, pp. 177–9. Thompson 1984 was unavailable to me. The older view, represented by Bury 1923, I, p. 202, that Honorius reasserted control over Britain after 410, has been generally abandoned, but see Jones, 1964, I, p. 191. See also P. Bartholomew, 'Fifth-Century Facts', *Britannia*, 13 (1982), 261–70.
187 See items in n. 184 above and, for the word 'Bagaudae' see Clifford E. Minor, '*Bagaudae* or *Bacaudae*?'. *Traditio*, 31 (1975), 318–22. See Zosimus, VI, 5, 2. See also John Drinkwater, 'Peasants and Bagaudae in Roman Gaul', *Echos du monde classique: Classical Views*, 28 (1984), 349–71.
188 It is not clear that the Eastern emperor in the early fifth century maintained a regular standing fleet since there is no indication of it (as there is for the West) in the *Notitia Dignitatum*. The best discussion of naval power in the fifth century is by J. R. Moss, 'The Effects of the Policies of Aëtius on the History of Western Europe', *Historia*, 22 (1973), 722–8, who cites other pertinent works. See also Jones 1964, pp. 610, 640, 679.
189 Goffart 1980. For the standard view see Oost 1968, pp. 151–5. See also O'Flynn 1983, pp. 73, 173 (n. 37), and 198 (n. 55), and E. A. Thompson's essay, 'The Settlement of the Barbarians in Southern Gaul' (first published in 1956), reprinted in Thompson 1982, pp. 23–37, who argues that the Visigoths were settled in Aquitaine to control the Bagaudae. That was probably one of the results, rather than the cause, of the settlement. See also Demougeot 1979, pp. 475–7.
190 Bury 1923, I, p. 211.
191 Gibbon (Bury ed., 1909–14), III, p. 417.
192 Jones 1964, I, pp. 191–2.
193 On this knotty problem see Jones 1964, I, pp. 195–9, and Goffart 1980, App. A, 'How Many Vandals Invaded Africa?', who concludes that the actual number of Vandals 'continues to be anybody's guess'.
194 On this point see my comments in Ferrill 1985, p. 10.
195 On the date of Vegetius see W. Goffart, 'The Date and Purpose of Vegetius' *De Re Militari*', *Traditio*, 33 (1977), 65–100, and T. D. Barnes, 'The Date of Vegetius', *Phoenix*, 33 (1979), pp. 254–7. Goffart argues for a date in the reign of Valentinian III (425–55) and Barnes for a date in the reign of Theodosius I (378–95). Both authors cite many previous works on those two possibilities. Although my

respect for Barnes' scholarship is great, on this point Goffart's arguments are cogent and convincing. See also Goffart 1980, p. 252 (n. 1), and C. D. Gordon, 'Vegetius and his Proposed Reforms of the Army', in Evans 1974, pp. 35–58. See also Spaulding 1937.

196 Phillips 1940, pp. 9–10. About 150 manuscript copies of this work have survived from the Middle Ages, and it had been translated into English, French, and Bulgarian even before the invention of printing (p. 68). Between 1473 and 1489 it was printed in five different countries including a printing by Caxton in England (1489). The decline of interest in the nineteenth and twentieth centuries is best illustrated by the fact that the only English translation readily available is one by John Clark (London, 1767), reprinted (not in its entirety) in Phillips 1940, pp. 73–175.

197 *De Re Militari*, III, 26: 'Concerning cavalry there are many maxims, but since this branch of the army has progressed [rather than declined] in drill, arms and in the quality of mounts, I believe there is nothing to be learned from books. Present practices are sufficient' (translation mine).

198 On this point see Goffart (n. 195, above), pp. 82–3.

199 *Ibid.*, p. 68 (n. 15).

200 *De Re Militari*, II, 5.

201 Goffart (n. 195, above), pp. 93–4.

202 *De Re Militari*, II, 2. On the importance of integrated armies in ancient warfare see Ferrill 1985, *passim*.

203 *De Re Militari*, I, 20 (translation mine).

204 Jones 1964, p. 1038.

205 *De Re Militari*, I, 6.

206 *De Re Militari*, XVII.

207 See the translation and introduction of Dennis 1984. For other Byzantine works see A. Dain, 'Les stratégists byzantins', *Travaux et Mémoires*, 2 (1967), 317–92.

208 For a translation and commentary see Thompson 1952 and Hassall and Ireland 1979. See also R. P. Oliver, 'A Note on the *De Rebus Bellicis*', *Classical Philology*, 50 (1955), 113–18, and Barry Baldwin, 'The *De Rebus Bellicis*', *Eirene*, 16 (1978), 23–39.

209 *De Rebus Bellicis*, XX (translation Thompson 1952).

Chapter Seven

210 On Galla Placidia see Oost 1968 and Sirago 1961. See also Holum 1982.

211 The expression is that of Procopius. See Bury 1923, I, p. 300, n. 3, who cites and discusses the appropriate passage.

212 Oost 1968, pp. 171–2, gives a psychological explanation of Honorius' affection for his sister that allows too much credence in the scandal.

213 On Castinus see Martindale, *PLRE*, II, pp. 269–70.

214 Oost 1968, p. 179.

215 For John see Martindale, *PLRE*, II, pp. 594–5 (under Ioannes 6).

216 Oost 1968, p. 187, is surely correct in arguing against those historians who see Visigothic intervention as a direct attempt to help Placidia.

217 See Martindale, *PLRE*, II, pp. 21–9. On Aëtius as hostage see Clover 1971, pp. 56–7. Zecchini 1983 was unavailable to me.

218 See Moss (n. 173, above).

219 See Oost 1968, p. 221, n. 46, for the extensive bibliography on this subject. On Aëtius' rank in Gaul see O'Flynn 1983, p. 78. See also Vera Paronetto, 'La crisi politica in Africa all vigilia della invasione vandalica', *Miscellanea greca e romana*, 4 (1975), 405–52.

220 See T. D. Barnes, '*Patricii* under Valentinian III', *Phoenix*, 29 (1975), 155–70.

221 O'Flynn 1983, p. 80.

222 On the Vandals see Courtois 1955 and Belda 1969. On naval power see n. 173, above. See also Clover 1966, and Demougeot 1979, pp. 508–13.

223 E. A. Thompson, 'The Foreign Policies of Theodosius II and Marcian', *Hermathena*, 76 (1950), 58–75.

224 Randers-Pehrson 1983, p. 153.

225 C. M. Wells, 'The Defense of Carthage', in Pedley 1980, pp. 51–61. See also F. M. Clover, 'Carthage in the Age of Augustine', in Humphrey 1978, p. 9.

226 Clover (n. 225, above), p. 14, based on the account of Quodvultdeus, which he cites. See also Clover's article, 'Carthage and the Vandals', in Humphrey 1982, pp. 1–22, and Claude Bourgeois, 'Les vandales, le vandalisme et l'Afrique', *Antiquités Africaines*, 16 (1980), 213–28.

227 See O'Flynn 1983 for a judicious statement of this view. See also Wardman, (n. 29, above).

228 See the important discussion by Thompson (n. 37, above). On Ostrogothic warfare see Burns 1984, pp. 184–201. See also Delbrück 1921, II, pp. 39–56.

229 On the importance of the No-Man's zone in battle generally see Griffith 1981.

230 Quoted in Hackett 1983, p. 161.

231 On the Huns see Maenchen-Helfen 1973, Thompson 1948, and Altheim 1969. See also Demougeot 1979, pp. 369–93 and 521–57.

232 See the excellent discussion by Rudy Paul Lindner, 'Nomadism, Horses and Huns', *Past and Present*, 92 (1981), 1–19. On the warfare of the Huns see Maenchen-Helfen 1973, pp. 201–58.

233 Claudian, *Against Rufinus*, I, 329–31 (quoted in Hodgkin 1892, II, p. 2).

234 Ammianus Marcellinus (as quoted by

Hodgkin 1892, II, pp. 32–4, with modifications suggested by Maenchen-Helfen 1973, pp. 201–2).

235 Gibbon, Bury ed., 1909–14, III, pp. 442–3. For the passage in Jordanes on which this is based see Gordon 1960, p. 61. Jordanes' account was based on Priscus, a fifth-century Byzantine writer. On the date of Attila's accession see Maenchen-Helfen 1973, pp. 91–4.

236 See the persuasive essay by Lindner (n. 232, above). See also John Eadie, 'City and Countryside in Late Roman Pannonia: The *Regio Sirmiensis*', in Hohlfelder, New York 1982.

237 Linder (n. 232, above), p. 15, citing (in n. 47) among others, R. W. and M. L. Settle, *The Story of the Pony Express*, London 1974, pp. 37–9.

238 Lindner (n. 232 above), pp. 14–15, provides the bases for these estimates.

239 Ibid., p. 19.

240 For the barbarians see Thompson (n. 37, above).

241 On the Hunnic helmet see Maenchen-Helfen 1973, pp. 251–3.

242 Maenchen-Helfen 1973, pp. 241–51.

243 O'Flynn 1983, pp. 95–6. See also Briggs Twyman, 'Aetius and the Aristocracy', *Historia*, 19 (1970), 480–503.

244 Bachrach 1973, 1973, pp. 63–4.

245 On Attila and the East see, in addition to the items cited in n. 231, above, Ronald A. Bleeker, 'Aspar and Attila: The Role of Flavius Ardaburius Aspar in the Hun Wars of the 440s', *Ancient World*, 3 (1980), 23–8, and on the interrelationships of Vandal and Hun history see Frank M. Clover, 'Geiseric and Attila', *Historia*, 22 (1973), 104–17.

246 From Priscus (translation mine), quoted also in Bury 1923, I, p. 279, and Gordon 1960, p. 74. See also E. A. Thompson, 'Notes on Priscus Panites', *Classical Quarterly*, 41 (1947), 61–5, and Barry Baldwin, 'Priscus of Panium', *Byzantion*, 50 (1980), 18–61.

247 See Clover (n. 245, above) for a careful examination of this tradition.

248 For a thorough study of the sources and the strategy (but not the tactics) of the conflict see Ulf Täckholm, 'Aetius and the Battle on the Catalaunian Fields', *Opuscula Romana*, 7 (1969), 259–76. The battle of Châlons is the only battle of the Late Roman Empire included in Creasy's *Fifteen Decisive Battles of the World* (1851). See also the account in Fuller 1954, I, pp. 282–301; Gibbon, Bury ed., 1909–14, III, pp. 489–91; Bachrach 1973, pp. 66–7; Thompson 1948, pp. 140–3, and Dahmus 1983, pp. 17–54.

249 On the date see Bury 1923, I, p. 289 (n. 2) and on Honoria generally, Martindale, *PLRE*, II, pp. 568–9.

250 The exact location of the battle is unknown. See Bury 1923, I, p. 293 (n. 1), who refers to it as the battle of the Mauriac plains near Troyes. Maenchen-Helfen 1973, p. 131, says that searching for the battlefield is 'a favourite hobby of local historians and retired colonels'. The actual site of many ancient battles (for example, Zama) is disputed.

251 Täckholm (cited above, n. 248), p. 267, fails to understand this skirmish, because he sees Châlons as a cavalry battle. There is no agreement among modern authors whether the Romans fought on the right or left, but all agree that the hill or high ground was near the Roman position and that the Visigoths faced Attila's Ostrogothic allies. As a result there is general agreement about the tactical flow of the battle.

252 Täckholm (cited above, n. 248), p. 262.

253 Gibbon, Bury ed., 1909–14, III, p. 493.

254 O'Flynn 1983, pp. 97–8, and most modern historians do not even consider this possibility.

255 Bury (1923), I, pp. 293–4. Bury was simply disingenuous in arguing that the siege of Orléans was the decisive engagement. If Attila had won the battle of Châlons, he would surely have moved rapidly back against a defenceless Orléans. On the name of the battle see A. Alföldi, 'Les Champs Catalauniques', *Revue des études hongroises*, 6 (1928), 108–11.

256 For the invasion of Italy, and the disintegration of Attila's Empire see Maenchen-Helfen 1973, pp. 132–68, who defends Aëtius against his ancient and modern detractors, as does O'Flynn 1983, pp. 98–103. Although I generally agree with Maenchen-Helfen and O'Flynn, it does not seem necessary to reject the cogent criticisms of Aëtius' grand strategy, particularly with respect to Africa and to naval power, made by Moss (n. 173, above). O'Flynn's arguments (p. 183, n. 54) against Moss, that 'all the barbarian peoples settled within the empire were equally responsible for the erosion of its structure, the Vandals no more than the rest . . .' is strategic nonsense. Even a general who is 'interested primarily in his own career' sometimes has to make decisions on military rather than political grounds, and Aëtius was sometimes wrong (though not in 451–2).

257 Bury (1923), I, p. 296.

Chapter Eight

258 O'Flynn 1983, p. 100.

259 From Jordanes, quoted by Täckholm (n. 248, above), p. 267. Whether Attila actually gave this speech or not is irrelevant. It must describe a historical reality in any event.

260 For that army see A. Müller, 'Das Heer Justinians', *Philologus*, 71 (1912), 101–38.

261 Jones 1964, I, p. 612 (see also pp. 200–2).

262 Martindale, *PLRE*, II, pp. 749–51.

Notes

263 On Eudocia see Martindale, *PLRE*, II, pp. 407–8. Clover 1971, p. 25 (n. 96), argues that Maximus' son married Placidia, another of Valentinian's daughters. See also S. I. Oost, 'Aëtius and Majorian', *Classical Philology*, 59 (1964), pp. 27–8.

264 Bury 1923, I, p. 324 and n. 2, cites the evidence and calls the story 'credible, though it is not certainly true'. See also O'Flynn 1983, pp. 90–1, and p. 180 (n. 12).

265 Ralph Mathisen, 'Avitus, Italy and the East in AD 455–456', *Byzantion*, 51 (1981), 232–47. See also Demougeot 1979, pp. 573–90.

266 On the disputed question of Majorian's recognition by Leo see Kaegi 1968, pp. 31–4, who argues against it and Helmut Meyer, 'Der Regierungsantritt Kaiser Majorians', *Byzantinische Zeitschrift*, 62 (1969), 5–12, who argues for it. For additional discussion see O'Flynn 1983, pp. 185–6, n. 18. See also Gerald E. Max, 'Political Intrigue during the Reigns of the Western Roman Emperors Avitus and Majorian', *Historia*, 28 (1979), 225–37.

267 S. I. Oost, 'D. N. Libius Severus P.F. Aug.', *Classical Philology*, 65 (1970), 228–40.

268 In addition to Oost's article cited above (which is much longer than the existing evidence on Severus can justify!) see the brief listing in Martindale, *PLRE*, II, pp. 1004–5.

269 Frank M. Clover, 'The Family and Early Career of Anicius Olybrius', *Historia*, 77 (1978), 169–96.

270 Bury 1923, I, pp. 336–37.

271 'The Visigoths from Fritigern to Euric', *Historia*, 12 (1963), 126. See also Demougeot 1979, pp. 622–49, and R. W. Mathisen, 'Emigrants, Exiles, and Survivors: Aristocratic Options in Visigothic Aquitania', *Phoenix* 138 (1984), 159–70.

272 Jones 1964, I, pp. 244–6; Bury 1923, I, pp. 346–7. On the end of Noricum see Thompson 1982, pp. 113–33.

273 On Gundobad see O'Flynn 1983, pp.

129–31, and Demougeot 1979, pp. 661–71.

274 For the disappearance of the Roman army after the death of Aëtius see Jones 1964, I, p. 244.

275 See Bruce Macbain, 'Odovacer the Hun?' *Classical Philology*, 78 (1983), 323–7. Martindale, *PLRE*, II, p. 791, gives Odovacer a Hunnic father. See also R. L. Reynolds and R. S. Lopez, 'Odovacer: German or Hun?' *American Historical Review*, 52 (1946), 36–54.

276 Examples: E. T. Salmon, *A History of the Roman World from 30 B.C. to A.D. 138*, London, 1966; Chester G. Starr, *The Roman Empire: 27 B.C.–A.D. 476*, New York 1982; Fergus Millar, *The Emperor in the Roman World* (31 BC–AD 337), Ithaca 1977. Colin Wells, *The Roman Empire*, Stanford 1984, p. 1, describes his book as one 'on the Roman Empire from 44 BC to AD 235'.

277 For discussion see E. Demougeot, 'Bedeutet das Jahr 476 das Ende des römischen Reiches im Okzident?' *Klio*, 60 (1978), 371–81, who prefers the year 488. See also Brian Croke, 'AD 476: The Manufacture of a Turning Point', *Chiron*, 13 (1983), 81–119, and Wes 1967.

278 For an interesting discussion see Paul Kennedy, *Strategy and Diplomacy 1870–1945*, London 1983, esp. pp. 197–218, entitled 'Why Did the British Empire Last So Long', who discusses a 'downhill-all-the-way' approach, a tendency to identify the 'beginning of the decline of the British Empire . . . in the age of Marlborough or Cromwell'. See also A. Demandt, 'Das Ende des Altertums im metaphorischer Deutung', *Gymnasium*, 87 (1980), 178–204.

279 Kennedy (n. 278, above), p. 197, speaking of the British Empire.

280 Ibid., p. 202.

281 Hackett 1983, p. 162.

282 Delbrück 1920, I, p. 509 (translation Renfroe).

283 For du Picq see n. 49, above.

Select Bibliography

This bibliography contains books only. Articles are cited in full in the notes and are not listed separately here.

Adams, John P., *Logistics of the Roman Imperial Army: Major Campaigns on the Eastern Front in the First Three Centuries AD*, diss., Yale U., New Haven 1976.

Adcock, F. E., *The Greek and Macedonian Art of War*, Berkeley 1957.

Altheim, Franz, *Niedergang der alten Welt; eine Untersuchung der Ursachen*, Frankfurt 1952.

—— *Geschichte der Hunnen*, 2 vols., Berlin 1969.

Ammianus Marcellinus (translation J. C. Rolfe), 3 vols., Cambridge, MA (Loeb Classical Library) 1935.

Aricescu, Andrei, *The Army in Roman Dobrudja*, Oxford 1980.

Arnold, C. J., *Roman Britain to Saxon England*, London 1984.

Austin, N. J. E., *Ammianus on Warfare*, Brussels 1979.

Bachrach, B. S., *Merovingian Military Organization 481–751*, Minneapolis 1972.

—— *A History of the Alans in the West*, Minneapolis 1973.

Baldwin, Barry, *The Roman Emperors*, Montreal 1980.

Barnes, Timothy D., *Constantine and Eusebius*, Cambridge, MA 1981.

—— *The New Empire of Diocletian and Constantine*, Cambridge, MA 1982.

Baynes, Norman H., *Byzantine Studies and Other Essays*, London 1955.

Belda, Morales, *La marina vandala*, Barcelona 1969.

Bell, H. I., Martin, V., Turner, E. G., and van Berchem, D., *The Abinnaeus Archive: Papers of a Roman Officer in the Reign of Constantius II*, Oxford 1962.

Birley, Anthony, *Septimius Severus The African Emperor*, Garden City 1972.

—— *The People of Roman Britain*, Berkeley 1980.

Birley, E., *Research on Hadrian's Wall*, Kendal 1961.

Bitter, Norbert, *Kampfschilderungen bei Ammianus Marcellinus*, Bonn 1976.

Blockley, R. C., *The Fragmentary Classicising Historians of the Later Roman Empire: Eunapius, Olympiodorus, Priscus and Malchus*, Liverpool 1981.

Boak, A. E. R., *Manpower Shortage and the Fall of the Roman Empire in the West*, Ann Arbor 1955.

Bowder, Diana, *The Age of Constantine and Julian*, London 1978.

Bowersock, G. W., *Julian the Apostate*, Cambridge, MA 1978.

Bowersock, G. W., Clive, John, and Graubard, Stephen R., *Edward Gibbon and the Decline and Fall of the Roman Empire*, Cambridge, MA and London 1977.

Brauer, George C., *The Age of the Soldier Emperors: Imperial Rome, AD 244–284*, Park Ridge, NJ 1975.

Breeze, David J., *The Northern Frontiers of Roman Britain*, London 1982.

Bregman, J., *Synesius of Cyrene: Philosopher-Bishop*, Berkeley 1982.

Brisson, Jean-Paul, ed., *Problèmes de la guerre à Rome*, Paris 1969.

Brown Peter, *The World of Late Antiquity AD 150–750*, London and New York 1971.

—— *Society and the Holy in Late Antiquity*, Berkeley 1982.

Browning, Robert, *The Emperor Julian*, London 1975.

Burns, Thomas S., *The Ostrogoths*, Wiesbaden 1980.

—— *A History of the Ostrogoths*, Bloomington 1984.

Bury, J. B., *History of the Later Roman Empire*, 2 vols., London and New York 1957 (reprint of 1923 ed.).

—— *The Invasion of Europe by the Barbarians*, New York 1967 (reprint of 1927 ed.).

Butler, R. M., ed., *Soldier and Civilian in Roman Yorkshire*, Leicester 1971.

Callu, J. P., *La Politique monétaire des empereurs romains de 238 à 311*, Paris 1969.

Cameron, Alan, *Claudian, Poetry and Propaganda at the Court of Honorius*, Oxford 1970.

—— *Circus Factions: Blues and Greens at Rome and Byzantium*, Oxford 1976.

Campbell, J. B., *The Emperor and the Roman Army 31 BC–AD235*, Oxford 1984.

Cantarelli, Luigi, *La diocesi italiciana de Diocleziano alla fine dell impero occidentale*, Rome, 1964 (reprint of 1903 ed.).

Chambers, Mortimer, *The Fall of Rome: Can It Be Explained?*, New York 1963.

Chastagnol, Andre, *La fin du mondes antique*, Paris 1976.

Cheesman, G. L., *The Auxilia of the Roman Imperial Army*, Chicago 1975 (reprint of 1914 ed.).

Chevallier, Raymond, ed., *Melanges d'archeologic et d'histoire offerts à Andre Piganiol*, 3 vols., Paris 1966.

Christiansen, P. G., *The Use of Images by Claudius Claudianus*, The Hague and Paris 1969.

Claudian (the works of), trans. by M. Platnauer, 2 vols., Cambridge, MA (Loeb Classical Library) 1922.

Clauss, Manfred, *Der magister officiorum in der Spätantike (4.–6. Jahrhundert)*, Munich 1980.

Clemente, Guido, *La 'Notitia Dignitatum'*, Cagliari 1968.

Clover Frank M., *Geiseric the Statesman: A Study of Vandal Foreign Policy*, U. Chicago (Ph.D. diss.) 1966.

—— *Flavius Merobaudes: A Translation and Historical Commentary*, Philadelphia 1971.

Connolly, Peter, *Greece and Rome at War*, London 1981.

Courcelle, Pierre, *Histoire litteraire des grandes invasions germaniques*, 3rd ed., Paris 1964.

Courtois, Christian, *Les Vandales et l'Afrique*, Paris 1955.

Creasy, Sir Edward, *The Fifteen Decisive Battles of the World*, New York 1892 (originally pub. 1851).

Croke, Brian, and Emmett, Alanna, eds., *History and Historians in Late Antiquity*, Sydney 1983.

Crump, Gary A., *Ammianus Marcellinus as a Military Historian*, Wiesbaden 1975.

Dahmus, Joseph, *Seven Decisive Battles of the Middle Ages*, Chicago 1983.

De Blois, Lukas, *The Policy of the Emperor Gallienus*, Leiden 1976.

Delbrück, Hans, *History of the Art of War Within the Framework of Political History*, Vol. II: *The Germans* (translation W. J. Renfroe), Westport, CT 1980; also Vol. I: *Antiquity*, 1975. (3rd ed. originally published in German, 1920–21).

Demandt, Alexander, *Der Fall Roms*, Munich 1984.

Demougeot, Emilienne, *De l'unite à la division de l'empire romain 395–410*, Paris 1951.

—— *La formation de l'Europe et les invasions barbares: Des origins germaniques a l'avènement de Dioclétien*, Paris 1969.

—— *La formation de l'Europe et les invasions barbares, II: De l'avènement de Dioclétien (284) à l'occupation germanique de l'empire romain d'Occident*, Paris 1979.

Dennis, George T., *Maurice's Strategikon: Handbook of Military Strategy*, Philadelphia 1984.

Diesner, Hans-Joachim, *Der Untergang der römischen Heerschaft in Nordafrika*, Weimar 1964.

—— *The Great Migration: The Movement of Peoples Across Europe, AD 300–700* (translation C. S. V. Salt), London 1982.

Domaszewski, A. von, *Die Rangordnung des römischen Heeres*, 2nd ed. revised by Brian Dobson, Cologne 1967 (original ed. 1908).

Ducrey, Pierre, ed., *Gibbon et Rome à la lumiere de l'historiographie moderne*, Geneva 1977.

Dudden, F. Homes, *The Life and Times of St. Ambrose*, Oxford 1935.

Duff, J. Wight, *A Literary History of Rome in the Silver Age from Tiberius to Hadrian*, 3rd ed. New York 1964.

Earle, E. M., ed., *Makers of Modern Strategy*, Princeton 1943.

Engels, Donald W., *Alexander the Great and the Logistics of the Macedonian Army*, Berkeley 1978.

Evans, J. A. S., ed., *Polis and Imperium: Studies in Honour of Edward Togo Salmon*, Toronto 1974.

Ferrill, Arther, *The Origins of War: From the Stone Age to Alexander the Great*, London and New York 1985.

Fitz, J., ed., *Limes: Akten des XI. internationales Limeskongresses*, Budapest 1977.

Frank, R. I., *Scholae Palatinae; The Palace Guards of the Later Roman Empire*, Papers and Monographs of the American Academy in Rome, vol. 23, Rome 1969.

Frank, Tenney, ed., *An Economic Survey of Ancient Rome*, 6 vols., Baltimore 1940.

Frézouls, Edmond, ed., *Crise et redressment dans les provinces européennes de l'Empire (milieu du IIIe–milieu du IVe siecle ap. J.-C.)*, Strasbourg 1983.

Fuller, J. F. C., *The Decisive Battles of the Western World*, 2 vols., London 1954.

Gibbon, Edward, *The History of the Decline and Fall of the Roman Empire* with Introduction, Notes and Appendices by J. B. Bury, 7 vols., London 1909–14. There is an earlier Bury edition, 1896–1900.

Goffart, Walter, *Caput and Colonate: Towards a History of Late Roman Taxation*, Toronto 1974.

—— *Barbarians and Romans AD 418–584, The Techniques of Accommodation*, Princeton 1980

Gold, Barbara K., *Literary and Artistic Patronage in Ancient Rome*, Austin 1982.

Goodburn, R., and Bartholemew, P., eds., *Aspects of the Notitia Dignitatum*, Oxford 1976.

Gordon, C. D., *The Age of Attila*, Ann Arbor 1960.

Gossman, Lionel, *The Empire Unpossess'd: An Essay on Gibbon's Decline and Fall*, Cambridge 1981.

Grant, Michael, *The Climax of Rome*, London and Boston 1968.

—— *The Army of the Caesars*, London 1974.

—— *The Fall of the Roman Empire – A Reappraisal*, London 1976.

Griffith, Paddy, *Forward into Battle; Fighting Tactics from Waterloo to Vietnam*, Chichester 1981.

Grosse, Robert, *Römische Militärgeschichte von Gallienus bis zum Beginn der byzantinischen Themenverfassung*, Berlin 1920.

Hart, B. H. Liddell, *Strategy*, New York 1954.

Hassall, M. W. C., and Ireland, R., *De Rebus Bellicus*, 2 parts, Oxford 1979.

Haupt, D., and Horn, H. G., eds., *Studien zu den Militärgrenzen Roms*, Cologne 1977.

Haywood, R. M., *The Myth of Rome's Fall*, New York 1958.

Head, Constance, *The Emperor Julian*, Boston 1976.

Hodgkin, Thomas, *The Dynasty of Theodosius*, Oxford 1889.

—— *Italy and Her Invaders*, 2 vols., 2nd ed., Oxford 1892.

Hoffmann, Dietrich, *Das spätrömische Bewegungsheer und die Notitia Dignitatum*, 2 vols., Düsseldorf 1969.

Hohlfelder, R., ed., *City, Town and Countryside in the Early Byzantine Era*, New York, 1982.

Holder, P. A., *The Roman Army in Britain*, New York 1982.

Holum, K., *Theodosian Empresses: Women and Imperial Dominion in Late Antiquity*, Berkeley 1982.

Humble, Richard, *Warfare in the Ancient World*, London 1980.

Humphrey, J. H., ed., *Excavations at Carthage 1976 Conducted by the University of Michigan*, vol. IV, Ann Arbor 1978.

——, ed., *Excavations at Carthage 1978 Conducted by the University of Michigan*, vol. VII, Ann Arbor 1982.

James, Edward ed., *Visigothic Spain*, Oxford 1980.

Johnson, Stephen, *The Roman Forts of*

the Saxon Shore, New York 1976.

Jones, A. H. M., *The Later Roman Empire 284–602*, 4 vols., Oxford and 2 vols., Norman, OK 1964, reprinted 1975.

—— *The Decline of the Ancient World*, Harlow and New York 1966, reprinted 1975.

—— Martindale, J. R., and Morris, J., *The Prosopography of the Later Roman Empire, Vol. I AD 260–395*, Cambridge 1971.

Jordan, David P., *Gibbon and His Roman Empire*, Urbana 1971.

Jordanes, *The Gothic History*, translated by C. C. Mierow, New York, 2nd ed. 1915, reprinted 1960.

Kaegi, Walter Emil, *Byzantium and the Decline of Rome*, Princeton 1968.

—— *Byzantine Military Unrest 471–843*, Amsterdam 1981.

—— *Army, Society and Religion in Byzantium*, London 1982.

Kagan, Donald, *The End of the Roman Empire: Decline or Transformation*, 2nd ed., Lexington, MA 1978.

Katz, Solomon, *The Decline of Rome and The Rise of Medieval Europe*, Ithaca 1955.

Keegan, John, *The Face of Battle*, London and New York 1976.

Keppie, Lawrence, *The Making of the Roman Army*, London 1984.

Kienast, Dietmar, *Untersuchungen zu den Kriegsflotten der römischen Kaiserzeit*, Bonn 1966.

King, Anthony, and Henig, Martin, *The Roman West in the Third Century*, 2 vols., Oxford 1981.

Klein, Richard, ed., *Julian Apostata*, Darmstadt 1978.

Lot, Ferdinand, *The End of the Ancient World and the Beginnings of the Middle Ages* (trans. by P. and M. Leon), New York 1931.

Luttwak, Edward N., *The Grand Strategy of the Roman Empire From the First Century AD to the Third*, Baltimore 1976.

McCartney, Eugene S., *Warfare by Land and Sea*, New York 1963.

MacMullen, Ramsay, *Soldier and Civilian in the Later Roman Empire*, Cambridge, MA 1967.

—— *Enemies of the Roman Order: Treason, Unrest, and Alienation in the Empire*, Cambridge, MA 1967.

—— *Roman Government's Response to Crisis AD 235–337*, New Haven and London 1976.

Maenchen-Helfen, Otto J., *The World of the Huns*, Berkeley 1973.

Martindale, J. R., *The Prosopography of the Later Roman Empire, Vol. II AD 395–527*, Cambridge 1980.

Maspero, Jean, *Organisation militaire de l'Egypte byzantine*, Paris 1912.

Matthews, John, *Western Aristocracies and Imperial Court, AD 364–425*, Oxford 1975.

Maurice, *Strategikon* (translation George V. Dennis), Philadelphia 1984.

Mazzarino, Santo, *Stilicone: La crisi imperiale dopo Teodosio*, Rome 1942.

Maxwell, Valerie, *The Military Decorations of the Roman Army*, London 1981.

Millar, Fergus, ed., *The Roman Empire and Its Neighbours*, London and New York 1967, reprinted 1981.

Minor, Clifford E., *Brigand, Insurrectionist and Separatist Movements in the Later Roman Empire*, Seattle (unpublished Ph.D. dissertation, U. of Washington) 1971.

Mommsen, Theodor, *Gesammelte Schriften*, VI, 3, Berlin 1910.

Morris, John, *The Age of Arthur*, New York 1973.

Musset, Lucien, *The Germanic Invasions*, University Park, PA 1975.

O'Flynn, John Michael, *Generalissimos of the Western Roman Empire*, Edmonton 1983.

Oman, Charles, *A History of the Art of War in the Middle Ages*, 2 vols., 2nd ed., London 1924.

Oman, Charles W., *The Art of War in the Middle Ages AD 378–1515*, Ithaca 1953 (reprint of the 1885 ed.).

Oost, Stewart I., *Galla Placidia Augusta*, Chicago 1968.

Papini, Annunziata Maria, *Ricimero. L'agonia dell'Impero romano d'occidente*, Milan 1959.

Paribeni, Roberto, *Da Diocleziano alla caduta dell'impero d'occidente*, Bologna 1941.

Parker, H. M. D., *The Roman Legions*, Cambridge 1958 (reprint of 1928 ed.).

Paschoud, Francois, *Roma aeterna: Études sur le patriotisme romain dans l'Occident latin à l'époque des grandes invasions*, Rome 1967.

—— *Cinq études sur Zosime*, Paris 1975.

—— *Zosime, Histoire Nouvelle*, 2 vols., Paris 1971 and 1979.

Pastorino, Agostino, *La prima spedizione di Alarico in Italia (401–402 d.C.)*, Turin 1975.

Patlagean, Evelyne, *Pauvrété économique et pauvrété sociale à Byzance*, 4ᵉ–7ᵉ siècles, Paris and The Hague 1977.

Pavan, M., *La politica gotica di Teodosio*, Rome 1964.

Pedley, John Griffiths, ed., *New Light on Ancient Carthage*, Ann Arbor 1980.

Phillips, Major Thomas R., *Roots of Strategy*, Westport, CT 1982 (reprinted from 1940 ed.).

Piganiol, Andre, *L'Empire Chrétien (325–395)*, 2nd ed., Paris 1972.

Randers-Pehrson, J. D., *Barbarians and Romans*, Norman, OK 1983.

Richmond, Ian A., *The City Wall of Imperial Rome*, College Park, Maryland 1971.

Robinson, H. R., *The Armour of Imperial Rome*, London 1975.

Rostovtzeff, Michael I., *Social and Economic History of the Roman Empire*, 2 vols., Oxford 2nd ed. 1957.

Runkel, F., *Die Schlacht bei Adrianopel*, Berlin 1903.

Scullard, H. H., *Roman Britain: Outpost of the Empire*, London and New York 1979.

Seeck, Otto, *Geschichte des Untergangs der antiken Welt*, 6 vols., Stuttgart 1920–21.

—— *Notitia Dignitatum*, Frankfurt 1962 (reprint of 1876 ed.).

Selkirk, Raymond, *The Piercebridge Formula*, Cambridge 1983.

Senger und Etterlin, Fridolin von, *Neither Fear Nor Hope* (translation George Malcolm), New York 1964.

Seston, William, *Diocletien et la tétrarchie*, Paris 1946.

Simons, Gerald, *Barbarian Europe*, New York 1968.

Sirago, Vito Antonio, *Galla Placidia e la trasformazione politica dell'Occidente*, Louvain 1961.

Sitwell, N. H. H., *Roman Roads of Europe*, New York 1981.

Snyder, Jack, *The Ideology of the Offensive: Military Decision Making and the Disasters of 1914*, Ithaca 1984.

Spaulding, Oliver L., *Pen and Sword in Greece and Rome*, Princeton 1937.

Speidel, Michael P., *Guards of the Roman Armies*, Bonn 1978.

—— *Roman Army Studies*, Amsterdam 1984.

Stark, Freya, *Rome on the Euphrates: The Story of a Frontier*, New York 1966.

Starr, Chester G., *Civilization and the Caesars: The Intellectual Revolution in the Roman Empire*, Ithaca 1954.

—— *The Roman Imperial Navy 31 B.C.–A.D. 324*, Cambridge 1960 (reprint of 1941 ed.).

—— *The Roman Empire 27 B.C.–A.D. 476: A Study in Survival*, Oxford 1982.

Ste Croix, G. E. M. de, *The Class Struggle in the Ancient Greek World from the Archaic Age to the Arab Conquests*, London 1981.

Stein, Ernst, *Histoire du Bas-Empire* 2 vol. in 3, Amsterdam 1968 (originally published as *Geschichte des spätromischen Reiches*, Vienna 1928).

Temporini, Hildegard, ed., *Aufstieg und Niedergang der römischen Welt*, Berlin and New York.

Thompson, E. A., *A History of Attila and the Huns*, Oxford 1948.

—— *A Roman Reformer and Inventor*, Oxford 1952.

—— *The Visigoths in the Time of Ulfila*, Oxford 1966.

—— *The Goths in Spain*, Oxford 1969.

—— *Romans and Barbarians*, Madison 1982.

—— *Saint Germanus of Auxerre and the End of Roman Britain*, 1984.

Todd, Malcolm, *The Northern Barbarians, 100 BC–AD 300*, London 1975.

Tsangadas, B. C. P., *The Fortifications and Defence of Constantinople*, New York 1980.

Van Berchem, Denis, *L'armée de Diocletien et la réforme constantinienne*, Paris 1952.

Vegetius, *Flavi Vegeti Renati Epitoma Rei Militaris*, ed. by C. Lang (Teubner Texts), Leipzig 1885.

Vogt, Joseph, *The Decline of Rome*

(translation J. Sondheimer) New York 1967.

Waas, Manfred, *Germanen in römischen Dienst im 4. Jahrhundert n.C.*, Bonn 1965.

Walbank, F. W., *The Awful Revolution: The Decline of the Roman Empire in the West*, Liverpool 1969.

Wallace-Hadrill, J. M., *The Barbarian West 400–1000*, 3rd ed., London 1967.

Warry, John, *Warfare in the Classical World*, London and New York 1980.

Watson, G. R., *The Roman Soldier*, London and New York 1969.

Webster, Graham, *The Roman Imperial Army*, London 1969.

Wells, Colin, *The German Policy of Augustus*, Oxford 1972.

—— *The Roman Empire*, London and Stanford, CA, 1984.

Wells, C. M., ed., *Roman Africa: The*

Vanier Lectures 1980, Ottawa 1982.

Welsby, Derek A., *The Roman Military Defence of the British Provinces in its Later Phases*, Oxford 1982.

Wes, Marinus, *Das Ende des Kaisertums im Westen des römischen Reichs*, The Hague 1967.

White, Lynn, *The Transformation of the Roman World*, Berkeley and Los Angeles 1966.

Wightman, Edith Mary, *Roman Trier and the Treveri*, London 1970.

Williams, Stephen, *Diocletian and the Roman Recovery*, London 1985.

Wolfram, Herwig, *Geschichte der Goten*, Munich 1979.

Zecchini, G., *Aezio. L'ultima difesa dell' Occidente Romano*, 1983.

Zosimus, *Historia Nova* (translation James J. Buchanan and Harold T. Davis), San Antonio 1967.

Sources of Illustrations

Line drawings

All battle plans by Martin Lubikowski and also drawings on pp. 22, 44; the following drawings by Schelay Richardson: frontispiece, pp. 48, 49, 143, 144; all maps by H. A. Shelley except p. 100 (after M. Grant (ed.) *The Birth of Western Civilization* 1964). Other credits: after A. Banks *Atlas of Ancient and Medieval Warfare* 1973: p. 148; after Browning 1975: p. 53; after Connolly 1981: frontispiece, p. 48 (left); after Diesner 1982: p. 42; after P. Dixon *Barbarian Europe* 1976: pp. 24, 162–3; after M. Grant 1964: p. 100; after Grant 1968: p. 11; after Hodgkin 1892: p. 72; after Luttwak 1976: p. 44; after M. Mackenzie *De Rebus Bellicis* BAR International Series 63, 1979: p. 131; after E. C. May and G. P. Stadler *Ancient and Medieval Warfare* 1980: p. 61; after O'Flynn 1983: p. 89; after Robinson 1975: p. 50; after Simons 1968: endplate; after Warry 1980: pp. 48 (right), 49, 143, 144.

Plates

Alinari 18; Anderson 5; Aosta Cathedral 18; Barletta 17; Peter Chèze-Brown 1; Hirmer Fotoarchiv 11, 12, 13, 14, 17, 19, 21; Istanbul Arkeoloji Müzeleri/Deutsches Archäologisches Institut 23; Leningrad: Hermitage Museum 15; London: British Museum 12; Courtauld Institute of Art 2; Madrid: Academia de la Historia 16; Martin Hürlimann 3; Monza: Cathedral Treasury 19; Oxford: Bodleian Library 20; Paris: Bibliothèque Nationale 24, 26, 27; Musée du Louvre 21, 25; Rome: Deutsches Archäologisches Institut 4, 6, 7; Museo Nazionale delle Terme 5; Palazzo dei Conservatori 13, 14; Tanjug 10; Venice: Piazza San Marco 11; Vienna: Kunsthistorisches Museum 22; 9 after M. Rostovtzeff, 'L'Art Gréco-iranien', *Revue des Arts Asiatiques*, Vol. VII, 1931–1932.

Index

Page numbers in italic refer to illustrations; numbers in bold refer to plates

Index

Index

Index